THE
100 BEST
Internet Stocks

TO OWN FOR THE LONG RUN

Investing in the Internet Economy
and the Companies That Make It Click

Gene Walden • Tom Shaughnessy

DEARBORN™
A **Kaplan Professional** Company

Dedicated to the memory of Walter and Clara Gingery

Associate Publisher: Cynthia A. Zigmund
Senior Managing Editor: Jack Kiburz
Interior Design: Lucy Jenkins
Cover Design: Jody Billert, Billert Communications
Typesetting: Elizabeth Pitts

Library of Congress Cataloging-in-Publication Data

Walden, Gene.
    The 100 best internet stocks to own for the long run: investing in the internet econ-omy and the companies that make it click / Gene Walden, Tom Shaughnessy.
        p.   cm.
    Includes index.
    ISBN 0-7931-3850-7 (6×9 pbk.)
    1. Internet industry—Finance—Directories. 2. Online information services indus-try—Finance—Directories. 3. Investments—United States—Directories. 4. Stocks—United States—Directories. I. Title: Hundred best internet stocks to own for the long run. II. Shaughnessy, Tom. III. Title.

    HD9696.8.U62 W35   2000
    332.63'2—dc21   00-029433

Contents

Alphabetical Listing of the 100 Best Internet Stocks

Preface

No phenomenon of modern times demarcates the turn of the millennium more fittingly than the Internet revolution. This global economic metamorphosis represents a sea change so rapid and dramatic that dozens of exciting new innovations are hitting the market every single day—and promising young companies are going public every week. In fact, the vast majority of the companies featured in this book first issued their stock in 1999 or 2000.

The Internet economy is a subject so vast, so new, and so complex that it would have been virtually impossible to cover it in an accurate and timely manner without the help of others. That's why my coauthor, Tom Shaughnessy, a veteran of the high-tech industry, was so valuable in helping to develop the book, evaluate the companies, and cover the technical aspects of the Internet economy. We also enlisted the services of stat specialist Larry Nelson, who compiled the financial tables, stock growth graphs, and other material for this book, as he has for nearly all the *100 Best Stocks* books.

The purpose of this book is to provide investors with a comprehensive yet easy-to-understand overview of the Internet economy, including its technologies, its business models, its future trends, and, of course, its leading stock prospects.

The Internet economy is here to stay. I hope this book will help you build a portfolio of dynamic young stocks that will grow and prosper for years to come.

—Gene Walden

Acknowledgments

A number of people have contributed to this book in one way or another. I'd like to thank my close friends who helped introduce me to Internet investing, Dennis Kleve, Steve Daffer, and Richard Jacobs.

Thanks also to the staff at Dearborn for their assistance in shaping, editing, and publishing the book, including Cynthia Zigmund, Jack Kiburz, Paul Mallon, Sandy Holzbach, and my many other friends at Dearborn. They're true professionals.

—Gene Walden

Introduction: Now Entering $yberspace

To the casual observer, the Internet economy represents little more than a fledgling collection of online retailers noted most for their heavy losses and inflated stock prices. Many believe that Internet investment opportunities have, by and large, had their day, that the early bird has already gotten the worm and the growth of the sector is all but over.

That's why millions of investors, brokers, and money managers are still on the sidelines waiting for this speculative fad to run its course.

They could be waiting for a long, long time.

The Internet has spawned an economic revolution that is changing civilization as we know it. It is radically affecting the way we live, learn, interact, and do business. And we are still very, very early in the game. New Internet technologies and concepts will continue to feed the growth of the sector for years to come. This is the proverbial ground floor opportunity for an entirely new economic order, and those investors still watching the parade go by may be passing up the greatest broad-based investment opportunity of their lifetime.

In fact, it is the broad-based, multidimensional nature of the Internet that distinguishes it from other speculative markets of the past. From the tulip bulb craze of 17th century Holland, to the biotech stocks and junk bond funds of the early 1980s, to the Japanese crash of the late 1980s, most of the boom-to-bust markets of the past have involved investments of a single narrow segment.

By contrast, the Internet represents a transformation of nearly the entire global economic system—communications, infrastructure, science and technology, media, entertainment, financial services, retailing, marketing and advertising, business-to-business commerce, and even governmental services. And its reach is worldwide and border-free. Over the next two decades, the Internet will continue to change our lives in ways we simply cannot yet imagine.

Think of the early days of the automobile. Initially the only obvious source of revenue was the manufacture and sale of the cars themselves—and even that seemed dubious. The earliest models were expensive, difficult to start, prone to frequent breakdowns, and largely inadequate at maneuvering the rugged dirt and mud roads of the day. Yet from that narrow and speculative sector emerged a broad, new economic order that changed the world forever. Not only did the automobile alter the way people lived, worked, and spent their free time, it also fueled the exponential growth of the worldwide oil, steel, and rubber industries and gave birth to heavy manufacturing, road construction, auto insurance, trucking, and a multitude of other related industries.

Still in its infancy, the Internet is already beginning to have that same type of explosive impact on the economy. In fact, the more than $500 billion the Internet generates annually in the United States already far exceeds the total revenue of the entire U.S. automotive industry.

LEARNING TO LIVE WITH VOLATILITY

The uninitiated may question how we can discuss with such confidence a speculative run already infamous for its volatile swings. Indeed, some Internet stocks have soared 20- to 30-fold in less than a year—while others have plummeted from precarious highs by 70 to 90 percent.

No question, the Internet market is as turbulent as any sector of the past century. The share price of online retailer ValueAmerica, for instance, soared quickly from its 1999 initial public offering price of about $25 to more than $70 a share—then tumbled to under $5 after the company reported disappointing returns. Even companies that have stayed on track financially, such as E*Trade, Ameritrade, and Priceline.com, have seen their share prices dip 60 to 70 percent from their earlier highs before edging back up. It's not unusual for some of the biggest, most successful names on the Net—Amazon.com, Yahoo!, and Commerce One, among others—to experience occasional dips of 30 to 50 percent.

But let's put those perilous dives into perspective. Even after a 47 percent drop in its share price in early 2000, Commerce One was still up 1,600 percent from its 1999 low. Yahoo! also has had its ups and downs, but a $10,000 investment in that stock three years ago would have already grown to $1.5 million! Who needs Powerball! Volatility is the price you have to pay for a chance to earn truly spectacular returns.

The question many market observers wonder about is how Internet stocks with no profits can post such phenomenal gains. There is a very compelling reason: the revenue of those companies is growing at cyberspeed. Companies that didn't even exist three years ago are already posting annual revenues of $10 to $100 million, with strong prospects for raising those levels another tenfold over the next two to three years. As the revenue and assets of a company grow, its value—and stock price—increase, as well.

Some market observers also question how the few Internet stocks that *do* earn a profit can justify their astronomical price-earnings ratios (PE).

Wall Street uses PE ratios (stock price divided by earnings per share) to determine whether a stock is fairly priced relative to the market. The higher the PE, the pricier the stock. But while the PEs of traditional blue chip stocks have generally fallen in the 10 to 35 range, the PEs of many high-tech and Internet stocks have soared to well over 100. Many analysts believe those inflated PEs are an unmistakable sign that the sector is over-priced. But the growth of many Internet companies tends to make their high PEs irrelevant. CNET is a good example. In 1998, the Web operation had earnings of 4 cents a share, with a PE ratio that ranged from 158 to 503. But in 1999, CNET's earnings grew from 4 cents a share to $4.92, sending its PE down to under 10. So instead of being grossly overpriced, CNET was suddenly underpriced compared to the market averages. Because of the incredible growth of these young companies, traditional fundamental stock measures don't always apply.

Across the board, the Internet economy is growing at an astounding rate. While the U.S. economy has been growing at a sizzling 4 to 5 percent per year—fast enough to convince Federal Reserve Chairman Alan Greenspan to do all he could to slow things down—the Internet economy has been surging at an unfathomable 70 percent per year! No other segment of the economy even comes close.

SECTORS WITHIN A SECTOR

Although some see the Web as a broad blur of similar stocks, in truth, Internet stocks are not created equally. They don't trade in tandem, they don't share the same growth prospects, and they offer vastly different products and services.

There are nine fairly distinct sectors within the Internet economy. In other words, this is not just one ground floor investment opportunity, but nine separate significant opportunities. Savvy investors will try to buy stocks that represent most if not all of those subsectors, providing diversification within this broad market. This book will help you differentiate the sectors and evaluate the leading stocks within each sector.

The nine sectors include:

1. Infrastructure (equipment such as routers and switches used to operate the Internet)
2. Software
3. Internet service providers (ISPs) and portals
4. Business services (such as Web site development, operation, and order fulfillment)

5. E-commerce (business to business)
6. E-tailing (retailer to consumer)
7. Online financial services (such as banking and investing)
8. Media and entertainment
9. Internet holding companies

We offer a detailed overview of the key technologies, market niches, economic business models, and future trends of each of those sectors beginning on page 1.

HOW TO INVEST IN THE INTERNET MARKET

Rule 1: There are no tried-and-true rules for investing in Internet stocks.

If someone should try to tell you, in all earnestness, that they can show you exactly when to buy and when to sell an Internet stock, do yourself a favor and kindly walk away. No one really knows yet how to value these stocks. It's way too early in the game. All we have are preliminary theories on how best to invest in the Internet for the long term.

Here's our strategy: Internet stock investing is simply a matter of making a continuing series of small bets. Since it is impossible at this point to determine with any certainty a fair market value for the vast majority of Internet stocks, they will continue to experience broad price swings. But by making a series of small bets in a wide range of companies—buying a few shares now, a few shares later, and still more down the road—you will accomplish your most important goal. That goal is to acquire a growing stake in the burgeoning Internet economy while it is still in its early stages.

Here is our step-by-step approach:

1. Buy quality. Because we can't put a fair value on these stocks, the most important thing is to buy stocks that are either leaders in their sector or upstarts with strong growth momentum. As the Internet continues to expand in the years ahead, the best stocks will mirror or exceed the overall growth of the Internet economy.

2. Diversify. Try to build a diversified portfolio by buying a few shares of several stocks. Considering there are nine distinct sectors within the Internet economy—all of which have potential for outstanding long-term growth—your goal should be to eventually own shares from most, if not all, of those sectors.

3. Buy a few shares at a time. Take a gradual accumulation approach through a series of small bets. By buying a few shares at a time, you can spread your risks and minimize the effects of the market volatility. For the market-leading companies, start with a few shares and add more later—regardless of whether the stock price has climbed or dropped.

4. Don't worry about high share prices. Internet stocks can cost as much as $300 to $400. While the high prices scare away some investors, that's a mistake you don't want to make. Otherwise, you will be passing up most of the best stocks of the Internet economy. With all stocks, you tend to get what you pay for, and if you want the best, you have to pay the price. If a stock costs $200 and you only have $1,000 to invest, buy five shares. There's no shame in buying small lots, and with online brokerage commissions as low as $8 a trade, your commission costs are a nonfactor. And best of all, if you've chosen the right stock, it will soon split, climb, and split again, boosting your holdings to a multiple of your original lot.

5. Start immediately. There's no reasonable rationale for putting off Internet investing. Begin investing in Internet stocks as soon as you can raise the money. If you already have large investments in stocks of other segments—but no investment in Internet stocks—you should consider selling a portion of your position in some of those other stocks to reinvest in Internet companies. Otherwise, use some of the money from your regular earnings to begin building your Internet portfolio.

Either way, it is important to get involved as soon as possible while the Internet market is in its infancy. This is a market that will be growing and evolving for years to come. Even conservative investors should buy some Internet stocks for the sake of diversification so that their portfolio more accurately represents a cross-section of the overall economy. The sooner you get started, the lower your price of entry, and the greater your potential for long-term returns.

6. Look for buying opportunities. From time to time, Internet stocks fall out of favor and may drop 20 to 50 percent. That's a good time to snap up shares of the top companies. Don't worry about whether the shares are going to fall further. If the stock is already down 25 percent from its high, you're 25 percent ahead of the game. On the other hand, don't be afraid to invest in stocks that are setting new highs. Momentum investing has been very lucrative for Internet investors. The Internet is not for value investors. Internet stocks that have been going up often tend to keep going up. Buying winners can be a very successful strategy.

7. Accumulate—don't buy and sell. Find good stocks and build a position in them. Don't sell out with the first quick run-up — and don't kick yourself when the inevitable happens: the stock blasts to a new high, then drops 25 percent. That's life in the stock market. But the good stocks will continue to bounce back. Imagine the investor who bought Microsoft in 1988 and sold out shortly thereafter with a 25 percent gain. That may have been a great short-term success, but over the next ten years the stock climbed almost 10,000 percent. A $10,000 investment in Microsoft in 1989 would have grown to about $1 million by 2000. That's what you want in the Internet—long-term home runs. A rapid buy-and-sell approach, in fact, is a poor strategy for investing in any type of stock. A recent study of consumer investing trends showed that the households that traded the most frequently over the past five years had the lowest annual rate of return— about 13 percent—while households that traded the least had the highest rate of return—about 18.5 percent. And by holding for the long term, investors also avoid capital gains taxes and brokerage commissions.

8. Never say never (when to sell). You bought the stock because the company was growing quickly. Now you learn that revenue growth is flat, and the company's fortunes are waning. Good time to sell the stock. The other time to sell is if you learn of another company from the same segment that is taking market share from a stock you hold. Go with the market leaders and the upstarts with momentum and dump the companies that lose their edge.

9. Use this book to find prospects. Think of this book as a catalog for investment shoppers. To select your portfolio of Internet stocks, read through the 100 profiles and narrow your choices to 10 to 12 good prospects. The profiles will help you understand what the company does and how it's positioned within its niche. The financial tables and stock growth graphs will give you a snapshot of their past performance. Once you've selected 10 to 12 favorites from the book, use other sources, such as the Internet, the library, or recent publications to find out more about how those companies are doing now. Follow their stock prices for a few days to get a feel for their trading range, and then begin making relatively small investments in the stocks that you feel are the best bets at the time. You also can follow many of these stocks (as well as stocks from the other *100 Best Stocks* books) at our free Web site <www.Allstarstocks.com>.

10. One more step—finding winners in the IPO after-market. One of the most exciting aspects of the Internet market is that promising new stocks continue to go public week after week. If you want to invest in some of the hottest new stocks, you'll need to do some additional homework, but good sources are readily available. Unless you have a good broker, you probably won't be able to get your hands on any of the best initial public stock offerings (IPOs) as they're issued. But you can still profit by buying the best stocks immediately following their IPOs—before the institutional money managers, mutual fund managers, and other individual investors have started to accumulate the stock for their portfolios. Where can you learn about new IPOs? There are several good *free* sources:

- <www.internet.com>. This site offers a wealth of information about both old and new Internet stocks. It has a special section on Internet IPOs. Recent IPOs are listed—including projected issue dates—as well as recent IPOs. The site also provides profiles and other information about each of the stocks.
- <www.hoovers.com>. A very large and comprehensive financial Web site, Hoovers offers detailed information on all upcoming IPOs (Internet companies as well as all other types of stocks). Hoovers also includes profiles and other information on each company, and it gives projected IPO issue dates.
- <www.ipofinancial.com>. The site offers a calendar of upcoming IPOs. It also gives a price recap that details the trading range for recent IPOs.
- <www.Onmoney.com>. In my regular weekly column at Onmoney, I occasionally cover old, new, and soon-to-be-issued Internet stocks. The site also has other features on stock market investing and a wealth of detailed research on thousands of stocks and mutual funds.

SELECTING THE 100 BEST INTERNET STOCKS

Traditional stock screening methods that work for other sectors of the market are of little relevance in selecting top-quality Internet stocks. Historical performance means nothing, because most Internet stocks have very short histories. In fact, the vast majority of the 100 stocks featured in this book were not even publicly traded until 1999—and a couple went public in 2000. Instead, we had to resort to another very time-consuming technique—brutally long, hard, tedious research.

Step one was to compile an initial list of candidates. To gather the list, we looked at the stock holdings of all of the top performing Internet-related mutual funds, reviewed the "best stock" lists from magazines and newspapers, scanned the Web for news stories on Internet stocks, talked to a few money managers and analysts, and dug up information on all Internet IPOs dating back to 1998.

In all, we compiled a list of several hundred prospects that appeared to have solid potential. (Many of the stocks that didn't make our top 100 appear in an honorable mention list at the back of this book.) We tried to limit our list to companies that derived (or soon would derive) most of their revenue from Internet-related activities. As a result, many outstanding stocks that are involved in the Internet but generate most of their revenue elsewhere were not considered, including companies such as Microsoft, Sun Microsystems, EMC, Intel, AT&T, IBM, Nortel Networks, and Oracle.

We carefully analyzed all the companies on our list, looking at their products and services, their position within their sector, their revenue growth, their stock growth and stability, their management, their customers and strategic allies, and their leading investors. We checked their Web sites, read recent news reports about each company, viewed analysts' recommendations, and evaluated the industry niche of each of the more than 300 stocks.

Even after all of our analysis, there were still about 150 stocks on the list that we felt could easily land in the top 100. Unfortunately, some excellent stocks were left off the list, but the final 100 is a select group of exciting young companies that are pioneering the latest Internet innovations and technologies. Not all will reach phenomenal success, but many will be market leaders for years to come.

RANKING THE STOCKS

In the Internet economy, with its young, unproven stocks and uncharted industries, constructing an objective and accurate system for ranking companies is about as easy as ranking the speed of 100 bullets all fired at once.

While the 100 companies featured here all boast outstanding short-term growth records, most have been in business less than three years and have no earnings. And the vast majority have been publicly traded less than two years. That doesn't give us a lot to go on in comparing and rating stocks based on past performance. As objective as we tried to be, the system is far from perfect—and that's what makes this whole process so exciting.

That's also why you should view the rankings strictly as a loose guideline. Make your choices based on your own knowledge, analysis, selection criteria, and—let's face it—gut feeling.

As you can see in the chart below, the ranking system features these key points:

- Five categories
- Four points maximum per category
- Twenty points maximum total score

Earnings Progression	★ ★ ★ ★
Revenue Growth	★ ★ ★ ★
Stock Growth	★ ★ ★ ★
Consistency	★ ★ ★ ★
Stability/Vulnerability	★ ★ ★ ★
Total Points	**20 points**

These were the factors we weighed in awarding points for each category:

- **Earnings progression.** Companies with strong, consistent earnings growth through three or four years would earn the maximum four points. (Shorter histories received fewer points.) Stocks that had no earnings but showed a positive progression from heavy losses to smaller losses or to positive earnings also could earn the maximum four points. Lesser growth (or progress) meant fewer points. Companies with increasing losses received no points.
- **Revenue growth.** Nearly every stock in the book has had outstanding revenue growth. Companies with strong, sustained revenue growth for three or four years received the maximum four points. Strong two-year growth was worth three points, and very strong one-year growth was worth two points.
- **Stock growth.** Companies with strong, sustained three- or four-year growth (over 40 percent per year) received the maximum of four points. Younger stocks could get three points for strong two-year growth, two

points for strong one-year growth, and one to two points for 1999 IPOs with strong growth in the months after going public.

- **Consistency.** Companies with three or four consecutive years of increased earnings and revenue would receive the maximum four points. Companies with a "positive earnings progression"—with losses steadily declining or changing to positive earnings—also could score the four-point maximum. Companies with shorter histories or less consistent growth would receive fewer points.
- **Stability/Vulnerability.** In this subjective category, we looked at the company's history, its growth momentum, its future potential, the potential of its sector, its competition, its position within its niche, its customers and alliances, and other related factors. Stocks we felt were best-positioned for success based on all of those factors received the highest rating. Very few companies received a perfect four.

YOUR FINAL STEP

It's nearly time to enter $yberspace. But before you begin investing in any of the 100 stocks featured in this book, you may find it helpful to learn the essentials of the key sectors of the Internet economy.

The following section offers an overview of each of the nine Internet sectors (infrastructure, ISPs and portals, software, business services, business-to-business e-commerce, e-tailing, online financial services, media and entertainment, and holding companies).

You'll learn about the key technologies, market niches, economic business models, and the future prospects and trends of each of the nine sectors. By understanding the strengths, weaknesses, and fundamentals of each sector, you should be better prepared to build an all-star portfolio—and to uncover the most promising opportunities on the Net.

Here's hoping you pick only winners!

 **Infrastructure**

In the 1980s, the computer revolution was in full force, but there was one missing ingredient—the ability of all of those computers to communicate with each another.

This critical shortcoming was not lost on two academics at Stanford University. In 1984, husband-wife team Len Bosack and Sandy Lerner noticed students and researchers still had to physically exchange floppy disks in order to communicate—even with thousands of state-of-the-art computers on campus. Bosack and Lerner saw this "sneaker net" arrangement as a gaping hole in the fabric of the computer age. A technology called *local area networks* (LANs) enabled users to connect to the same cable to freely share data, printers, and messages. But there was still no easy way to share data between different LANs, prompting complaints that these new "islands of automation" were holding back progress.

Bosack and Lerner also saw that a big payoff was in the offing for whoever developed a technology that would allow computers to easily exchange information. The couple invented a device called the *router,* a combination of hardware and software designed to automatically move "packets" of data between LANs. Soon they had the Stanford campus wired with their routers, linking all the computers into an "inter-network" that connected departments and labs. That was the birth of internetworking.

Bosack and Lerner went on to found Cisco Systems and build it into a highly profitable company. An industry giant with a market capitalization of about $200 billion, Cisco Systems has been a pioneer in the development of the Internet, helping make the Web accessible to hundreds of millions of users around the world. The company is the dominant player in the Internet infrastructure sector, commanding about an 80 percent share of the market for the routers used to move data packets around the Internet.

Many other key manufacturers have joined Cisco to help string this complex global data communications system together.

HOW THE INTERNET WORKS

Put simply, the Internet is a decentralized collection of computers bound together by an intricate networking scheme called the Internet Protocol (IP). IP enables users to communicate with each other regardless of the make, model, or operating system of their computers. IP works its magic through two basic technologies:

1. A standardized "digital packet format" that can transport data across any local area network hooked to the Internet

2. An "addressing system" that directs packets of data anywhere on the Internet, with a minimum number of hops along the way

The Internet Protocol was invented by the U.S. Department of Defense to enable its contractors in industry and academia to share research and development data more easily. But right away people started using the fledgling IP network for such things as freewheeling discussion groups and e-mail. Word soon spread that IP was the unifying networking system the world had been waiting for, because anybody could use it regardless of where they were or what kind of computer they had.

The Internet is anarchy by design. There is no central authority controlling Internet operations—in part because no central management team could possibly administer something of such size and dynamism. The closest thing to a central authority is a group called the Internet Society, based in Reston, Virginia. This not-for-profit organization coordinates such things as technical standards and the task of doling out IP addresses and domain names. But once you've got your name and address, it's an open playing field where users can do pretty much as they see fit as long as they comply with the various Internet standards. The basic rule is that if other users can't locate your address or understand your data packets, you're out of the game. Internet standards are enforced by market forces, which is how the Internet has been able to sustain such awesome growth and still hold together.

There is no dividing line between private organizations hooked to the Internet and the Internet itself. They are one and the same. The Internet is a "network of networks" through which traffic freely travels, but each network is independently owned and operated. Homes and small businesses link up to Internet service providers (ISPs) via dial-up connections, while larger companies have routers permanently connected to their ISPs. Larger companies operate private internetworks—called *intranets*—that are kept mostly inaccessible to Internet traffic. At the Internet's core is a "backbone" composed of ISPs freely exchanging traffic between themselves across very high-speed links. (A *backbone* is a network that only has other networks connected to it, rather than user devices such as PCs or servers. This lets backbones operate at much higher speeds than regular LANs.)

This universe of home and small business users, corporate intranets, and Internet service providers adds up to the Internet as we know it.

KEY TECHNOLOGIES

In physical terms, computers on the Internet are connected by a global lattice of network devices and telecom links collectively called the *infrastructure*. Although Internet infrastructure is an engineering field unto itself, the investor should understand three basic concepts:

1. **The infrastructure must grow with traffic volumes.** The demand for infrastructure products increases as the amount of traffic flowing over the Internet goes up. Given the Internet's phenomenal growth rates, the network equipment market looks to stay hot for years to come.
2. **The infrastructure's technology defines what the Internet can do.** The level of technology in the devices making up the infrastructure dictate what is possible over the Internet. The visionary plans for the multimedia over the Web will require substantial investment in new Internet equipment to work.
3. **Internet equipment is based on open standards.** Internet infrastructure products must be able to work with those manufactured by other companies.

You've probably heard the term *bandwidth* used in connection with Internet speed. Bandwidth is the measure of how much raw data can be moved over a network link. The type of cable a network link uses can give it more bandwidth in much the same way that having eight lanes along a stretch of Interstate will move traffic faster than four lanes.

Although a fiber-optic cable designed to move 2 billion bits of data per second is going to outperform a copper telephone line rated for 56,000 bits, the equipment connecting Internet links has just as big an effect as the media. In other words, a fiber-optic link won't do any good if the equipment at each end of the link is slow.

The manufacture and sale of infrastructure equipment has been the most profitable sector of the Internet economy so far, although some online businesses have also started to post impressive profits. With the Internet still in its infancy, demand for infrastructure-related gear has been growing rapidly. The Internet is tied together through several key hardware components.

Routers

The most important piece of Internet equipment is the *router*, the device that reads IP addresses in data packet headers to steer traffic to the correct destination. The router is the Internet's enabling technology.

You might think of the Internet as a global telephone system that handles data instead of sound waves. When you dial a phone, your call is switched between hard-wired circuits to find a path to the number you dialed. By contrast, when you send an Internet message, you turn your data packets over to a nearby router and leave it to that device to figure out how to get the packets to the destination. This is called "best effort" forwarding, which means that the routers handling your data packets will do the best they can to deliver your data packets under the current circumstances.

Although Web surfers generally use domain names like Allstarstocks .com to move around, network devices translate them into numerical addresses, such as 209.22.234.19. Routers use the numerical IP address—not the domain name—to locate the computer it represents. The development of the Internet Protocol system into a worldwide network made it possible for the first time for any computer user to communicate with virtually any other user.

Routers know the best routes to take at any given moment, because they exchange updates on the status of nearby network links every few minutes. Send a message to the same IP address five minutes later, and your data packets may take a different route based on changing traffic patterns, a link gone down, a new link brought up, or some other factor.

Physically, most routers look like VCRs, although the big ones resemble dormitory refrigerators or even full-sized ones. Like all network devices, routers are "black boxes" with no monitor, keyboard, or other peripherals. In fact, network devices don't even have disks for the simple reason that their sole mission is to move data to the "next hop" along the way, not to store it.

Switches

The data switch is closely related to the router in that both are used to move data between LANs. Switches are dumber than routers, but they work a lot faster. Unlike routers, switches don't read IP addresses and don't exchange information on the best routes to take between locations. They simply keep a running list of what was recently sent from point A to point B.

Relieved of the need to compute routes makes the switch lightning fast. But using them pays off only in situations where there is a high proportion of repeat traffic, such as within a corporate intranet or between end points along an Internet backbone link.

Demand for switches is booming. In fact, switching technology is now being integrated into routers to help speed things up by making it unnecessary to read IP addresses, except for data packets headed to new or faraway destinations.

Firewalls

A *firewall* is a kind of router that specializes in security. It works by forming an intentional bottleneck in the flow of traffic between an intranet and the Internet. As traffic flows through the firewall, each data packet is inspected to enforce security rules programmed by the company's Network Manager. The security rules focus on what source addresses may send packets into the intranet, the kind of traffic allowed, and so on. Inspecting traffic also slows it down, of course, so tighter security rules means slower Internet performance for corporate users.

Access Servers

The most prevalent Internet technology is the *access server,* a device that answers calls from users logging in by phone. Internet service providers use banks of access servers to connect home subscribers, and companies use them to connect telecommuters. The trend in access servers is to build more intelligence into them, especially to provide better front-end security, and to do a better job of routing calls between the telephone network and the intranet.

Network Media

Sometimes called "bandwidth" or "pipe," this is the technology that moves data through physical space. Although simple twisted-pair copper is used in most office LANs, the future is in *fiber optics*. Fiber-optic technology passes data as light waves over glass or plastic strands instead of as electrical pulses over metal. Nearly all Internet backbones are now fiber, and all office LAN backbones soon will be. Thousands of times faster than metal cable, the only thing holding fiber optics back are the electronic devices terminating the cables. Tens of billions of dollars are now being invested in improving the electronic devices used to operate fiber-optic networks.

Another network medium of note is *wireless technology*. Wireless LANs are already in use where workers must be mobile, such as in warehouses and hospitals. The major drawback to current wireless technology is that it is slower than home Internet dial-up modems. Billions of dollars are being invested in wireless technology for both mobile LANs and satellite-based wide area networks used to bypass telephone network distribution.

Customer Premises Equipment

The old adage that a chain is only as strong as its weakest link is also applicable to the Internet. On the Internet, a connection is only as fast as its slowest network link, almost always somewhere between the home or small business and the ISP. This is the so-called last mile of the Internet—the final stretch where speeds drop from millions or even billions of bits per second to mere thousands.

If you're connecting via telephone, this final stretch spans from a neighborhood "central office" to your home. Even today, most telephone circuits use old-fashioned copper wires, so the problem is trying to pack more speed over the same old copper. Phone companies are doing this by putting better switches into the central offices and then selling customers fancier devices to use between their PCs and the telephone outlet. These devices, referred to as *customer premise equipment,* can turn a normal phone line into a digital line by improving the equipment at each end.

Network Appliances

Network appliances is a catchall name used to describe any specialized piece of network hardware dedicated to performing a single function. It is the hottest area of innovation in the Internet infrastructure, with young companies coming up with new uses that reach beyond traditional Web applications. Examples include biometric devices that verify a user's fingerprint or retinal pattern before allowing log-in; so-called load-balancers, which shuffle traffic in and out of servers more efficiently; and credit card readers attached to home PCs.

Network Management Systems

Managing internetworks has always been a tough proposition. But as networks have gotten bigger and more complicated, most network management teams now scramble all the time. An entire industry has sprung up to create network hardware and software to design, operate, and manage internetworks. These products, used by large companies and ISPs, are becoming increasingly important. Users are demanding more reliability from the network services they use, and it's no longer possible to deliver quality service without using sophisticated network management tools.

MARKET POSITIONING

The Internet infrastructure market is dominated by a mix of big, integrated manufacturers with soup-to-nuts product lines and an army of niche players and start-ups. Whatever the vendor type, they all sell to infrastructure equipment end-user markets that can be broken into four groups:

1. **The "Enterprise" customer.** Fortune 500 companies and large government customers are starting to demand the same kind of integrated service from their network equipment makers as they get from IBM and Hewlett-Packard for their computing needs. Enterprise customers buy a wide range of services in addition to hardware, especially for network security and management.
2. **Tier 1 Internet service providers.** These are the "backbone providers" who operate ultra-high-speed fiber-optic links throughout metro areas, between cities, and even across oceans. These companies make heavy use of high-end switches, routers, and fiber-optic equipment. Tier 1 ISPs sell bandwidth to smaller ISPs and to corporations operating big intranets.
3. **Tier 2 Internet service providers.** These companies deal predominately with home or small business "retail" subscribers.
4. **The SOHO niche.** The small office/home office (SOHO) market niche has recently come into the industry's crosshairs. The SOHO market is booming because small companies and telecommuters need more than just a modem and an Internet account to compete in the Internet economy. Equipment manufacturers are expanding their product lines downward to fit the budgets of this burgeoning market.

Whatever the market niche, all products manufactured by infrastructure companies must comply with open technical standards, the most important being the Internet Protocol. For example, products made by Cisco Systems must be able to exchange IP packets with equipment manufactured by Juniper Networks, 3Com, Nortel, and everybody else. This is important because it becomes much tougher to gain the level of market dominance achieved by Microsoft and Intel with their "Wintel" duopoly.

ECONOMIC BUSINESS MODELS

The business models of network equipment manufacturers haven't inspired the controversy seen in most other Internet segments. Physical products are sold for cash on the barrelhead, usually followed by a steady stream of replacement parts and upgrades. The infrastructure model is more or less the same as that in the computer industry, where a commodity hardware distribution model is followed, with products primarily sold through distributors or value-added resellers (VARs).

Distributors help network equipment makers buffer their inventory levels with demand and keep their direct sales forces lean. VARs sell integration services along with the equipment sale, further enabling network equipment makers to minimize their field personnel.

PROSPECTS AND TRENDS

The infrastructure business will continue to track the growth of the Internet, primarily because the infrastructure *is* the Internet. The prospects for infrastructure equipment makers also should receive a boost from the fundamental changes in the Internet currently taking place. Not only are more people connecting, they're also starting to use the Web in different ways. Even if Internet growth stopped today, the infrastructure would still need to quadruple in power just to handle the new network applications coming online. And there is no shortage of technologies competing for the honor.

This makes the decision to invest in Internet infrastructure a simple one. The trick is picking which technology will flourish and which companies within that technology will lead the way.

Media convergence on the Net. If you have an Internet account, surf around for a while and take note of the kinds of traffic you're looking at. Virtually all of it is some combination of text, still photos, and drawings in the Web pages you're downloading. If you think about it, the Web hasn't changed much in its early years of existence. It is still mostly pages filled with text and static graphics.

That will change sooner than you might expect. Other media are beginning to converge on the Internet in order to exploit its reach and power. Videoconferencing, television, radio, and other media have already taken a foothold on the Web, and they'll need far more bandwidth than the Internet infrastructure currently offers. Multimedia convergence has huge implications, not only for Internet infrastructure equipment makers, but for all telecommunications companies.

The battle for the last mile. The technology used to connect homes and small businesses must be upgraded, and everybody knows it. The only debate is over whether the connection should go to the neighborhood telephone central office, the local cable TV office, or uplink to a satellite sitting in stationary orbit. With such a huge potential payoff, hundreds of billions of dollars are being wagered to win the last mile, and media convergence is the reason why.

IP telephony. In much the same way network equipment makers ambushed the world with their routers 15 years ago, "Internet telephones" are now being quietly rolled out. That's right, the Internet wants to swallow up all media, even the telephone business! You can make a call over the Internet now, but service is limited and quality is poor. However, that will change dramatically in the near future. IP telephony is the next big "killer app" for the Internet.

Virtual Private Networks. Big companies and governmental agencies have traditionally used private lines leased from phone companies to run their wide area networks (WANs). But under the latest technology, a company can now set up a Virtual Private Network (VPN) that does the same job but at a third of the cost. By 2003, nearly two-thirds of all corporate WANs are expected to be run over VPNs, another boom Internet market.

Quality of Service (QoS). Leaving traffic management decisions up to routers has been the bedrock of Internet architecture to date. This "best effort" philosophy is widely recognized as the reason the Internet has been able to sustain its stupendous growth without falling apart. But best effort is no longer good enough to accommodate media convergence. For example, inadequacies in today's Internet service results in video image jerking and phone conversations with people talking over one another. Not surprisingly, those technological short-comings are limiting demand for these services.

The wave of the future is Quality of Service routing, or QoS, which will dramatically improve the speed and quality of Internet traffic routing. This is an emerging technology that lets the routers and switches involved in a connection guarantee minimum quality levels. For example, QoS would line up the necessary service resources before starting a videoconference or placing an Internet phone call. QoS is an "enabling technology" of critical importance to media convergence.

ISPs and Portals

As you enter the Web, the first stop is your Internet service provider, or *ISP*. Put simply, an ISP connects users to the Internet. ISPs handle modem phone calls from home users and "always-on" dedicated connections from businesses.

The second stop is a *portal*, which downloads the first page in your Web browser after a connection to the Internet is established. Portals are more than just an initial stop; it is a complete Web environment offering surfers everything from free e-mail to search engines, chat rooms, messaging, news, weather, and other free services to lure Internet surfers into using its site as their "home on the Web."

To put the pieces into place, think of the Internet this way: the infrastructure provides the roads and bridges over which all traffic travels. ISPs own and operate most of the public part of the Internet infrastructure (big corporations and governments operate subject internetworks too, but much of that is private). ISPs serve as the feeder streets and on-ramps that funnel traffic, and the biggest ISPs operate high-speed highways between cities called Internet "backbone" links. Finally, portals provide the road signs, directions, rest stops, and recreation areas along the way.

But while both ISPs and portals play a key role in the make-up of the Internet, don't let their complementary roles fool you—they are very different in their technology and business models.

KEY TECHNOLOGIES

ISPs are basically network operators. An ISP operates "points of presence" by placing equipment in metropolitan areas they serve. By contrast, portals operate big Web sites—not networks. In fact, portals *are* ISP customers, buying bandwidth from them to speed traffic to their Web sites.

ISP Technology

In addition to networking equipment, ISPs use various kinds of digital telecom link technologies, both for making local Internet connections with subscribers and for moving data over high-speed backbone links. All equipment used by ISPs must be compatible with the Internet Protocol (IP).

Network equipment. ISPs make heavy use of three kinds of network devices: access servers, routers, and data switches. Access servers answer modem phone calls from home and small business subscribers. Once a dial-up connection is made, the surfer's IP data packets pass out the back side of the access server and enter a router, which charts a path to the destination and forwards the packets on their way. Most bigger companies have routers at their sites, which maintain a permanent connection with the ISP's router to form an always-on connection.

Routers and switches move traffic beyond the data closet. Routers are placed where destinations are less likely to be known, because they have the intelligence to figure out fast routes to unknown IP addresses. Switches, which are faster but have cruder pathfinding capability, tend to be used to send traffic over backbone links.

Because they move most Internet traffic, ISPs have emerged as major telecom players. This has happened at both ends: ISPs operate access networks in cities where they maintain a point-of-presence end, and they run long-haul backbone links between cities they serve.

"Last mile" telecom technologies. A chain is only as strong as its weakest link, and the Internet can only be as fast as the infrastructure serving the user. The bottleneck holding back Internet performance is the "last mile" separating the ISP from its home and business subscribers.

Most subscribers still dial into the Internet via a plain old telephone line, a pair of copper wires from the phone set all the way to a "central office" operated by the telephone company in the neighborhood.

Until recently, most central offices had only telephone switches designed to handle voice. Because they can't recognize data, phone switches simply forward modem analog signals to the ISP's data closet, where the transmission is converted into a higher speed digital format.

But data switches are now being placed in neighborhood central phone offices. They can be used to set up digital links from a home or business to the Internet. The most popular data switch technology is called Digital Subscriber Line (DSL). A DSL switch at the central phone office and a DSL "modem" on your home PC changes a plain old copper telephone line into a digital circuit capable of moving data dozens of times faster. The DSL equipment at both ends finesses a lot more speed out of the copper circuit.

Phone companies are deploying DSL equipment into their central offices as fast as possible. And so are ISPs, which, thanks to the telecom deregulation, are able to "co-locate" DSL switches in locked cages in central offices operated by regulated regional Bell operating companies.

Another contender for Internet traffic over the last mile is the cable modem, which bypasses the phone network altogether. Cable television companies are now putting special data switches into their offices and encouraging subscribers to put cable modems on their PCs. The equipment at both ends transforms the cable TV system from a one-way video network into a two-way Internet Protocol network.

Internet-enabled cable TV systems have the potential to run even faster than DSL circuits, because the cable plant they use is a lot thicker than the thin copper wire pairs phone circuits use. However, DSL proponents argue that the ultimate speed cable modems will attain is unknown, because cable TV systems must also handle television signals and were never meant to serve as an interactive medium.

The newest contender for the last mile is a wireless technology called Microwave Multipoint Distribution System (MMDS). Originally developed to move cable TV signals around the country, MMDS was recently certified by the Federal Communications Commission (FCC) for two-way traffic, opening the way to use it as a communications platform for Internet access. MMDS was a key motive behind MCI WorldCom's $115 billion buyout of Sprint, which had been busily snapping up local MMDS licenses from the FCC.

Backbone technologies. Most Internet backbones now run over fiber-optic cable plant, as does nearly all long distance voice traffic. Indeed, any real difference between voice and data barely exists in network backbones now, with big fiber network operators reporting in 1999 that data had finally surpassed voice as the majority of traffic.

Advances in backbone technologies have been coming at a breakneck pace. Only a few years ago, the original fiber links ran at 155 million bits per second, or Mbps. The current state of the art is 2.5 Gbps—for *billions* of bits per second. Links of 40 Gbps have just started to go online, and optical technology approaching 100 Gbps will begin appearing as early as 2003. This leapfrogging will result in a nearly thousandfold increase in backbone speeds in a decade.

The next big improvement in backbones will have to do with flexibility, not speed. A new technology called *intelligent optical networking* will soon make it possible for Internet backbone operators to offer bandwidth on demand. Right now, it takes weeks or months for a technician to go into the field and configure new customer circuits into the fiber-optic hardware. Intelligent optics will make it possible to do the same tasks "in software" from a computer console in minutes.

Portal Technologies

Portals are low-tech operations compared to ISPs. In physical terms, they are basically large, sophisticated Web sites. They have powerful computers called "servers" dedicated to handling requests from visitors and "disk farms" to store information to download.

Portals add value to the Internet with their software and data. Initially, most Web portals were search engines used to find other Web sites, but now that's just a small part of what they offer. Nowadays, portals provide free services for just about anything a surfer might need: e-mail, shopping, news, and stock market information.

ISP MARKET POSITIONING

The ISP marketplace is segmented into two levels: big companies that operate fiber-optic backbone links between cities or even undersea links between continents, and at the retail end of the market, ISPs that sell to subscribers, operate their Internet connections, and provide customer service.

Today, there are thousands of ISPs, but that's changing. Years of mergers, acquisitions, and internal network expansion have ushered in a new class of national ISP that has the marketing clout and economy of scale to squeeze out the little guys. There are three basic kinds of ISPs:

1. **Retail ISPs.** These companies run integrated operations with local access networks and national backbone links of their own. Their access networks must be in enough metropolitan areas to cover many households. The biggest ISP of all, America Online, with more than 20 million subscribers, fits this description. So does number two, EarthLink Networks, with over 3 million subscribers.

2. **Business ISPs.** Business ISPs focus on corporate and government customers and also operate substantial access networks, but to cover businesses instead of households. The two best-known business ISPs are PSINet and Verio. They distinguish themselves with reliability, secure networking, and added services such as Web site hosting. Business ISPs also sell bandwidth to smaller retail ISPs.

3. **Internet backbone providers.** A little-known type of ISP is the Internet backbone provider. These companies primarily sell bandwidth to big corporations and other ISPs. A good example of this

is Global Crossing, which operates a web of high-speed links beneath oceans and across continents. Most other Internet backbone providers are still thought of as telecom companies, because most of their traffic is still voice. These include MCI WorldCom, AT&T, and others.

The lines separating these three types is blurring fast. It's relatively easy to set up Web hosting computers in their data centers, so AOL and EarthLink have begun aggressively pursuing business customers, which account for about 60 percent of all ISP revenues.

PORTAL MARKETING

Portals fight for market positioning mostly by relentless promotion. Only Yahoo! and one or two other established players got into the game early enough to simply grow along with the Internet boom. Portals measure their market share in the form of visits, especially by unique individuals. The way the game is played now, growth in portal traffic can come by either horizontal or vertical marketing:

- **Horizontal marketing.** Big players like Excite, Lycos, and Yahoo! go after the mainstream marketplace with pervasive name recognition and portal services anybody can use.
- **Vertical niche marketing.** Latecomers are targeting niches with services and data specific either to demographic populations or to entire economic sectors. Good examples of this are Healtheon/WebMD's focus on health care and LookSmart's targeting of women.

There are endless variations on these two themes, of course. For example, Lycos is building a horizontal empire by acquiring such content providers as Angelfire, Tripod, and Wired Digital. CMGI is using the same strategy, having taken control of AltaVista and several other Web properties. Both companies hope to attain a critical mass where a good portion of surfers spend much of their online time moving between the company-owned Web sites.

Portals are more vulnerable to competition than ISPs. Although ballooning marketing costs have made it very expensive for upstart portals such as Go Network to seize market share, users can be fickle. The best analogy is that portals are like radio or TV stations.

The good news in the comparison is that portals serve worldwide markets instead of just a region; the bad news is that there can be as many new portals as there are venture capitalists writing checks for start-ups. Unlike radio and TV, however, no artificial limit is put on the number of portals in the form of FCC licenses.

ECONOMIC BUSINESS MODELS

The business models used by portals and ISPs differ sharply. Portals are basically media properties operating in an unregulated environment. ISPs are also unregulated, but they own and operate chunks of physical infrastructure.

ISP Business Models

The source of revenue varies according to type of ISP, and in some cases even the company.

Retail ISPs rely on subscriptions as their primary revenue stream. The current standard is to charge between $15 and $20 per month for unlimited access. Most retail ISPs also operate Web portals of their own from which they garner banner ad revenue. The best-known example of this is America Online, but it's the exception.

Business ISPs also sell subscriptions, but pricing varies according to the speed of the connection and how many employees the customer has. Business ISPs also get revenue from services they offer in addition to Internet connectivity. Web site hosting, for example, costs a business between $100 per month and thousands of dollars, depending on the amount of data and visitor traffic. Business ISPs also have gone into the business of operating Virtual Private Networks (VPNs), which are basically private networks over the Internet.

Internet backbone providers write complicated contracts that charge corporate or ISP customers a monthly minimum in exchange for certain performance guarantees, and then assess incremental fees thereafter based on the amount and type of data traffic.

Because of the time and expense involved in building a network, ISPs are by nature more vulnerable to acquisition than to destruction. It's easier for bigger ISPs to simply buy a smaller competitor's network infrastructure and subscriber base than to compete for it.

Portal Business Models

Portals are media properties because they rely on advertising as their primary source of revenue. Specifically, portals collect money according to the number of visitor "hits" on a page containing an advertiser's banner ad.

A *banner* is a graphical object on a Web page that can move and even respond to users. A *targeted banner ad* is one that selectively appears according to the reason for a person's visit to a site. For example, it's possible to make a car banner ad appear on a page downloaded from a search for online auto want ads. When clicked, most banners take the user to the Web site of the advertiser paying for the ad.

Portals charge only a tiny fraction of a penny for simply displaying a banner ad. If the ad is clicked, the advertiser pays the portal a few cents, higher if the Web surfer has desirable consumer demographics or actually buys something at the advertiser's site.

Obviously, portals need huge traffic volumes to make money at such rates. The good news here is that, portal operating expenses are low. The bad news is that 60 percent or more of a portal's budget is spent on marketing, mostly in the form of mass advertising.

The combination of high expenses and razor-thin margins has goaded Web portals to cash in on their traffic by also operating e-stores at their sites. To date, most portal e-stores are "virtual" operations, with another company actually holding product inventory and fulfilling orders.

PROSPECTS AND TRENDS

Traffic and technology are conspiring to wreak big changes in how ISP and portal businesses operate. While companies in both categories stand to gain with each new Internet user, both Internet sectors are likely to be transformed in the near future.

ISP consolidation continues. The last few years have seen thousands of mergers and acquisitions in the American ISP industry alone. The economy of scale lends itself to providing Internet connectivity, a capital-intensive business because of the high cost of installing and operating network infrastructure and supporting customers. The cost per customer acquisition is also going up, making the value of a national brand an increasingly important asset.

Residual price points for basic ISP access. Dial-up service for home users will continue to plummet. Some companies have already flirted with offering free service, although it's hard to see how that can be made to work economically. Unlimited monthly access for under $10 will become commonplace, creating more pressure for smaller Tier 2 ISPs to either sell out or outsource local infrastructure from Tier 1 vendors and concentrate on marketing and support.

There is no free lunch, at least not a good one. Free ISPs such as Net-Zero will have trouble making it. It's hard to balance the unavoidable costs of network operations and marketing with income from banner ads. Free Internet service is slower, lower in quality, and rife with catches. Consumers want broadband speed and reliability more than saving a lousy $15 a month. That consumer demographics by definition is worse for free ISPs will make things even tougher for them.

The coming backbone bandwidth glut. Thousands of miles of ultra-high-speed optical technology is now being installed in North America and Europe. Much of this new fiber cable will remain "unlit" until demand increases to the point where the expense of gearing it up can be justified, and that will be delayed by the choke hold of slow last mile technology, for the time being at least. There's an old rule that applications will always change in a way that soaks up newly available speed, but this time it looks as if it'll be backbone billing rates that take the soaking.

On-demand bandwidth. "Intelligent optical" technology will make it possible for ISPs and corporate backbone users to purchase bandwidth almost on the fly. It will soon be possible to dynamically configure, test, and deliver backbone services on a spot market basis. This will reduce financial risk to Web site operators and will help make multimedia Internet applications such as IP telephony possible.

Telephony and the Internet finally converge. The process is already well underway where big Internet backbone networks are integrating with long distance telephone networks. Given that voice and Internet data traffic are now about equal in volume, convergence will have tremendous effects on economies and competition. It will finally become possible to weave interactive talk into applications running on computer screens to enhance online meetings, business negotiations, remote training, and myriad other uses.

Media crossover will continue. Traditional media companies—publishers, motion picture studios, TV networks, record companies—will continue to invest heavily in Internet properties. Remember, so far the Web has mostly been used to publish text. But the MP3 Internet music format had immediate and far-reaching impact on the music business, and media moguls in movies and television are bracing to take their hit next. It's only a matter of time and bandwidth.

Fear and loathing over audience metrics. Media properties need a fairly reliable method for audience measurement to work well. The long-standing yardstick is that if Madison Avenue thinks it's good enough, then it's good enough. But does anybody really know who's going where in a medium with 80 million Web sites, and whether a visitor is viewing an entire page or instantly "clicking out" before the banner has even appeared? A big part of the Internet economy is waiting for the other shoe to drop on the "metrics" issue.

Smarter online advertising technology. Web surfers hate banner ads because they slow things down. A new generation of online ad technology is emerging that is both polite and intelligent. These new ads quietly announce themselves and invite the viewer to activate them for a truly interactive advertising experience. The theory is that the advertiser makes a better impression even if the polite ad isn't clicked.

Cable television changes the ISP industry. Although DSL and wireless are coming on strong, cable modem technology is so fast that it will secure a big chunk of the last-mile market. A new breed of ISP will emerge that is able to weave together home entertainment, Internet surfing, and even phone service into a single package. America Online had this in mind when it merged with Time Warner and picked up Time Warner Cable in the deal. The attractions of "cable Internet" are so compelling that GTE is making a federal case out of it with a lawsuit, arguing that cable operators should grant all ISPs use of their networks.

 # Software

A fast-growing, multi-billion-dollar industry, the Internet software market is made up of a dizzying array of technologies, product categories, and vendors. It represents a vital second layer of the Internet infrastructure that facilitates the open exchange of information among hundreds of millions of home PCs, office networks, Internet service providers (ISPs), and Web servers.

There are three broad categories of Internet software:

1. **Web site software.** Used to build and operate e-stores, portals, and other kinds of Internet sites.
2. **Internet distribution software.** Helps connect users with sites with tools to search the Web, "push" information out to interested users, cache data at strategic locations to speed downloads, and perform other connection tasks.
3. **Surfer software.** Includes e-mail, instant messaging, file transfer, and other standard Web surfing applications.

The Internet is divided into two parts: The general Internet handles such applications as streaming video, chat, e-mail, and file transfer. The World Wide Web, which is a subset of the Internet (the part visible through a browser), is where most users spend their time. The Web browser is the dominant application of the Internet. There are software applications for every category of Internet use.

KEY TECHNOLOGIES

When you click a button in your Web browser, your computer "uploads" a small number of Internet Protocol (IP) data packets to a Web server somewhere. That server, usually a large computer sitting in a distant computer room, fields your request and "downloads" hundreds or thousands of IP packets containing the Web page you requested.

A Web page is downloaded in pieces that are assembled by your browser. You might be surprised to know that these pieces usually come from different sources. For example, if you visited the financial portal OnMoney.com and asked for a stock chart, its server would download most of the page, BigCharts.com would send the financial charts from its server in Minnesota, and New York Internet ad agency DoubleClick.com would choose banner ads that fit your interests or the site profile and insert them into your page as it loads.

Protocols

Much of the software technology used to run the Internet is built on *protocols,* which are standard formats for moving data between two devices. There are dozens of protocols at work in the Internet, each filling a specific role.

Lower-level software protocols are part of the infrastructure. These include IP to handle packets, the Transmission Control Protocol to manage user connections, and many more. But it's the higher-level "application" protocols that allow people to use the Internet. Let's quickly review the most important ones:

- **HyperText Transfer Protocol (HTTP).** This protocol makes the World Wide Web possible by telling servers and browsers how to exchange and display data.
- **File Transfer Protocol (FTP).** When you download a software product for trial use, for example, the server sending it and your PC behave according to FTP standards.
- **Simple Mail Transfer Protocol (SMTP).** This sets the format and rules for exchanging e-mail.
- **HyperText Markup Language (HTML).** HTML is a programming tool used to define the structure and layout of Web pages.
- **eXtensible Markup Language (XML).** This tool complements HTML by letting programmers "mark up" Web pages with tags to describe their contents and make information easy to find and compare.

Dozens of other protocols exist to use the Internet for such purposes as instant messaging, music, and video. All Internet software products are based on at least one protocol, usually more.

"Run-Time" Platforms

Although protocols make the free exchange of information possible, additional technologies are needed to make the Internet more powerful, especially the Web. Platforms are used for *run time,* the term for Internet applications in operation.

Java. Both a programming language and a "platform" that will execute a program on a computer, Java code is compatible with virtually any kind of computer. Conceived by Sun Microsystems in the early 1990s, Java can make Web pages as interactive as a Windows programs on your PC, which is a necessity for most e-commerce applications. Java is now an open technology standard, with products offered by Microsoft, IBM, and many others in addition to Sun.

Application Server Platforms (ASP). Once an e-commerce program is ready, it must be hooked up with the internal computer systems of the company running it. Corporate systems for credit approval, sales order entry, and inventory aren't Internet-compatible. The easiest way to hook them up is to use an "application server" computer to translate between Web site visitors and these back-end systems. Instead of "hard wiring" internal applications and databases to the various Internet Protocols, which takes a great deal of custom programming, everything is handed off to an ASP platform product to map from one side to the other.

Customer Relationship Management platforms (CRM). The inter-activity of Web software makes it possible to automate aspects of a company's interaction with customers. Over the past few years, technology has emerged to "personalize" what a Web site visitor sees according to a personal profile in order to maximize sales. CRM packages also have been developed to help provide customer assistance and deliver other services.

MARKET POSITIONING

The Internet is by definition a cooperative system. Software companies must comply with open technical standards or their products won't be able to communicate over the Internet. That's why the role of standards is so important on the Internet, because they define most Internet software market niches.

The Internet's inherent openness makes it very difficult to establish a proprietary standard in the market. So if you're looking for the next great *de facto* standard like Microsoft Windows, forget it. Internet products must be designed to fit published specifications that any competitor can obtain.

Internet software companies must compete for market share by other means of differentiation. The most common strategy is to stake out a functional niche and concentrate on being best at that. Another is to make a product comply with a standard's requirements but to "extend" it by adding custom capabilities that are proprietary.

Web Site Software Positioning

There are two kinds of Web site software: packages and development tools. Both are used to create the Web server applications that download content to site visitors, capture information input by them, and execute e-commerce transactions.

The line is blurred between the two product types, because both come with prefabricated screens, logic modules, reports, and other features. Both also come with integrated development environments with tools for programming in various languages (HTML, XML, and Java) to create, test, and operate Web site programs. The differences are a matter of degree.

Web site packages from such companies as BroadVision and Open Market come nearly complete, requiring only that they be "built out" to fit the particular customer's needs. The customization is generally done by a team of programmers who work on the Web site's screens and content and hook up internal systems that are not Internet compatible. Because they're sophisticated and expensive, Web site packages are used primarily by large corporations and well-heeled pure Internet companies.

Web development tools are used by companies that decide to take the "roll your own" site development strategy. These are low-end products that are usually licensed per programmer, or according to the volume of site visitors to be handled. The best-known development tools are from Macromedia and Allaire, whose products are used by hundreds of thousands of small businesses and by programming staffs in large corporate computer departments.

Microsoft also sells a variety of development tools, including its Visual InterDev programmer toolkit and the consumer-oriented HTML tool Front Page.

Internet Distribution Software Positioning

There are separate Internet applications for distributing content in and out of Web sites. These products also are sold to Web site operators, but fulfill such narrow functions as Internet searching, managing links directories, data caching, and "pushing" data out to users who have subscribed to selected subject interest groups.

The best-known Internet distribution software makers are Inktomi and Akamai. Inktomi's search engine is used by hundreds of major Web sites. Akamai is well known for its streaming media products used for broadcasting audio and video over the Internet.

Internet Surfer Software Positioning

There are hundreds of Internet software companies that make surfer software products. Consumers use these packages for everyday tasks ranging from sending e-mail to finding great shopping deals with "software agents" that constantly check e-stores throughout the Web.

Companies selling this type of Internet software tend to be minor players, partly because so many of them have been acquired by bigger operations. The software giants also make the surfer software business tough. The biggest surfer product of all—Web browsers—are distributed free by Microsoft and AOL/Netscape Communications. The same is true for instant messaging software, the latest Internet craze.

ECONOMIC BUSINESS MODELS

Most Internet software companies use business models that are traditional to their respective niche.

Because high-end packages are capable of handling very high traffic volumes and big database sizes, they cost hundreds of thousands of dollars. Like non-Internet software companies, Web site package vendors charge 15 to 20 percent of the packages list price in fees for annual maintenance.

Most Web site development products are licensed at between $500 and $2,000 per programmer desktop. The price of their run-time platforms usually depends on the number of site visitors or the amount of Web site data to be stored.

Vendors of Internet distribution software have more options. They, too, license their products but sometimes also loan them to Web sites in exchange for a portion of the revenues generated using them. For example, Inktomi gets a cut of referral fees a Web site collects from e-stores for referrals made using a loaned copy of the Inktomi Shopping Engine.

Most Internet surfer software makers use the "shareware" business model. *Shareware* is a business strategy where a free version of a product can be downloaded for trial use. The goal is to lure the free user into becoming a paying customer in order to obtain a newer or more complete version of the package that's not free. The trouble is, most surfers stick with the freebie, which is why many surfer software companies also rely on banner ad revenues to survive.

PROSPECTS AND TRENDS

The Internet software industry will only get bigger. It won't just grow along with the exploding population of Web sites and surfers, it also will expand by taking on more functional tasks as the Internet permeates things around us.

Web software lines will blur. The demarcation between the Internet and internal computer systems is still fairly clear, but it won't be for long. In the not too distant future, all software will be Internet compatible. This opens the door for the most successful Internet software vendors to encroach on in-house turf now held by traditional software companies.

Internet development software goes commodity. In a related trend, products now used to construct Web sites will be licensed in even greater numbers as corporate computer departments transition client-server applications to internal "intranet" Web sites. Prices will drop as one or two big Internet tools companies take on Microsoft "on the inside."

Internet distribution software gets even more sophisticated. Software made to find and move content around the Internet will take on even greater responsibility as Web sites look for ways to further refine information delivery. The new software will ensure that employees, customers, and even computers receive information on specific subjects quickly and easily.

A more powerful breed of surfer software emerges. The Internet will soon be propelled into its second phase. Broadband capacity bandwidth will set loose a torrent of new software applications filled with content in various media, such as audio, video, and telephony. Corporate software makers have already geared up for this, but individual Internet surfers will need "viewers" and other tools in order to use the advanced options.

Internet Business Services

Most Web businesses get by with a lot of help from their friends. Using outside vendors to handle the increasingly technical tasks of building and maintaining an e-commerce site allows companies to concentrate on the parts of their business that they do best.

The list of contract services in the Internet economy is a long one, but they can be broken down into three basic groups:

1. **Internet consulting firms.** These companies design and install Web sites, connect them to internal databases, set up security, and sometimes consult on Web marketing and public relations.
2. **Web hosting services.** Most Internet companies don't even run their own computer systems; they farm them out to Web hosting services. Big customers locate their own servers inside locked steel cages in the host's computer room; smaller customers rent space on servers the hosting service owns.
3. **Internet business services.** Specialty companies provide various services that help customers run their e-businesses. Whether it's placing banner ads, tracking visitor demographics, or some other repetitive task, there's a service company on the Web ready to help—for a fee, of course.

The services sector is booming right along with the Internet itself. Market researcher Dataquest estimates that Internet business services accounted for about $10 billion in sales in 1999 and will grow to nearly $60 billion by 2003. That's a lot of opportunity.

KEY TECHNOLOGIES

Generally speaking, Internet services aren't necessarily technology-oriented. Most service companies don't make the hardware and software that power the Web, they just use it to solve customer problems.

Internet Consulting and Technology

A consulting firm's principal technology asset is the expertise of its people. Strategically, a consulting company must stay abreast of technologies that are popular with clients. Otherwise, not only will it lose business, it also will eventually lose consultants to competitors. Internet consulting firms must balance between their current skills and the need to stay on the cutting edge. They are constantly reviewing emerging technologies and training personnel to keep pace with technological advances.

Web Hosting and Technology

Web hosting companies aren't technology companies either. They're technology-intensive, though. These companies configure and operate data centers and networks outfitted with the latest tools for system management, performance tuning, and security. Large hosts run multiple data centers strategically located throughout the world and connected by dedicated high-speed links. For example, Exodus Communications runs 16 world class computer centers that host Yahoo!, eBay, and other major Web sites. By outsourcing to a hosting company like Exodus, Web companies can stay out of the computer operations business, a demanding field best left to the experts. Web hosting services also must stay abreast of technology. Their focus is on understanding server hardware, operating systems, databases, and system management tools. Although hosting services don't create any of this technology, they do master it.

Internet Business Services and Technology

Unlike consultants and Web hosts, many providers of Internet business services develop their own technology to do business. In fact, using proprietary technology as a competitive weapon is commonplace in this niche. The best example of this is the Internet advertising business. Internet ad firms such as DoubleClick and 24/7 differ starkly from their real world counterparts, mostly because of how the Web works. When you download a page, the banner ads on it are downloaded from an "ad server" system that decides which ad to run based on your personal profile. This is sophisticated software that each Internet advertising company creates and operates on its own. Another example of Internet business service technology is identity verification. A company called VeriSign issues and manages "digital certificates" that individuals use as electronic ID cards on the Internet. The company created high-tech technology that makes its certificates tamperproof. Microsoft and Netscape embed VeriSign's technology into their Web browsers.

MARKET POSITIONING

Because each is a distinct industry unto itself, market mechanics differ significantly among Internet consulting, hosting, and servicing. To understand how each market works, it's best to review them separately.

Internet Consulting Firms

There are tens of thousands of Internet consulting firms. Most are tiny shops that do work for small and medium-sized clients within a metropolitan area. Then there are a dozen or so national Internet consulting firms. These are young companies—Scient, Razorfish, and Cysive among them —that only undertake high-profile Internet projects. Most Internet consulting firms carve themselves into several distinct "practices" that specialize in customizing and installing a particular product. For example, many firms have a "BroadVision practice" with a team that works year-round with BroadVision's e-commerce software package. Traditional firms such as Andersen Consulting and EDS also work on Internet projects and have Internet practices. But the bulk of their projects still have to do with internal systems.

Web Hosting Services

Web hosting companies come in three basic types. There are a few big standalone outfits like Exodus whose only business is running highly efficient and secure data centers. These top-tier hosting companies run almost all the well-known Web sites. Most Internet service providers (ISPs) offer Web site hosting of some type. Big ISPs like PSINet and Verio run Web sites for thousands of medium-sized businesses. Traditional technology companies also are eyeing the hosting market to help lock in customers and tap into its growth potential. Forrester Research, the market research firm, projects that the hosting market will grow from $2 billion in 1999 to nearly $15 billion by 2003. That's why two traditional technology powerhouses, Intel and MCI WorldCom, each recently announced its intent to enter the Web hosting fray.

Internet Business Services

Providers of Internet business services do all the things Internet sites can't do themselves. They steer traffic between sites, execute e-mail marketing campaigns, track visitors, and perform dozens of other mundane, repetitive tasks. Internet service markets are aligned by niche. The biggest service niche is Internet advertising, where a half dozen or so companies have built "advertising networks" that automatically help clients buy and sell ad space—not surprising, given that Web site traffic is all-important in the Internet economy. There are plenty of other service niches: Network Solutions registers Internet domain names, Media Metrix measures Internet traffic and site visitor demographics, VeriSign hands out digital certificates, and so on. Being a "first mover" is especially critical in the Internet business services sector because setting up far-flung service networks becomes more difficult each day. On top of that, the growing number of participating customers enhances the service itself. For example, 24/7's giant advertising network makes it an attractive place to try to peddle Web site ad space.

ECONOMIC BUSINESS MODELS

Internet services companies have something we all like: recurring revenue. Companies in this sector operate on a fee-for-service basis, but sharply different business models are used, depending on the type of Internet service.

Internet Consulting Firms

Most Internet consulting companies charge clients by the hour. They calculate the hourly equivalent of a consultant's salary, add a gross profit margin of 100 percent or so, and invoice customers with weekly time sheets. Rates vary based on the consultant expertise level and the length of the engagement. A two-week engagement requiring a hot competency like Java programming could command upwards of $250 per hour, half that for a long engagement. There are basically two types of Internet consultants: Web designers who piece together Web pages using HTML coding or some other easy-to-learn Web tool and true programmers who write complicated software using Java or other powerful programming languages. Consulting is a hand-to-mouth business. Firms must pay consultants every other week but often must wait three months to collect from clients. This leaves many firms strapped for cash and can hinder expansion even in a favorable market. The biggest constraint on growth is recruiting and retaining consultants. A consultancy can grow only as fast as it can hire, and the computer programming market is one of the tightest labor markets ever. It can cost $20,000 or more in expenses to hire a consultant, and hiring competition has forced firms to set aside as much as 10 percent of revenues for employee retention programs such as personal training budgets. Consulting firms must use a traditional high-cost selling model, with offices in major cities housing sales teams that prospect for customers and bid on projects. The goal in Internet consulting is to capture long-term projects in accounts big enough to cross-sell follow-on projects. A recent trend in Internet consulting has been towards fixed bid contracts, which provide an opportunity for savvy consulting firms to fatten margins. It also introduces the risk of project losses that didn't exist under traditional time-and-materials billing arrangements.

Web Hosting Services

There are two types of customers who outsource to hosting services: big customers that own their servers and those that share space with other service customers on a server owned by the service. Depending on the level of service, a shared server Web site costs several hundred to several thousand dollars per month. Dedicated service can cost as much as several hundred thousand dollars per month—especially for companies that want their Web sites hosted in multiple facilities to speed response time experienced by visitors. Hosting companies must invest heavily to compete. The major host companies are constantly under construction, building new data centers as fast as possible to keep up with soaring demand. The data centers themselves are expensive and equipped with such features as earthquake countermeasures, redundant power systems, and security that would make a military man blush with envy. The absence of any significant labor constraint has let Web hosts expand rapidly. Companies like Exodus, Verio, and PSINet are building heavy-duty data centers that will be needed to handle the increased traffic that broadband Internet services will generate over the next few years.

Internet Business Services

The Internet business services arena largely operates on a "per click" basis. In other words, customers are charged pennies for each task performed, but there are millions of them to do. Internet business services are largely automated processes that take place between two computers with little or no human involvement. This lets service companies grow rapidly. After investing years and millions of dollars to develop a proprietary service technology, a service company need only add computer capacity and operations staff to expand. Most Internet business service companies use a low-cost Web sales model, where demand is driven through both online and real world advertising, and customers are acquired and serviced largely through the Internet, instead of through regional offices.

PROSPECTS AND TRENDS

Economics and market maturity will drive change in the Internet business services sector. The need for marketing clout and operational economies will cause the steady stream of mergers and acquisitions to continue unabated. Also, companies are becoming more savvy about using the Internet and will push vendors to improve service levels.

Beware the "dot-com consultants." A number of traditional companies have "dot-commed" their images in the hopes of jacking up their stock prices. Software consulting firms are among the leading culprits. But Wall Street is pretty good at distinguishing between the real e-companies and the impostors. The bottom line is, consulting firms steeped in traditional computer technologies aren't necessarily positioned to grow along with the Internet.

Many consulting firms lose their way. Those who paid top dollar for shares of an Internet consulting firm may be in for a letdown. Stratospheric market caps can pay off only if steady long-term growth is attained. But it's hard for small consulting firms to grow large. EDS and Computer Sciences had the advantage of large government contracts, and the Big Five all started as multinational accounting firms. In the long run, firms will need to do more than just recruit employees. They will need to develop their own project control technologies to boost quality and cut costs. Firms that grow through acquisitions will need proprietary project technology, because a consulting firm's sense of identity tends to be diluted with each acquisition.

Watch for hosting business burnout. It's a corporate tradition for the big dogs to wander into somebody else's yard when attracted by the promise of fat profit margins. The Web hosting business seems simple enough: build state-of-the-art computer rooms, fill them with the best technology, and hire a competent staff. But a glut of Web hosting capacity is possible in a few years. However, the best pure Web hosting companies will flourish, and the others will move on to something else.

A few dominant customer networks emerge. The barriers to market entry will soon become formidable in certain niches. DoubleClick and 24/7 are building huge customer rosters that attract still more customers wishing to join their ad exchanges. The more the merrier, unless you're caught on the outside looking in. The ultimate goal is for an Internet service to become so ubiquitous that Internet users come to regard it almost as a public utility. For example, VeriSign is trying hard to make its digital certificates the driver's license of the Web, where customers go to them without questioning why.

The surfers fight back. Advances in technology always seem to outpace the ability to deal with their consequences. Web ad networks have already come under fire for snooping on Web surfers, and new technologies are emerging that block banner ads from downloading with Web page content. As popular as that might be with Web surfers, it is a technology that threatens the very underpinnings of the Internet economy. The Web marketing industry will be forced to develop more surfer-friendly advertising techniques to continue to flourish. Otherwise, "blocker" technologies and even politicians may make things difficult.

 # E-commerce

Electronic commerce between businesses is the bedrock of the Internet economy. It dwarfs e-tailing in size, accounting for about 80 percent of all electronic business with sales of about $500 billion a year in the United States alone.

Companies are flocking to business-to-business e-commerce—usually called *B2B* or *e-procurement*—because trading online saves time and money and eliminates paperwork. The benefits of B2B are so great that it's not a question of whether most companies will do their buying over the Internet, but *when.*

How fast is B2B growing? It accounted for only 2/10 of 1 percent of the trade between U.S. businesses in 1997. By 2003, it should account for at least 10 percent—a 5,000 percent increase in just six years. Forrester Research, the market analysis firm, predicts that e-commerce will account for well over $1 trillion in trade by 2003.

Growth rates of this magnitude are almost unprecedented, but these startling projections seem reasonable in light of B2B's compelling benefits:

- **Lower transaction costs.** Processing a purchase over the Web can reduce administrative overhead by up to 70 percent.
- **Shorter purchasing cycles.** The average time between placing and filling an order is reduced from over seven days to less than two.
- **Improved inventory control.** Some early adopters of B2B report inventory carrying costs reduced by one quarter to one half.
- **Lower prices paid.** Increased bidding competition lowers the prices by up to 10 percent.

Collectively, these operational benefits can reduce procurement costs by up to 15 percent. Some companies are reporting a 300 percent return on their investment in e-procurement in the first year alone.

Numbers like these mean two things: a boom market in B2B software and explosive growth of the digital marketplaces where all this e-commerce between businesses will take place.

KEY TECHNOLOGIES

B2B e-commerce needs special software to operate by providing a format and a "place" on the Web where paperless purchasing transactions can take place. Four types of software are used to conduct B2B e-commerce:

1. **Digital marketplace platforms.** These are large computer "server" software packages used to set up online markets where

purchase requisitions are posted, products are offered for sale, bids are submitted, and deals are closed.

2. **B2B desktop software.** Individuals and small companies use special "client" software packages to participate in digital marketplaces.

3. **Electronic data interchange (EDI) software.** Standard computer formats have been created for such business forms as purchase orders and invoices that can be understood by virtually any computer.

4. **Supply chain software.** These packages are used by large corporations and their suppliers to handle such logistics as order scheduling, transportation, change orders, and quality control.

One other key B2B technology is XML—eXtensible Markup Language—which enables all e-commerce companies to interact. Much as Internet Protocol (IP) allowed all makes of computers to exchange data packets, and HTML code enabled all computer screens to display the same graphics and information, XML allows e-commerce buyers and sellers to interact seamlessly.

EDI: THE BIRTH OF E-COMMERCE

B2B has been around since long before the Internet. Companies started conducting business over private networks about 20 years ago, using the electronic data interchange, or EDI, format. EDI was the first broadly accepted format for enabling otherwise incompatible computers to communicate.

Not only did EDI lay the groundwork for business-to-business e-commerce, it still dominates the market. Used primarily for such core business transactions as purchase orders and insurance claims, EDI accounted for about $200 billion of the $250 billion in B2B e-commerce in the United States in 1998. But that dominance is fading fast.

For all its benefits, EDI has some drawbacks that will lead soon to its demise. EDI systems can be difficult to set up, and they often require a team of programmers to operate. Because of its limitations, corporations have begun replacing EDI with Internet-based digital marketplaces as quickly as possible.

DIGITAL MARKETPLACES—THE NEW WAVE

A *digital marketplace* is a Web site that facilitates buying and selling among companies. Because they are Internet-based, digital marketplaces have some major advantages over EDI-based electronic commerce:

- **Market making.** Digital marketplaces can handle as many (or as few) participants as desired. More competition makes for better prices.
- **All purchasing can be automated.** For the first time, companies are able to do all procurement transactions electronically, not just the ones for which EDI has been set up.
- **Easier internal integration.** Most internal corporate systems are now compatible with the Internet Protocol and Web browsers, or soon will be. This makes it easier for a company to link its external market transactions with product catalogs, approval processes, production schedules, and other internal systems.
- **Purchasing from the desktop.** Running inside a Web browser means anybody can go to a digital marketplace and perform tasks from their PC. It cuts down on the need for internal paperwork, phone calls, and technical support associated with procurement.

Digital marketplaces are almost "frictionless" compared to traditional business-to-business markets. Geographical limits, bureaucratic delays, and incompatible systems that place a drag on market forces don't exist in digital marketplaces. Unfettered by artificial constraints, companies can seek the best deals in truly open markets.

ECONOMIC BUSINESS MODELS

There are three kinds of B2B e-commerce companies:

1. **B2B software companies.** They sell digital marketplace software platforms, supply chain packages, and EDI systems used to conduct e-commerce between businesses. Most also collect 15 to 20 percent of the purchase price from customers in annual fees for system maintenance.
2. **Market makers.** They connect buyer with seller, collecting a fee of 5 to 10 percent for small deals and under 1 percent for the big ones. They also generate revenue from banner advertising, marketing services, and other sidelines.

3. **EDI service bureaus.** They process EDI transactions for other companies, charging a fee for their services. As EDI gives way to the Internet, service bureaus could disappear.

MARKET POSITIONING

Competition is red-hot in all B2B e-commerce niches, and why not? Digital marketplace operators, eyeing more than a trillion dollars in bookings, are working overtime to get as big a share as possible.

Getting there first is one key to success in the B2B market. Commerce One and Ariba have an advantage in the B2B software platform market, because each conglomerate who uses their software nudges its smaller trading partners to buy the same package.

First is also best for market makers, because once a digital marketplace attains a "critical mass" of traffic, buyers and sellers will come to prefer trading there to find the best action.

Most digital marketplaces are part online auction and part portal. Their ability to gain and hold market share rests on their ability to generate sufficient trading traffic to operate an efficient marketplace. In other words, in addition to operating a virtual bidding pit, a market maker must create a vibrant online community for the industry it serves in order to attract traffic.

Digital marketplaces should have staying power. As eBay proved with online auctions, the more traffic you've got, the more you'll get. That self-reinforcing cycle is difficult for an upstart competitor to break.

FUTURE PROSPECTS AND TRENDS

B2B e-commerce is fast becoming one of the great boom markets of all time. With rapid paybacks and stellar long-term prospects, B2B is attracting a growing number of competitive young companies. Here are some trends you can look for.

The traditional corporate software makers will move in. Software companies that make the large Enterprise Requirements Planning corporate applications will release B2B software platforms of their own. Although they're late to market, SAP, PeopleSoft, Oracle, and Baan are among the traditional software makers who will fight back by retrofitting their traditional client-server software for B2B e-commerce.

Mergers and acquisitions will continue in B2B. To keep up with the blazing pace of innovation, B2B software makers have been buying technology in the form of whole companies. Recently, for example, Ariba acquired platform giant Tradex in order to match Commerce One's market making strategy. Market makers will also grow by acquiring other high traffic sites.

The migration from EDI will go faster than expected. It took decades for industries to implement EDI for their core procurement transactions. Look for the rate of digital marketplace adoption to be much quicker, because XML is more powerful and easier to operate.

 **E-tailing**

TEACHING OLD CONSUMERS NEW TRICKS

With its limitless selection and irresistible bargains, online retailing has captured the imagination of the buying public—and a growing share of its pocketbook.

Internet spending, estimated at more than $30 billion a year in the United States, is expected to grow by at least 100 percent per year over much of the next decade. But the growing dollar volume has not yet translated into profits for e-tailers, in part because what succeeds in a traditional brick-and-mortar store doesn't necessarily work for a Web site. E-tailers face several obstacles:

- **The low threshold for start-up e-tailers invites fierce competition.** A traditional retailer must invest millions in a building, staff, and on-site inventory just to enter one local market. For a much lower investment, e-tailers can acquire a *global* presence. But this apparent advantage—low start-up costs, low overhead, and limitless "virtual shelf space"—has proven to be a double-edged sword. Virtually every market niche is crowded with e-tailers, while brick-and-mortar stores only compete with other stores in the vicinity.

- **It's harder to differentiate.** Standing out from the crowd has always been a central problem in retail. That's what makes it such a cutthroat business. In traditional retailing, something as mundane as a location on the right street corner can make the difference between success and failure. But on the Web, consumers can choose between dozens or even hundreds of e-tailers with just a few clicks.

- **Less is known about what works.** Business schools and consulting firms turned retailing into a science over past decades—making the American consumer the most studied species in nature. E-tailing brings new dynamics to the marketplace that render much of this conventional business school wisdom obsolete.

- **Marketing costs can be exorbitant.** While set-up and overhead costs are low for e-tailers, grabbing market share can cost tens of millions of dollars for marketing and advertising. And even that is no guarantee of success—as Value America and other e-tailing failures attest.

Despite its pitfalls, the online retail market still holds vast potential. Currently, Internet sales account for only about 1 percent of the $5 trillion retail market. As that percentage increases, and as e-tailers reach out to consumers in Asia and Europe, the growth in e-tailing could be staggering.

WHAT WORKS IN E-TAILING?

A few years ago the talk was that e-tailing would kill off traditional retailing. Now some question whether e-tailing can ever turn a profit. Such a wild swing in perception shows that e-tailing is the most misunderstood sector of the Internet economy.

The fact is, e-tailing is every bit as varied as traditional retailing. But not every type of product translates to the Internet equally well. Here's what works well over the Internet:

- **Products with high middleman costs.** The higher the intermediary costs as a percentage of the total price, the more motivated consumers are to shop online for bargains. An airplane ticket is a good example.
- **Commodity products.** Products that vary little between individual units are more Web-friendly, because they require no prior physical inspection. Computers, CDs, sporting goods, books, office and school supplies, and other popular consumer products fit the bill.
- **Known commodities.** Products such as toiletries and consumer health products that are already well established with the buying public make sense for Internet bargain hunters.
- **Intellectual content.** Products or services composed of intellectual content, such as insurance policies, lend themselves to Web retailing, because information can be digitized and there's nothing physical to inspect.
- **Goods that lend themselves to shipping.** "Virtual" means not physically present. The corner gas station isn't a suspect for Web extinction, because it must be bought when needed, making overnight shipping unacceptable. Also, the cost of shipping makes e-tailing such inexpensive items as soap and candy less feasible.

The Internet is not the first market medium to allow consumers to order goods from their own home. In fact, Sears made the catalog a marketing staple almost a hundred years ago. But e-tailing enjoys some fundamental advantages over catalog marketing.

Whereas catalogs are mailed out to consumers at great expense, Web shoppers go to e-stores on their own—at a minuscule cost per shopper. In the future, nearly all households will be connected to the Web, providing e-tailers with access to an unlimited market base without spending a penny on postage.

One other advantage for Web shopping is that e-stores are active sales environments, while catalogs are dormant objects. Web pages respond to shopper input in ways far beyond merely turning pages, which enhances the shopping experience. They also can capture automatically demographic data on visitors to help sell more to them later.

The e-tailing industry has already dwarfed the catalog business, which is why savvy catalog operators such as Land's End have transformed themselves into world class e-tailers.

WHAT MOTIVATES ONLINE SHOPPERS?

A 1998 survey of online shoppers by the consulting firm Ernst & Young offers a glimpse of what motivates them to shop online. Here are the results:

Reasons to Shop Online		Discouraging Factors	
Save time	64%	High shipping costs	51%
Stores too crowded	56%	High prices	45%
24/7 e-store hours	52%	Need to try item for fit	38%
At-home shopping (no driving)	37%	Not appropriate for large items	36%
Items cost less	16%	Want to see and feel items	26%
Able to shop earlier in season	14%		
Easier to shop	12%		
Better selection	11%		

Source: Ernst & Young's Third Annual Online Retailing Report (1998).

Other potential barriers to shopping online include concerns with privacy and credit card security, fear of return hassles, and the lengthy waiting period to receive orders.

Perhaps the most surprising thing about e-tailing is that in most cases prices are no cheaper. This may be because most e-tailers are still young companies that can't match the purchasing volumes of the discount store giants. That may change over time, but for now e-tailers must compete on selection and convenience.

Online shopping will probably never fully replace traditional retailers for the simple reason that many people love to shop. For many, shopping is a form of entertainment. Surfing the Net can never replace the pleasure sport shoppers derive from handling merchandise, trying on or testing products, and interacting with sales clerks and other shoppers.

E-TAILING TECHNOLOGY

Setting up an e-store requires relatively little in terms of equipment and technology. The typical e-tailer setup includes a server (a big computer that sits between the Web and the e-tailer's database), a high-speed ISP hookup, and fairly sophisticated software. The back-end software components are usually the same as in brick-and-mortar store systems, such as inventory, credit, sales order entry, financial, and accounting.

E-tailers distinguish themselves more by their business plans and marketing programs than by their technology. They all use similar Web site software, which is why most e-stores tend to look and behave more or less the same. Software has been invented to help e-tailers suggest products shoppers are most likely to have an interest in, but even innovations can't be used to differentiate an e-store, because new e-tailing technologies are quickly adopted by everyone.

Generally speaking, it's the e-tailer's ability to drive traffic to the site and close sales—not technology—that differentiates one e-tailer from another.

E-TAILER MARKET POSITIONING

E-tailing is done largely by vertical market niche. A company sets up an e-store catering to a particular consumer need and attempts to drive as much high-quality visitor traffic as possible to the e-store Web site.

As you've probably noticed on TV, most e-tailer marketing efforts rely on mass media advertising programs to drive traffic. But a less visible marketing technique is the use of affiliations. An e-tail *affiliate* is a related Web site that contracts to deliver visitor traffic to an e-store in exchange for a cut of the action, usually a few percentage points. Nearly all e-tailers have affiliation programs in place.

But the trend is actually *away* from vertical specialization. E-tail giants like Amazon.com and eBay have steadily expanded their product categories to take on more market niches. This is because in e-tailing, where traffic is everything, it's easier for a big name Web site to draw visitors, whether by mass advertising or through affiliate programs.

Another misconception about e-tailing is that it's dominated by pure Internet companies. Although few accurate statistics exist on the subject, most e-tailing revenues are probably captured by "click-and-mortar" companies—e-stores operated by companies that also operate a chain of physical stores. Walmart.com is a great example of this.

Click-and-mortar companies make natural e-tailers. The key to a successful e-tailing venture is brand recognition and effective back-office operations for such things as warehousing, order fulfillment, and customer service. Traditional retail giants have that out of the box. All they need to e-tail is to buy a Web site software package and hire a Web consulting firm to set up an e-store. There are even consultants to help set up affiliate marketing partner networks. So being early is less an advantage in e-tailing as in other sectors of the Internet economy.

ECONOMIC BUSINESS MODELS

There are three different kinds of e-tailer, each with distinct business models and revenue sources:

1. **E-stores.** You know the names: Amazon.com, HomeShopper .com, Beansnow.com and thousands more. Like traditional retail stores, these companies generate income on margins generated by buying low and selling high.
2. **Online auctions.** Open auctions bring buyer and seller together, using a variety of auction models. For instance, eBay uses the traditional auction model in which the seller names an asking price and accepts the highest bid. Priceline.com uses a reverse model in which the *buyer* puts an intended retail purchase up for grabs, letting interested vendors compete for the sale by naming their lowest price. But in the end, all online auctions rely on sales commissions as their primary source of revenue.
3. **Online agencies.** Online agents broker nonbid transactions on behalf of a third party source of a product or service. Agents rely on commissions from their client companies. For example, an online travel agency such as Travelocity.com receives a fee from the airline, cruise line, hotel, or rental car company for which it moves inventory.

Virtual e-tailers are online operations with no warehouse or order fulfillment infrastructure of their own. They merchandise products and take orders. They require very little capital to start, because they rely on traditional distributors to carry inventory and fulfill orders.

Physical e-tailers have their own warehouses, carry their own inventory, and handle order fulfillment through to customer delivery. For instance, Amazon.com is a physical e-tailer with a nationwide inventory and distribution network built around state-of-the-art warehouses millions of square feet in capacity.

Because they're so easy to set up, there are thousands of virtual e-tailers. Most are upstarts that probably harbor secret hopes of being bought out before they're crushed by the superior marketing clout and customer service of big physical e-tailers. Yahoo!, Lycos, and other giant portals also operate virtual e-stores at their sites, acting as a kind of "super affiliate" for companies that handle inventory and order fulfillment in the background.

FUTURE PROSPECTS AND TRENDS

Even by the wild standards of the Internet economy, the e-tailing industry is built on shifting sands. But winners will emerge—and the spoils will be great. Web efficiencies will become more of a factor, as more households connect to the Internet and consumers grow more comfortable with the idea of using credit cards on the Web. Several other key trends could also emerge.

Only the big will survive. E-tail consolidation will continue for several years. Distributors and traditional retailers will continue to enter the market to gain a presence and to exploit their physical assets, especially their product knowledge, manufacturing relationships, and inventory and distribution capabilities.

E-tailing will be cruel to losers. The only long-term assets an e-tailer has are its brand and its distribution center (if it has one). A fading brand could be a death knell for an e-tailer. In fact, young e-tail stocks may be the riskiest of all Internet stocks.

Pressure on prices will increase. Most Web shoppers tend to be fairly affluent now, but that could change as more consumers go online. Price will eventually become an important consideration for most online shoppers, much as it is today in brick-and-mortar outlets. That could drive e-tailers into razor-thin gross profit margins and reward Web sites that attract large traffic volumes and control costs.

Technology will become a factor. E-stores today all look and act pretty much the same. But as the novelty of online shopping wears off, consumers will demand better service. The sites with the best technology will have the best chance to retain customer loyalty, so creating innovative e-store software will become a much bigger factor than it is now.

The landscape will change. Look for the lines to blur between big portals and big e-tailers. The two will in fact probably merge, with the Amazons and eBays becoming portals and the likes of Yahoo! and Lycos continuing to enhance their e-stores.

Media and Entertainment

Someday soon, movies, radio, TV, and phone conversations will all flow together over the Internet, packaged into a single "pipe" that consumers can tap into any time, any place.

The debate still rages over what the preferred Internet "appliance" will be—the TV, the PC, or a new device yet to be conceived. Billions of dollars are being wagered on whether homes will be hooked up via digital phone lines, cable television networks, or even wireless connections. Few will argue, however, that most information will soon travel inside Internet Protocol (IP) packets instead of through the various transport media now used.

To understand the sector, a definition is in order. *Internet media and entertainment* is defined as: (1) content—information carried through a medium, including such things as shows, sporting events, and news; (2) media format—content must be put into a format that the hardware used to present it can understand (usually a software specification); (3) media services—companies are sprouting up to assist in the production and distribution of Internet content.

Internet media is the least mature sector of the Internet economy. It's also the most controversial.

KEY TECHNOLOGIES

Special technologies are required at both ends of the Internet media pipe. At the front end, content must be packaged into IP packet format for shipment. At the user's end, the information must be repackaged into whatever presentation format is being used.

IP is only the transport. Dozens of technical standards have been created to deal with packaging and presenting content. There are common standards for video, voice, audio, and other media forms. For example, the MP3 specification defines how to ship music over the Internet. As a result, hundreds of companies have designed MP3 into their products.

There also are enabling technologies that make Internet multimedia more practical. The most important is an emerging technology called Quality of Service, or QoS. In a nutshell, QoS enables all the routers and switches along an Internet connection's path to successfully complete a media connection. For example, Internet phone calls suffer from intermittent delays that cause people to talk over one another. To avoid that problem, QoS would guarantee that IP packets carrying voice would be delivered in a timely manner.

MEDIA ECONOMIC BUSINESS MODELS

Revenue sources vary according to the type of Internet media company. Most content publishers rely on banner advertising and, in some cases, subscriptions for "premium" content. They also include links to online retailers such as Amazon.com that pay the media companies a small referral fee for all sales generated from those links.

Media services companies operate more or less the same way as their real world counterparts. Net2Phone, for example, sells phone debit cards to consumers and markets discount phone services to businesses.

Media format companies encourage users to upgrade from free "shareware" versions of their software to ones with more functionality. The trouble is, almost everybody sticks with the free copy, which is why many are reinventing themselves as portals.

PROSPECTS AND TRENDS

Phone fares. Internet telephony could be a lucrative area, but most of the profits will probably go to such traditional players as MCI WorldCom and AT&T—not start-ups.

QoS is the key. QoS is an ambitious undertaking that's still in its infancy. Once it's implemented along the major backbones, media such as Internet telephony and videoconferencing will have a chance to succeed. Until then, companies involved in the technology—and investors who buy the stocks—may be in for some choppy waters.

Convergence is coming—but most won't notice. Eventually, the specialized hardware and software needed to run Internet media will be designed into such "appliances" as personal computers, cell phones, and TV sets. That could make the going tough for media format companies, although the best of the media companies may be acquired by traditional tech companies.

More free lunch? Web surfers have had the disturbing expectation that everything should be free. To survive, most media sites will have to follow the lead of commercial TV—generate revenue almost entirely from advertising. Some specialized sites may succeed on a subscription basis, but most will continue to live off their banner ads and proceeds from referrals to online retailers.

Online Financial Services

If you were to imagine the perfect business to build on the Web, certain criteria emerge: The business would involve no physical product, it would be information-intensive, and it would have traditional middleman fees that could be reduced or eliminated by going direct over the Web.

The financial services industry fits that bill perfectly. That's why the financial services sector has become one of the hottest markets of the Internet economy. Online financial services can be broken into three general categories: (1) online brokerages—online investment houses where individuals can trade stocks, options, mutual funds, and other securities; (2) market makers—the behind-the-scenes operations that guarantee market liquidity by being there to buy securities put up for sale, much like the men in the smocks on the floor of the NYSE; and (3) financial services retailers—consumers can shop the Web for the best rates on loans, mortgages, and even credit cards.

KEY TECHNOLOGIES

From a technology standpoint, think of online financial services as e-tailing on steroids. Most online financial services companies are basically Web sites with a lot of back-end data processing that even giant e-tailers like Amazon.com and eBay don't have.

That is particularly true for online brokerages, which must carefully perform several "transaction processing" steps in order to ensure that everything is perfect before a trade is executed. It's all done using software that is custom built by the online brokerages.

These systems also must handle housekeeping chores such as issuing account statements and billing customers. System availability and security are critical to any Internet business, but they're imperative to online financial services companies.

The systems market makers operate don't have the graphical customer interface of online brokerages. These systems list stocks online, constantly update a stock's going price, and electronically execute trades.

Nasdaq is a prime example. Its "trading floor" isn't a physical place, but rather a cluster of mainframe computers humming away in a computer room. Other market makers have custom built their systems along the same lines as Nasdaq.

MARKET POSITIONING

In general, online financial services companies are retailers. They mass market their services in the same manner as their real world counterparts.

The online brokerage business has already become crowded, and the field should continue to grow as traditional giants such as Morgan Stanley Dean Witter and Merrill Lynch go online. Online investing is here to stay, because investors enjoy trading online—with access to the same timely market information as a well-connected broker.

Online services measure themselves by active accounts. The two largest, Ameritrade and E*Trade, both have nearly a million accounts. Online brokerages seek to differentiate themselves by offering customers sophisticated tools for portfolio management.

ECONOMIC BUSINESS MODELS

Online brokerages make their money from four revenue streams:

1. Trading fees (the going rate is about $8 per trade)
2. Interest charged to account holders for credit extended
3. "Order flow" payments that market makers pay brokerages for sending trades their way
4. Interest earned on investment securities

Market makers such as Knight/Trimark earn the bulk of their money on the "bid/ask spread" between buyer and seller.

PROSPECTS AND TRENDS

The more things change . . . After spending several years in denial, the traditional brokerage houses are finally recognizing the need to add online trading to their mix of offerings. Otherwise, they risk losing customers by the thousands.

Will just "being there" still be good enough? Loan companies have always made a good part of their living by being down the street, available to review your paperwork and extend you a loan (if you're lucky). The tables have turned. The Web will eventually remove the geographical dimension from financial retailing entirely, forcing operators to chase online borrowers and take greater risks.

Will a "super exchange" emerge? The combined effect of online brokerages and online marketing could someday spawn a single world stock exchange. Nasdaq, which recently acquired AMEX, has already created online trading floor software. Could the NYSE be next?

Internet Holding Companies

The Internet economy holds such tremendous opportunity that it has engendered a new kind of business designed to cash in: an *Internet holding company* is a business with major ownership stakes in a collection of Internet companies.

Internet holding companies are similar to traditional venture capital (VC) firms, with a few key distinctions:

- **Later stage investment.** VC firms tend to invest in start-ups, while Internet holding companies are more likely to get involved later, when a young company is up and running and is entering the expansion stage.
- **Size of equity stake.** VC firms travel in packs and generally end up with a small percentage of outstanding shares. Internet holding companies like to be the biggest single shareholder of a property, often taking majority or even total ownership.
- **Publicly traded.** Although most VC firms are private, Internet holding companies are publicly traded in order to feed their voracious appetites for investment capital.
- **Operational involvement.** VC firms don't get involved in their companies on a day-to-day basis, while holding companies often provide marketing services, back office support, and management services.
- **Inter-company leverage.** The holding company business model has been around for decades, but an *Internet* holding company takes the concept a step further by directing firms in its portfolio to steer traffic to each other's sites—and even to share technology.

MARKET POSITIONING

The ability to share expertise across a portfolio gives Internet holding companies a strategic advantage in the marketplace. Most holding companies tend to specialize in specific niches. For instance, Internet Capital Group invests almost exclusively in the business-to-business (B2B) e-commerce sector, including stakes of about 20 to 40 percent equity in about 50 companies (with majority positions in a few others). It has a stake in Vertical-Net, the big B2B "market maker" that operates dozens of niche digital marketplaces (online trade communities), as well as e-commerce systems integrator Breakaway Solutions, e-procurement software maker Right-Works, and the e-commerce transaction processing service ClearCommerce.

CMGI, the biggest Internet holding company, has focused on portals and Internet business services. It controls Lycos and AltaVista, two of the Web's busiest portals. CMGI also has taken a strong position in the Internet advertising area. AdForce and Flycast give it a position in the booming "ad serving" business; Engage Technologies profiles Web site visitors to "personalize" the content each sees; and PlanetDirect provides local content for nearly 500 Internet service providers. CMGI has been aggressive in sharing resources among its properties; for example, its portals feed visitor information into Engage's profile database.

ECONOMIC BUSINESS MODELS

A big part of a holding company's time is spent looking for deals. The rest is spent helping portfolio companies grow.

The classic model is to grow a company for three to five years and then take it public. For example, CMGI invested about $6 million in GeoCities, nurtured it, and then took it public, earning about $1 billion on the IPO—not a bad payday.

PROSPECTS AND TRENDS

The double-edged sword. Internet Capital Group gained $170 million for its minority stake when Tradex was acquired by Ariba, but lost much of its digital-marketplace-making infrastructure in the process. Ideally, a holding company should try to accumulate a majority stake in its most important properties.

Being a visionary will get tougher. The impressive success of Internet holding companies will attract imitators. Competition is already heating up for stakes in emerging Internet companies, and the next round of "killer apps" may be tougher to spot.

The early bird gets the billions. Holding companies will have to invest in new Internet properties earlier than in the past. Otherwise, the best prospects will either be snapped up by someone else or become overpriced.

INFRASTRUCTURE

Cisco Systems, Inc.

170 West Tasman Drive
San Jose, CA 95134
408-526-4000
Nasdaq: CSCO
www.cisco.com

Chairman: John Morgridge
President and CEO: John T. Chambers

Earnings Progression	★ ★ ★ ★
Revenue Growth	★ ★ ★ ★
Stock Growth	★ ★ ★ ★
Consistency	★ ★ ★ ★
Stability/Vulnerability	★ ★ ★ ★
Total Points	**20 points**

Cisco Systems is the only truly indispensable component of the Internet economy. Take away any of the other Internet heavyweights—Yahoo!, Amazon, or AOL, among others—and the Web would still survive and thrive. But take away Cisco Systems and there is no Internet.

The World Wide Web is held together by Cisco routers, switches, and access servers. The company supplies more than 80 percent of all routers used on the Internet backbone. Nearly all the information on the Internet travels through Cisco Systems products.

Cisco is also the world's leading supplier of networking products for corporate intranets in addition to the global Internet. The San Jose, California operation markets its products to four types of buyers, including:

1. Large organizations with complex networking needs, such as corporations, government agencies, and universities

2. Major network operators, such as telecommunications carriers, cable companies, and Internet service providers
3. Volume markets, such as small businesses and home office users
4. Other suppliers who license features of Cisco technology for inclusion in their products or services

Under Cisco's corporate growth strategy, dubbed "technical agnosticism," the company adopts competing technologies instead of fighting them. It pursues this strategy mostly by acquiring the most promising start-up technology companies (about a half-dozen each year). This keeps Cisco at the cutting edge of technology and also prevents the management team from growing inbred and stale.

One of Cisco's most notable strengths is its product architecture. Its entire product line runs the company's IOS operating system, which is perhaps second only to Microsoft Windows in importance. Customers like the fact that its technicians need learn only a single computing environment to do almost any task—which helps lock in Cisco's market position.

Cisco's management track record is unrivaled over the past decade. The company has been able to relentlessly absorb new technologies and corporate acquisitions without missing a beat, while still maintaining a high level of customer satisfaction.

The next challenge for Cisco is promoting Internet telephony. If Internet phone calling becomes routine, Cisco could see its revenues grow fivefold.

Cisco sells its products through a direct sales force of 7,500 representatives and technical support personnel. Internationally, the company sells through about 120 distributors around the world. Foreign sales account for about 40 percent of the company's $12 billion in annual revenue.

Cisco was founded in 1984 by a husband-wife team working at Stanford University who set out to develop a way to tie the world's local networks together. The company brought its first product to market in 1986, and sales have been soaring ever since.

The company has about 21,000 employees and 20,000 shareholders. It has a market capitalization of about $400 billion.

EARNINGS PER SHARE PROGRESSION   ★ ★ ★ ★

Earnings growth past 4 years: 343 percent (45 percent per year)

REVENUE GROWTH   ★ ★ ★ ★

Past 4 years: 516 percent (58 percent per year)

STOCK GROWTH   ★ ★ ★ ★

Past 4 years: 1,192 percent (90 percent per year)
Dollar growth: $10,000 over 4 years would have grown to $129,200.

CONSISTENCY   ★ ★ ★ ★

Increased earnings per share: 4 consecutive years
Increased revenue: 4 consecutive years

STABILITY/VULNERABILITY   ★ ★ ★ ★

There is no company in the Internet economy more solid than Cisco.

CISCO SYSTEMS AT A GLANCE

Fiscal year ended: July 31
Revenue in $ millions

	1995	1996	1997	1998	1999	4-Year Growth Avg. Annual (%)	Total (%)
Revenue ($)	1.98	4.10	6.44	8.49	12.2	58	516
Earnings/share ($)	0.14	0.23	0.34	0.42	0.62	45	343
PE ratio range	23-62	23-50	29-60	41-117	73-174		

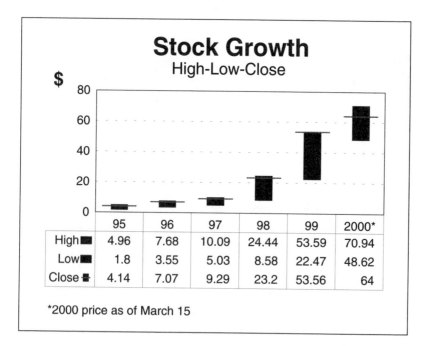

Stock Growth
High-Low-Close

	95	96	97	98	99	2000*
High	4.96	7.68	10.09	24.44	53.59	70.94
Low	1.8	3.55	5.03	8.58	22.47	48.62
Close	4.14	7.07	9.29	23.2	53.56	64

*2000 price as of March 15

2

Yahoo! Inc.

3420 Central Expressway
Santa Clara, CA 95051
408-731-3300
Nasdaq: YHOO
www.yahoo.com

Chairman and CEO: Timothy Koogle

Earnings Progression	★ ★ ★
Revenue Growth	★ ★ ★ ★
Stock Growth	★ ★ ★ ★
Consistency	★ ★ ★ ★
Stability/Vulnerability	★ ★ ★ ★
Total Points	**19 points**

Yahoo! must be doing something right. After all, 120 million Web surfers use the Internet portal service for news, online shopping, and search engine services, making Yahoo! the most popular spot on the World Wide Web. On average, Yahoo! logs more than 450 million page views per day and is the leading Internet portal in terms of traffic, advertising, and household and business user reach.

The Santa Clara, California operation offers a comprehensive online navigational guide to the Web utilizing a subject-based directory of Web sites. The Yahoo! online directory includes more than a million Web sites organized under 14 principal categories: arts and humanities, business and economy, computers and Internet, education, entertainment, government, health, news and media, sports, reference, regional, science, social science, and society and culture. Each category is broken down further by scores of subcategories to make it easier for users to pinpoint the exact type of site they want. Users also can search the Web by entering key words that direct them to a variety of Web site choices.

The Yahoo! site includes current information and reference material from such leading content providers as Reuters, Associated Press, Deutche Presse, ESPN, *The Sporting News,* the Weather Channel, and *The Wall Street Journal.* The site also includes printed and audio news, sports, business, stock quotes, entertainment news, and weather. It has auctions, Yellow Pages, maps, driving directions, classified listings, online shopping, chats, message boards, and personal calendars and address book options.

Yahoo! has established a prominent global presence on the Web. Yahoo! Japan attracts more than 40 million page views per day, and Yahoo! Europe gets about 17 million views per day.

The company went public with its initial stock offering in 1996. It has about 800 employees and a market capitalization of about $82 billion.

EARNINGS PER SHARE PROGRESSION ★ ★ ★

The company has gone from losses to increasing profits.

REVENUE GROWTH ★ ★ ★ ★

Past 4 years: 36,687 percent (338 percent per year)

STOCK GROWTH ★ ★ ★ ★

Past 3 years: 15,199 percent (435 percent per year)
Dollar growth: $10,000 over 3 years would have grown to $1,528,900.37.

CONSISTENCY ★ ★ ★ ★

Positive earnings progression: 2 consecutive years
Increased sales: 4 consecutive years

STABILITY/VULNERABILITY ★ ★ ★ ★

With more than 450 million page views per day, Yahoo! is the most popular spot on the Web. And, it makes money—what a unique concept!

YAHOO! AT A GLANCE

Fiscal year ended: Dec. 31
Revenue in $ millions

	1995	1996	1997	1998	1999	4-Year Growth Avg. Annual (%)	Total (%)
Revenue ($)	1.6	19.7	70.5	231.7	588.6	338	36,687
Earnings/share ($)	-0.01	-0.02	-0.08	0.03	0.10	233*	233*
PE ratio range	NA	NA	NA	126-1254	534-2175		

*Earnings per share growth figures reflect 1-year growth.

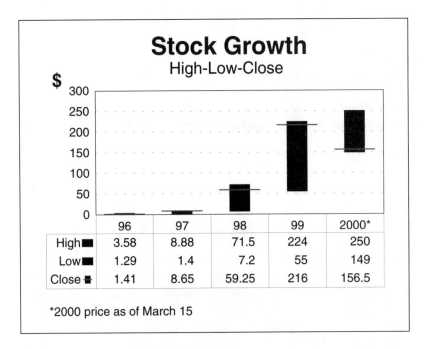

Stock Growth
High-Low-Close

	96	97	98	99	2000*
High	3.58	8.88	71.5	224	250
Low	1.29	1.4	7.2	55	149
Close	1.41	8.65	59.25	216	156.5

*2000 price as of March 15

CMGI, Inc.

100 Brickstone Square, First Floor
Andover, MA 01810
978-684-3600
Nasdaq: CMGI
www.cmgi.com

Chairman, President, and CEO: David S. Wetherell

Earnings Progression	★ ★ ★ ★
Revenue Growth	★ ★ ★ ★
Stock Growth	★ ★ ★ ★
Consistency	★ ★ ★
Stability/Vulnerability	★ ★ ★ ★
Total Points	**19 points**

CMGI has quickly amassed an Internet empire unrivaled by any other company in the world. The firm has acquired a stake in dozens of Internet-related companies. As the Internet grows, CMGI is virtually guaranteed to grow with it.

The Andover, Massachusetts operation owns a number of Internet companies outright and has heavy investments in many others. CMGI invests in emerging growth companies through its venture capital affiliate, @Ventures.

Among its majority-owned operating companies are AltaVista, Engage Technologies, NaviSite, 1stUp.com, Activate.net, Adsmart, Magnitude Networks, NaviNet, FlyCast, Signature Network, and German-based Adtech Advertising Service.

Through @Ventures, the company has investments in Lycos, Critical Path, Silknet, HotLinks, Visto, Boatscape.com, and a number of other Web companies.

In all, the CMGI network includes more than 50 companies. CMGI leverages the technologies, content, and market reach of its network of companies to foster rapid growth and market leadership.

CMGI also provides fulfillment services through three subsidiaries: SalesLink, InSolutions, and On-Demand Solutions. Among its services are product and literature fulfillment, turnkey outsourcing, telemarketing, and sales lead inquiry management. It also offers traditional mailing list services through its CMG Direct subsidiary.

Through its NaviSite subsidiary, the company provides high-performance Internet outsourcing services (including Web hosting and server management) for a growing number of companies in search of a Web presence. NaviSite monitors and supports its customers' servers around the clock and provides customers with detailed reports covering the performance, availability, and activity of their Web sites.

CMGI has been a favorite investment of several prominent high-tech companies, including Compaq, Intel, and Microsoft, who all hold minority positions in CMGI.

Formerly known as CMG Information Services, CMGI initiated its first Internet venture fund in 1996. The company has about 1,000 employees and a market capitalization of about $35 billion.

EARNINGS PER SHARE PROGRESSION ★ ★ ★ ★
Past 4 years: 1,178 percent (89 percent per year)

REVENUE GROWTH ★ ★ ★ ★
Past 4 years: 1,464 percent (99 percent per year)

STOCK GROWTH ★ ★ ★ ★
Past 4 years: 4,674 percent (163 percent per year)
Dollar growth: $10,000 over 4 years would have grown to $477,400.

CONSISTENCY ★ ★ ★
Increased earnings per share: 2 of the past 4 years
Increased revenue: 4 consecutive years

STABILITY/VULNERABILITY ★ ★ ★ ★
With all of its subsidiaries and venture investments, CMGI is well established and well diversified within the Internet economy. This is a monster operation.

CMGI AT A GLANCE

Fiscal year ended: July 31
Revenue in $ millions

	1995	1996	1997	1998	1999	4-Year Growth Avg. Annual (%)	Total (%)
Revenue ($)	11.1	28.5	70.6	84.1	173.6	99	1,464
Earnings/share ($)	0.36	0.18	-0.29	0.19	4.60	89	1,178
PE ratio range	11-101	6-32	NA	11-112	7-70		

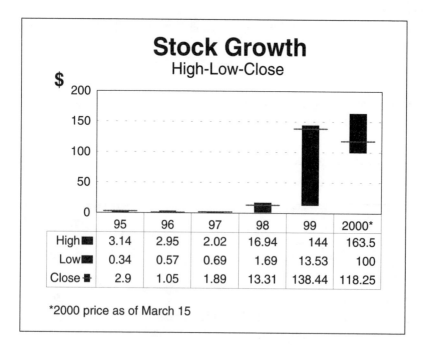

Stock Growth
High-Low-Close

$	95	96	97	98	99	2000*
High	3.14	2.95	2.02	16.94	144	163.5
Low	0.34	0.57	0.69	1.69	13.53	100
Close	2.9	1.05	1.89	13.31	138.44	118.25

*2000 price as of March 15

SOFTWARE

4

Check Point Software Technologies Ltd.

Three Lagoon Drive, Suite 400
Redwood City, CA 94065
650-628-2000
Nasdaq: CHKP
www.checkpoint.com

Chairman, President, and CEO: Gil Shwed

Earnings Progression	★ ★ ★ ★
Revenue Growth	★ ★ ★ ★
Stock Growth	★ ★ ★ ★
Consistency	★ ★ ★ ★
Stability/Vulnerability	★ ★ ★
Total Points	**19 points**

Several years ago, one wag observed that Internet security was so bad it resembled a leaky bucket filled with Swiss cheese. Things have improved a lot since then, thanks in no small part to Israel-based Check Point Software Technologies, the world leader in Internet security.

Check Point founder and CEO Gil Shwed invented the firewall and is revered as one of the Internet's true pioneers. E-commerce wouldn't be possible without firewalls, which are security gateways that protect internal networks from hackers.

The Israeli operation dominates the Internet security software market with more than 32,000 customers and over 100,000 installations. Its leading products include:

- **Security software.** FireWall-1, its flagship product, is augmented by several other security products.

61

- **Traffic control software.** The company expanded into products used to boost network performance and reliability. In addition to software, Check Point manufactures PC boards to make certain network applications run faster.
- **Virtual Private Network (VPN) software.** Companies use VPNs to run their internal networks over the Internet, and Check Point is the early leader in the VPN software market.

The company is well positioned for growth. Its VPN software is becoming increasingly popular as cost-conscious corporations dump their private leased-line networks. VPNs can save companies up to 60 percent on wide area networking costs. In addition, ISPs and corporations are turning to traffic control software to deliver the service levels that IP telephony and video conferencing need to operate effectively.

Check Point has fortified its market position through its OPSEC alliance, a group of manufacturers that sets technical standards for integrating Check Point technology into their products. Partners include IBM, Hewlett-Packard, Sun Microsystems, Microsoft, Netscape, Intel, MCI WorldCom, and others.

Check Point Software Technologies went public with its initial stock offering in 1996. The company has about 500 employees and a market capitalization of about $8 billion.

EARNINGS PER SHARE PROGRESSION ★ ★ ★ ★
Past 3 years: 427 percent (74 percent per year)

REVENUE GROWTH ★ ★ ★ ★
Past 4 years: 2,210 percent (120 percent per year)

STOCK GROWTH ★ ★ ★ ★
Past 3 years: 814 percent (101 percent per year)
Dollar growth: $10,000 over 3 years would have grown to $91,400.

CONSISTENCY ★ ★ ★ ★
Increased earnings per share: 3 consecutive years
Increased revenue: 4 consecutive years

STABILITY/VULNERABILITY ★ ★ ★
Most big players are intensively working on security products, but Check Point is one of the best, established Internet companies.

CHECK POINT SOFTWARE AT A GLANCE

Fiscal year ended: Dec. 31
Revenue in $ millions

	1995	1996	1997	1998	1999	4-Year Growth Avg. Annual (%)	4-Year Growth Total (%)
Revenue ($)	9.5	31.9	86.3	141.9	219.5	120	2,210
Earnings/share ($)	0	0.22	0.51	0.91	1.16	74*	427*
PE ratio range	NA	31-86	15-48	6-26	9-96		

*Earnings per share figures reflect 3-year growth.

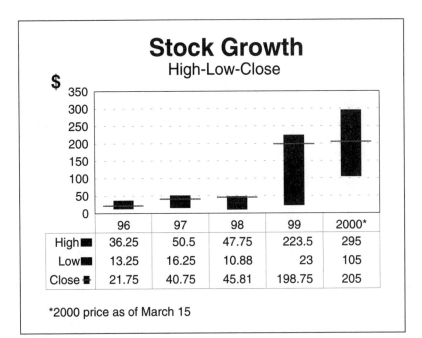

Stock Growth
High-Low-Close

$	96	97	98	99	2000*
High	36.25	50.5	47.75	223.5	295
Low	13.25	16.25	10.88	23	105
Close	21.75	40.75	45.81	198.75	205

*2000 price as of March 15

SOFTWARE

5
BroadVision, Inc.

585 Broadway
Redwood City, CA 94063
659-261-5100
Nasdaq: BVSN
www.broadvision.com

Chairman, President, and CEO: Pehong Chen

Earnings Progression	★ ★ ★ ★
Revenue Growth	★ ★ ★ ★
Stock Growth	★ ★ ★ ★
Consistency	★ ★ ★ ★
Stability/Vulnerability	★ ★ ★
Total Points	**19 points**

Companies need software to run their e-commerce sites, and BroadVision is selling more than its share.

Over the past few years, the company has built an impressive list of clients that include major corporations such as American Airlines, pure e-tailers such as Cyberian Outpost, "click and mortar" e-tailers such as Home Depot, and even government agencies such as the U.S. Postal Service.

BroadVision makes what it calls "personalized relationship management" software. The idea is to use personal profiles to filter out unwanted information, focusing instead on individual interests and priorities. This is an important feature because many Web sites have a tendency to inundate users with volumes of irrelevant information.

The Redwood City, California operation offers four key software products, including:

1. **One-to-One Enterprise.** This is the base software platform used to run an e-commerce Web site.

2. **One-to-One Commerce.** This software package for online sales is able to present products, take orders, track fulfillment, and do billing.
3. **One-to-One Financial.** This is a software package used by banks, brokerages, and other financial institutions to conduct secure on-line transactions.
4. **One-to-One Knowledge.** This software organizes information into "channels" customized to the needs of departments or even individuals.

BroadVision's status as a "best of breed" Web site software package vendor is evident in its strategic alliances with top companies, such as Cisco Systems, Hewlett-Packard, and other key players.

BroadVision averages about $350,000 per sale and does more than 40 percent of its business overseas. The international mix is a good sign for the long term, as Europe and Asia begin to catch up with North America in conversion to the Internet economy.

Pehong Chen founded the company in 1993. Earlier in his career he served as vice president of multimedia technology at the database software company Sybase. BroadVision has about 300 employees and a market capitalization of about $9 billion.

EARNINGS PER SHARE PROGRESSION ★ ★ ★ ★
Dwindling losses turned to growing earnings the past 4 years.

REVENUE GROWTH ★ ★ ★ ★
Past 4 years: 21,288 percent (281 percent per year)

STOCK GROWTH ★ ★ ★ ★
Past 3 years: 6,366 percent (301 percent per year)
Dollar growth: $10,000 over 3 years would have grown to $646,600.

CONSISTENCY ★ ★ ★ ★
Positive earnings progression: 3 consecutive years
Increased revenue: 4 consecutive years

STABILITY/VULNERABILITY ★ ★ ★
There's plenty of competition in the Web site software package business, but BroadVision is on a solid foundation.

BROADVISION AT A GLANCE

Fiscal year ended: Dec. 31
Revenue in $ millions

	1995	1996	1997	1998	1999	4-Year Growth Avg. Annual (%)	Total (%)
Revenue ($)	.54	10.9	27.1	50.9	115.5	281	21,288
Earnings/share ($)	—	–0.18	–0.12	0.05	0.22	340*	340*
PE ratio range	—	—	—	NA	42-828		

*Earnings per share growth figures reflect 1-year results.

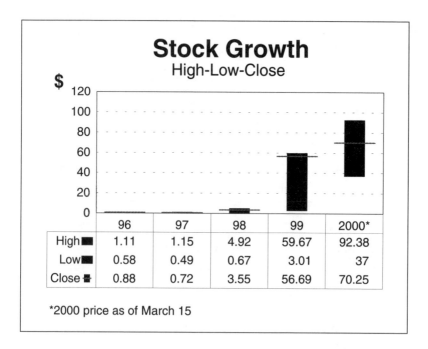

Stock Growth
High-Low-Close

$	96	97	98	99	2000*
High■	1.11	1.15	4.92	59.67	92.38
Low■	0.58	0.49	0.67	3.01	37
Close ■	0.88	0.72	3.55	56.69	70.25

*2000 price as of March 15

6

Broadcom Corporation

16215 Alton Parkway
Irvine, CA 92618
949-450-8700
Nasdaq: BRCM
www.broadcom.com

President, CEO, and Co-Chairman: Henry T. Nicholas III
Chief Technical Officer and Co-Chairman: Henry Samueli

Earnings Progression	★ ★ ★ ★
Revenue Growth	★ ★ ★ ★
Stock Growth	★ ★ ★
Consistency	★ ★ ★
Stability/Vulnerability	★ ★ ★ ★
Total Points	**18 points**

Don't you love it when somebody comes along and slaps conventional wisdom in the face? That's exactly what Broadcom has done in the networking microchips market.

Broadcom makes high-bandwidth ("broadband") chips designed for Internet connection devices. Among its leading customers are 3Com, AT&T, Sony, Hewlett-Packard, and Cisco Systems. It specializes in the "convergence" arena, in which voice, video, and data are merging on the Internet as one common medium. Among Broadcom's leading products are computer chips for:

- Cable set-top boxes and cable modems
- Digital broadcast satellites and terrestrial digital broadcast stations
- Digital Subscriber Line (DSL) modems and central phone office switches

67

- Broadband interface cards that connect PCs and larger computers to office networks

Attacking such a wide range of markets rarely happens in the chip business, especially with a small company. But Broadcom feels that serving diverse markets can be a real advantage, because it can transfer know-how learned in one broadband chip market to the others.

Broadcom's strategy seems to be right on target. Not only have its flagship cable products captured an 80 percent market share, but its other products also are compiling impressive results. Broadcom is the first manufacturer to develop single-chip products for three distinct technology applications: its chips are used for Internet connection devices, local networks, and cable modems.

Founded in 1991, Broadcom positioned itself at the ground floor of the convergence arena. The company went public with its initial stock offering in 1998. Broadcom has a market capitalization of about $22 billion.

EARNINGS PER SHARE PROGRESSION ★ ★ ★ ★
Past 3 years earnings growth: 1,700 percent (165 percent per year)

REVENUE GROWTH ★ ★ ★ ★
Past 5 years: 8,395 percent (204 percent per year)

STOCK GROWTH ★ ★ ★
Past year: 351 percent
Dollar growth: $10,000 invested over one year would have grown to $45,100.

CONSISTENCY ★ ★ ★
Increased earnings per share: 3 of the past 4 years
Increased revenue: 5 consecutive years

STABILITY/VULNERABILITY ★ ★ ★ ★
The company must dance through the feet of giants like Intel and Texas Instruments, but its blazing start and proven development methods should serve it well.

BROADCOM AT A GLANCE

Fiscal year ended: Dec. 31
Revenue in $ millions

	1995	1996	1997	1998	1999	4-Year Growth Avg. Annual (%)	Total (%)
Revenue ($)	6.1	21.4	36.9	211.9	518.2	204	8,395
Earnings/share ($)	0.00	0.02	-0.02	0.15	0.36	165*	1,700*
PE ratio range	—	NA	NA	60-173	64-401		

*Earnings per share data reflect 3-year results.

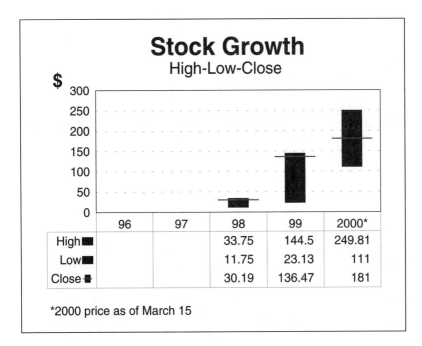

Stock Growth
High-Low-Close

$	96	97	98	99	2000*
High			33.75	144.5	249.81
Low			11.75	23.13	111
Close			30.19	136.47	181

*2000 price as of March 15

7

i2 Technologies, Inc.

909 East Las Colinas Boulevard
Irving, TX 75039
214-860-6000
Nasdaq: ITWO
www.i2.com

Chairman, President, and CEO: Sanjiv S. Sidhu

Earnings Progression	★ ★ ★ ★
Revenue Growth	★ ★ ★ ★
Stock Growth	★ ★ ★ ★
Consistency	★ ★ ★
Stability/Vulnerability	★ ★ ★
Total Points	**18 points**

When General Motors and Commerce One announced their blockbuster deal to create the online GM TradeXchange, they turned to software maker i2 Technologies to provide the brains behind the operation.

i2 makes "supply chain management" software, which is used by manufacturers to synchronize the flow of goods and services with suppliers. Managing events within a manufacturing company is hard enough, but complexity soars when coordinating across several companies.

But i2 has helped companies pull it off with their innovative software. The company, founded in 1988 by two engineers out of Texas Instrument's famed Artificial Intelligence Lab, came up with a breakthrough scheduling technology for managing business-to-business transactions.

i2's product, called Rhythm, enables companies to manage inventories and factory floors with greater precision. Rhythm has earned a reputation for delivering enormous efficiency gains to its customers.

Rhythm evolved into an Internet product, because digital marketplaces also need software to handle logistics in order to form online exchanges for complex products. With that in mind, i2 expanded Rhythm into a product suite with several modules:

- **Supply Chain Management (SCM).** The company's flagship product, Rhythm SCM, fine-tunes the business of e-commerce from bid through delivery.
- **Product Lifecycle Management (PLM).** Used to find reusable components and to identify potential production bottlenecks.
- **Rhythm eCustomer Marketing Suite.** This software is used to profile and target customers, configure and price complex products, and even schedule field technician service calls.

i2 went public with its initial stock offering in 1996. It has about 2,200 employees and a market capitalization of about $16 billion.

EARNINGS PER SHARE PROGRESSION ★ ★ ★ ★

Earnings growth past 4 years: 250 percent (37 percent per year)

REVENUE GROWTH ★ ★ ★ ★

Past 4 years: 2,105 percent (117 percent per year)

STOCK GROWTH ★ ★ ★ ★

Past 3 years: 916 percent (117 percent per year)
Dollar growth: $10,000 over 3 years would have grown to $101,600.

CONSISTENCY ★ ★ ★

Increased earnings per share: 3 of the past 4 years
Increased sales: 4 consecutive years

STABILITY/VULNERABILITY ★ ★ ★

Like most software companies, i2 Technologies faces intense competition, but its Rhythm software puts i2 among the world's elite.

i2 TECHNOLOGIES AT A GLANCE

Fiscal year ended: Dec. 31
Revenue in $ millions

	1995	1996	1997	1998	1999	4-Year Growth Avg. Annual (%)	Total (%)
Revenue ($)	25.9	87.9	213.7	368.3	571.1	117	2,105
Earnings/share ($)	0.04	0.06	0.03	0.07	0.14	37	250
PE ratio range	NA	115-284	229-500	35-161	66-810		

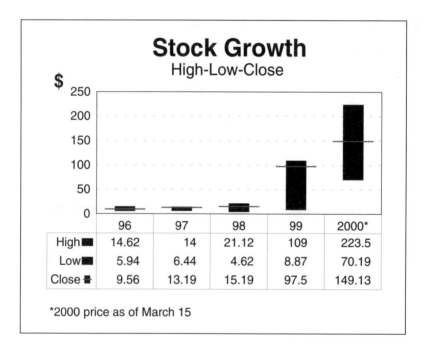

Stock Growth
High-Low-Close

$	96	97	98	99	2000*
High	14.62	14	21.12	109	223.5
Low	5.94	6.44	4.62	8.87	70.19
Close	9.56	13.19	15.19	97.5	149.13

*2000 price as of March 15

8

VeriSign, Inc.

1350 Charleston Road
Mountain View, CA 94043
650-961-7500
Nasdaq: VRSN
www.verisign.com

Chairman: D. James Bidzos
President and CEO: Stratton D. Sclavos

Earnings Progression	★ ★ ★
Revenue Growth	★ ★ ★ ★
Stock Growth	★ ★ ★
Consistency	★ ★ ★ ★
Stability/Vulnerability	★ ★ ★
Total Points	**17 points**

Does a 90 percent market share grab your attention? That's VeriSign's piece of the market for Web site trust services, making it one of the most important service companies on the Net.

The Mountain View, California operation issues and manages "digital certificates," which are computer files encrypted with virtually unbreakable codes. The certificates are essentially electronic ID cards used by computers to verify the identity of individuals and even other computers.

Knowing who you're dealing with is especially important in the faceless world of the Internet, and the level of security provided by passwords is far too weak for most e-commerce transactions. That's where VeriSign comes in. Its tamper-proof certificates are known only to the identified party and the e-commerce site. Its services include:

1. **Web site certificate services.** E-merchants use VeriSign not only to protect themselves, but also to give consumers a feeling of security for their Internet credit card transactions.
2. **Enterprise certificate services.** Organizations are turning to VeriSign to help guarantee security within their internal networks and in private extranet connections to trading partners.
3. **VeriSign affiliate certificate services.** VeriSign outfits affiliates with the software, data centers, and expertise to operate trust services for closed e-commerce and communications networks.

The company is well on its way to becoming the standard for online certificates. Microsoft and Netscape have embedded VeriSign software into their browsers and Web server packages, and Cisco Systems has incorporated VeriSign software into its routers.

VeriSign has about 320 employees and a market capitalization of about $20 billion.

EARNINGS PER SHARE PROGRESSION   ★ ★ ★
The company had its first gain in 1999, reversing a string of losses.

REVENUE GROWTH   ★ ★ ★ ★
Past 4 years: 22,099 percent (286 percent per year)

STOCK GROWTH   ★ ★ ★
Past year: 1,192 percent
Dollar growth: $10,000 over 1 year would have grown to $129,000

CONSISTENCY   ★ ★ ★ ★
Positive earnings progression: 2 consecutive years
Increased sales: 4 consecutive years

STABILITY/VULNERABILITY   ★ ★ ★
VeriSign's market position could hardly be more solid, but it must keep pace with technology advances in the arcane field of cryptography.

VERISIGN AT A GLANCE

Fiscal year ended: Dec. 31
Revenue in $ millions

	1995	1996	1997	1998	1999	4-Year Growth Avg. Annual (%)	Total (%)
Revenue ($)	.382	1.4	13.4	38.9	84.8	286	22,099
Earnings/share ($)	–0.21	–0.19	–0.28	–0.24	0.35	NA	NA
PE ratio range	NA	NA	NA	NA	NA		

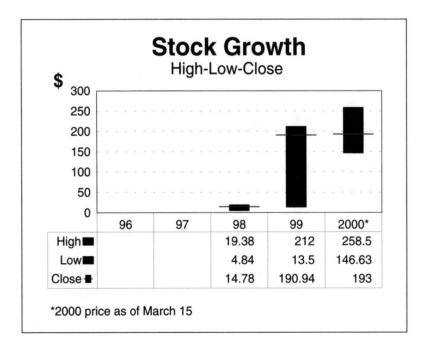

Stock Growth
High-Low-Close

$	96	97	98	99	2000*
High ■			19.38	212	258.5
Low ■			4.84	13.5	146.63
Close ■			14.78	190.94	193

*2000 price as of March 15

ONLINE FINANCIAL
SERVICES

9

Knight/Trimark Group, Inc.

Newport Tower, 29th Floor
525 Washington Boulevard
Jersey City, NJ 07310
201-222-9400
Nasdaq: NITE
www.knight-sec.com

Chairman: Steven L. Steinman
President and CEO: Kenneth D. Pasternak

Earnings Progression	★ ★ ★ ★
Revenue Growth	★ ★ ★ ★
Stock Growth	★ ★
Consistency	★ ★ ★ ★
Stability/Vulnerability	★ ★ ★
Total Points	**17 points**

No one has benefited more from the boom in online stock trading than Knight/Trimark Group.

The Jersey City operation is the market maker for several online brokerage companies, and the leading market maker for all Nasdaq stocks. As the market maker, it maintains bid and ask prices on securities and stands ready to buy those stocks if necessary to keep the market fluid. The company, which executes stock buy and sell transactions initiated by millions of investors, collects a very tiny percentage on every transaction it executes.

In all, Knight/Trimark makes the market for about 7,000 Nasdaq and over-the-counter securities and all NYSE and AMEX stocks when they are traded in the over-the-counter market.

Knight/Trimark has made rapid strides to become the market leader. In 1997, it ranked sixth among Nasdaq market makers, trading about 235 million shares a month. By the end of 1998, it ranked first among Nasdaq market makers, trading more than 600 million shares a month, including 250,000 separate trades each day. By early 2000, the company's volume had doubled again, executing about 500,000 separate trades each day.

The company has attracted a growing client base among brokerage firms because of its automated trading procedure and leading-edge services. Knight/Trimark was the first market maker to accept stop orders on all Nasdaq stocks.

Knight/Trimark's early growth came from the boom in online trading by individuals, but it has become increasingly popular among institutional traders, such as pension funds and money management firms. Institutional trading accounts for about one-third of total revenue.

Knight/Trimark Group went public with its initial stock offering in 1998. The company has about 500 employees and a market capitalization of about $4 billion.

EARNINGS PER SHARE PROGRESSION   ★ ★ ★ ★

Earnings growth past 4 years: 1,986 percent (113 percent per year)

REVENUE GROWTH   ★ ★ ★ ★

Past 4 years: 1,047 percent (84 percent per year)

STOCK GROWTH   ★ ★

Past year: 284 percent
Dollar growth: $10,000 over 1 year would have grown to $38,400.

CONSISTENCY   ★ ★ ★ ★

Increased earnings per share: 4 consecutive years
Increased sales: 4 consecutive years

STABILITY/VULNERABILITY   ★ ★ ★

Knight/Trimark is a strong company in a leadership position of a booming industry.

KNIGHT/TRIMARK GROUP AT A GLANCE

Fiscal year ended: Dec. 31
Revenue in $ millions

	1995	1996	1997	1998	1999	4-Year Growth Avg. Annual (%)	Total (%)
Revenue ($)	69.8	185.2	226.7	355.7	800.7	84	1,047
Earnings/share ($)	0.07	0.25	0.31	0.53	1.46	113	1,986
PE ratio range	NA	NA	NA	4-27	7-56		

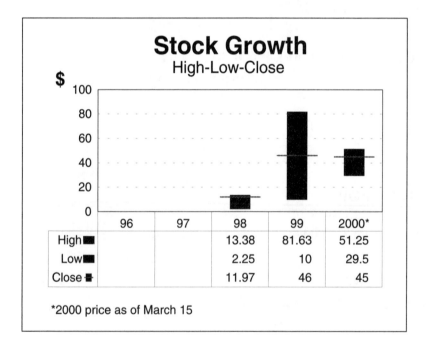

Stock Growth
High-Low-Close

$	96	97	98	99	2000*
High			13.38	81.63	51.25
Low			2.25	10	29.5
Close			11.97	46	45

*2000 price as of March 15

10
CNET, Inc.

150 Chestnut Street
San Francisco, CA 94111
415-395-7800
Nasdaq: CNET
www.cnet.com

Chairman and CEO: Halsey Minor

Earnings Progression	★ ★ ★
Revenue Growth	★ ★ ★ ★
Stock Growth	★ ★ ★ ★
Consistency	★ ★ ★
Stability/Vulnerability	★ ★ ★
Total Points	**17 points**

In a world of high-tech overload, CNET helps consumers make sense of new technology. The San Francisco firm operates a network of technology-related Web sites and produces several television shows that deal with technology issues.

CNET's Web sites are among the leading attractions on the Net in terms of both audience size and revenue. The company boasts millions of Web users each day. CNET does not sell any products but rather provides product information and reviews for high-tech consumers. The company's Web sites include:

- **CNET.com**—the leading site for product reviews and perspectives on developments in computers and the Internet
- **Builder.com**—a central source for Web-building product reviews and industry news
- **Computers.com**—the most comprehensive source for computer hardware information

- **News.com**—a timely technology news site
- **Shopper.com**—a consumer's source for determining where to buy computer products on the Internet. The site compares more than one million prices from 100 major resellers and contains data on more than 100,000 products.
- **Gamecenter.com**—which offers gaming news, reviews, tips, and downloads
- **Search.com**—an easy-to-use Web browser
- **Download.com**—a comprehensive software download services site

CNET first began to produce television shows in 1995. It now produces four weekly shows for the Sci-Fi Channel and one show, *TV.COM*, for syndication to other stations. The company also produces a series of daily technology inserts for local news broadcasts.

CNET's four Sci-Fi Channel shows include *CNET Central*, which covers news and feature stories regarding computer technology; *The Web*, which covers Web sites and technology; *The New Edge*, which covers new developments in technology; and *Cool Tech*, which covers new technology products.

CNET went public with its initial stock offering in 1996. It has about 500 employees and a market capitalization of about $4 billion.

EARNINGS PER SHARE PROGRESSION   ★ ★ ★
CNET progressed from large losses to annual 1999 earnings per share of $4.92.

REVENUE GROWTH   ★ ★ ★ ★
Past 4 years: 3,108 percent (138 percent per year)

STOCK GROWTH   ★ ★ ★ ★
Past 4 years: 2,091 percent (117 percent per year)
Dollar growth: $10,000 over 4 years would have grown to $219,000.

CONSISTENCY   ★ ★ ★
Positive earnings progression: 2 consecutive years.
Increased revenue: 4 consecutive years.

STABILITY/VULNERABILITY   ★ ★ ★
CNET is well established in its niche, and with a stake in both TV and the Internet, it is more diversified than many other Web stocks.

CNET AT A GLANCE

Fiscal year ended: Dec. 31
Revenue in $ millions

	1995	1996	1997	1998	1999	4-Year Growth Avg. Annual (%)	Total (%)
Revenue ($)	3.5	14.8	33.6	57.1	112.3	138	3,108
Earnings/share ($)	–0.23	–0.38	–0.46	0.04	4.92	12,200*	NA
PE ratio range	NA	NA	NA	158-503	2-16		

*Earnings per share growth figure reflects just 1 year.

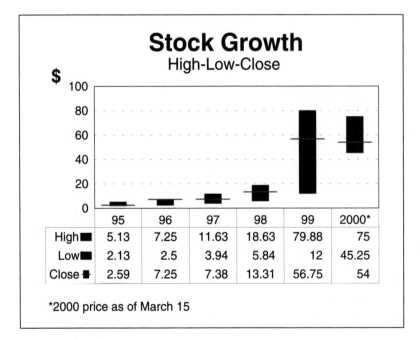

Stock Growth
High-Low-Close

$	95	96	97	98	99	2000*
High■	5.13	7.25	11.63	18.63	79.88	75
Low■	2.13	2.5	3.94	5.84	12	45.25
Close ■	2.59	7.25	7.38	13.31	56.75	54

*2000 price as of March 15

SOFTWARE

11
Mercury Interactive Corporation

1325 Borregas Avenue
Sunnyvale, CA 94089
408-822-5200
Nasdaq: MERQ
www.merc-int.com

Chairman, President, and CEO: Amnon Landan

Earnings Progression	★ ★ ★ ★
Revenue Growth	★ ★ ★ ★
Stock Growth	★ ★
Consistency	★ ★ ★ ★
Stability/Vulnerability	★ ★ ★
Total Points	**17 points**

A lot can go wrong on the World Wide Web—as anyone who has ever surfed the Net would quickly attest. Mercury Interactive software enables Internet companies to test their Web functions and isolate bad links, slow applications, and a host of other potential problems.

The Sunnyvale, California operation got its start prior to the emergence of the Internet, making software used by companies to test normal computer functions under UNIX or Windows. But in recent years, Mercury has focused increasingly on Internet testing.

Mercury's software is used by many of the world largest businesses, including America Online, Siemens, Alcatel, Federal Express, Hewlett-Packard, Citibank, Nabisco, and American Airlines.

The company's Internet testing software includes:

- **LoadRunner.** This Web load-testing tool is used to exercise the system just like real users would. It helps developers get an accurate view of system behavior and performance throughout the application development lifecycle.

- **WebTest.** This Internet testing software allows developers to measure response time to a browser request, to determine the maximum number of hits the server can support, and to validate the system's ability to function under various conditions.
- **Astra SiteManager.** This visual management tool scans an entire Web site, highlighting functional areas with color-coded links and URLs to create a complete visual map of the Web site. It pinpoints broken links or access problems, compares maps as a site changes, identifies key usage patterns, and validates dynamically generated pages.

Mercury Interactive has about 620 employees and a market capitalization of about $7 billion.

EARNINGS PER SHARE PROGRESSION ★ ★ ★ ★

Past 3 years: 500 percent (82 percent per year)

REVENUE GROWTH ★ ★ ★ ★

Past 4 years: 375 percent (48 percent per year)

STOCK GROWTH ★ ★

Mercury Interactive went public in 1999 and experienced strong gains after it's IPO.

CONSISTENCY ★ ★ ★ ★

Positive earnings progression: 4 consecutive years
Increased revenue: 4 consecutive years

STABILITY/VULNERABILITY ★ ★ ★

Mercury Interactive is a leader in the Web testing market. It has long been profitable, and its earnings have been rising rapidly.

MERCURY INTERACTIVE AT A GLANCE

Fiscal year ended: Dec. 31
Revenue in $ millions

	1995	1996	1997	1998	1999	4-Year Growth Avg. Annual (%)	Total (%)
Revenue ($)	39.5	54.6	76.7	121	187.7	48	375
Earnings/share ($)	-0.09	0.07	0.09	0.28	0.42	82*	500*
PE ratio range	—	34-86	24-72	19-57	25-133		

*Earnings per share growth is for 3 years.

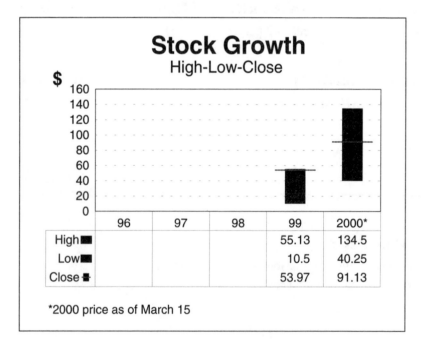

Stock Growth
High-Low-Close

$	96	97	98	99	2000*
High				55.13	134.5
Low				10.5	40.25
Close				53.97	91.13

*2000 price as of March 15

12

Carrier Access Corporation

INFRASTRUCTURE

5395 Pearl Parkway
Boulder, CO 80301
303-442-5455
Nasdaq: CACS
www.carrieraccess.com

Chairman, President, and CEO: Roger L. Koenig

Earnings Progression	★ ★ ★ ★
Revenue Growth	★ ★ ★ ★
Stock Growth	★ ★
Consistency	★ ★ ★ ★
Stability/Vulnerability	★ ★
Total Points	**16 points**

Talk about perfect market positioning. The three factors driving change in the "last mile" separating users from the Internet backbone—demand for more bandwidth, data/voice integration, and the Telecommunications Reform Act of 1996—all directly benefit Carrier Access Corporation.

The Boulder, Colorado operation manufactures digital media access devices, which, in a single box, connect a company to both the Internet and the telephone network.

Competitive local exchange carriers (CLECs), turned loose on the Baby Bells by deregulation, form the company's primary customer base, although Internet service providers (ISPs) are a growing source of business.

Founded in 1992, Carrier Access was first to recognize the need for smaller, simpler equipment to channel high-speed "T1" copper phone lines into businesses. While other manufacturers chased big customers, Carrier Access focused on selling cost-effective products to the seven million U.S. businesses too small to merit fiber-optic service to their buildings.

The company was a hit from the outset, because its products are easy to install and operate, yet packed with features that let CLECs offer flexible "carrier class" services on a par with the major corporations. As if the deregulated telecommunications market weren't hot enough, the explosive growth of the Internet has catapulted the company into the stratosphere.

Carrier Access products are placed at end-user sites, yet can be monitored and managed remotely. That's an important feature to CLECs and ISPs, which can't match the field technician forces Baby Bells have.

The company's products have kept up with technology advances having to do with technical standards for voice/data integration.

Carrier Access, which has 200 employees, made its initial public stock offering in 1998. It has a market capitalization of about $1 billion.

EARNINGS PER SHARE PROGRESSION   ★ ★ ★ ★

Past 2 years earnings growth: 1,760 percent (331 percent per year)

REVENUE GROWTH   ★ ★ ★ ★

Past 3 years: 1,776 percent (165 percent per year)

STOCK GROWTH   ★ ★

Past year: 95 percent
Dollar growth: $10,000 over 1 year would have grown to $19,500.

CONSISTENCY   ★ ★ ★ ★

Positive earnings progression: 3 consecutive years
Increased revenue: 3 consecutive years

STABILITY/VULNERABILITY   ★ ★

The company was smart and nimble enough to capitalize on the needs of the huge small business market, but competition is mounting.

CARRIER ACCESS AT A GLANCE

Fiscal year ended: Dec. 31
Revenue in $ millions

	1995	1996	1997	1998	1999	3-Year Growth Avg. Annual (%)	Total (%)
Revenue ($)	—	5.8	18.7	48.1	108.8	165	1,776
Earnings/share ($)	—	–0.03	0.05	0.23	0.93	331*	1,760*
PE ratio range	—	—	—	48-131	NA		

*Earnings per share data reflect 2-year growth.

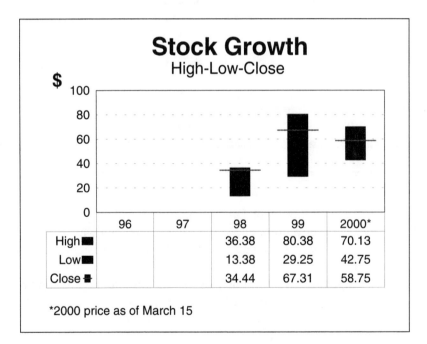

Stock Growth
High-Low-Close

	96	97	98	99	2000*
High■			36.38	80.38	70.13
Low■			13.38	29.25	42.75
Close ■			34.44	67.31	58.75

*2000 price as of March 15

13

Network Appliance, Inc.

495 East Java Drive
Sunnyvale, CA 94089
408-822-6000
Nasdaq: NTAP
www.netapp.com

Chairman: Donald T. Valentine
President and CEO: Daniel J. Warmenhoven

Earnings Progression	★ ★
Revenue Growth	★ ★ ★ ★
Stock Growth	★ ★ ★ ★
Consistency	★ ★ ★
Stability/Vulnerability	★ ★ ★
Total Points	**16 points**

The explosive growth of the Web has had the same effect on Internet traffic flow as the increased automobile volume has had on highway traffic—it has slowed down access to Web information, particularly during the busiest times of the day.

Network Appliance (NetApp) helps solve that problem by making a computer storage device called a "filer" that companies can use to store and retrieve data on their network quickly and efficiently.

The filers give organizations virtually unlimited data storage capacity. And because they are attached to the organization's network, all the computer users in the organization have easy access to store and retrieve data. The filers are built with a software system that optimizes file service task performance, providing faster and more dependable access than the general purpose computers traditionally used to store data.

Nine of the top ten Internet service providers worldwide use NetApp's storage devices, which range in price from $20,000 to $750,000. NetApp offers a variety of storage devices and related products:

- **SnapMirror and SnapRestore.** These products provide data backup and disaster recovery, allowing companies to minimize downtime and eliminate time-consuming backup routines.
- **NetApp C720S caching appliance.** This storage device is designed for smaller ISPs and company networks.
- **SecureAdmin.** This network security device allows administrators to conduct encrypted sessions over the Internet.

NetApp went public with its initial stock offering in 1995. It has about 800 employees and a market capitalization of about $25 billion.

EARNINGS PER SHARE PROGRESSION ★ ★

Earnings have bounced around the past four years after a loss in 1995.

REVENUE GROWTH ★ ★ ★ ★

Past 4 years: 1,855 percent (110 percent per year)

STOCK GROWTH ★ ★ ★ ★

Past 4 years: 1,554 percent (102 percent per year)
Dollar growth: $10,000 over 4 years would have grown to $165,400.

CONSISTENCY ★ ★ ★

Positive earnings progression: 2 consecutive years
Increased revenue: 4 consecutive years

STABILITY/VULNERABILITY ★ ★ ★

Network Appliance is a leader in this rapidly growing sector, and the company has been profitable since 1998.

NETWORK APPLIANCE AT A GLANCE

Fiscal year ended: April 30
Revenue in $ millions

	1995	1996	1997	1998	1999	4-Year Growth Avg. Annual (%)	Total (%)
Revenue ($)	14.8	46.6	93.3	166.2	289.4	110	1,855
Earnings/share ($)	–0.19	0.21	0.01	0.15	0.23	1.2*	9.5*
PE ratio range	NA	48-124	1328-4500	45-164	83-401		

*Earnings per share data reflect 3-year performance.

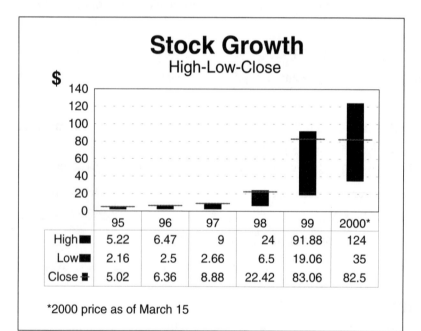

Stock Growth
High-Low-Close

$	95	96	97	98	99	2000*
High■	5.22	6.47	9	24	91.88	124
Low■	2.16	2.5	2.66	6.5	19.06	35
Close ■	5.02	6.36	8.88	22.42	83.06	82.5

*2000 price as of March 15

14

America Online Time Warner, Inc.

22000 AOL Way
Dulles, VA 20166
703-265-1000
NYSE: AOL
www.aol.com

Chairman: Steve Case
CEO: Gerald Levin
Vice Chairman: Ted Turner

Earnings Progression	★ ★
Revenue Growth	★ ★ ★ ★
Stock Growth	★ ★ ★ ★
Consistency	★ ★ ★
Stability/Vulnerability	★ ★ ★
Total Points	**16 points**

When America Online acquired Time Warner, it was a little bit like the mouse swallowing the elephant. AOL's annual revenue of about $5 billion was less than one-fourth that of Time Warner.

The merger created what is perhaps the world's most diversified media conglomerate. AOL is the world's leading Internet portal with more than 20 million subscribers. Time Warner commands the world's largest media empire, including an array of popular magazines, some leading cable television networks, and one of the world's leading music recording operations, Warner Music Group.

AOL operates two Internet services, America Online and CompuServe (with more than two million subscribers). The company also owns Netscape, which is one of the leading Internet browsers.

For a monthly fee of about $20, AOL members receive access to a variety of information and services, including breaking news, business and financial news, stock quotes, investment research, sports news, e-mail, Internet access, electronic magazines and newspapers, travel features and weather reports, online classes and conferences, an online encyclopedia, and a variety of children's games and information features. The company also offers online shopping through its site, a service that is growing rapidly. AOL subscribers spent about $10 billion shopping online in 1999.

AOL is expanding with similar services in Europe and Asia. It also owns about a 25 percent share of Hong Kong–based China.com.

The Virginia-based operation went public with its initial stock offering in 1992. With the Time Warner acquisition, AOL jumped from about 12,000 employees to nearly 80,000. Its market capitalization jumped from about $150 billion to about $250 billion.

EARNINGS PER SHARE PROGRESSION   ★ ★

AOL had earnings in 1999, but losses three of the previous four years.

REVENUE GROWTH   ★ ★ ★ ★

Past 5 years: 1,024 percent (83 percent per year)

STOCK GROWTH   ★ ★ ★ ★

Past 4 years: 3,121 percent (138 percent per year)
Dollar growth: $10,000 over 4 years would have grown to $322,100.

CONSISTENCY   ★ ★ ★

Positive earnings progression: 2 consecutive years
Increased revenue: 4 consecutive years

STABILITY/VULNERABILITY   ★ ★ ★

AOL is certainly stable, but the rapid growth it enjoyed may slow considerably now that it has become a diversified media conglomerate.

AMERICA ONLINE TIME WARNER* AT A GLANCE

Fiscal year ended: June 30
Revenue in $ millions

	1995	1996	1997	1998	1999	Avg. Annual (%)	Total (%)
						4-Year Growth	
Revenue ($)	425	1,323	2,197	3,091	4,777	83	1,024
Earnings/share ($)	–0.09	0.04	–0.58	–0.08	0.60	NA	NA
PE ratio range	NA	82-261	NA	NA	38-321		

*These figures do not include Time Warner numbers.

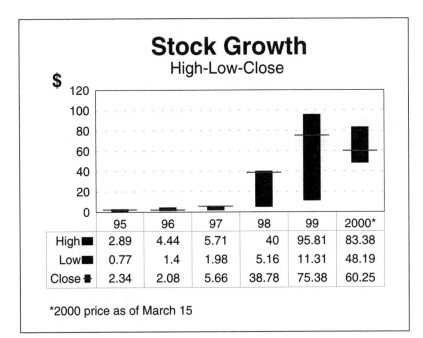

Stock Growth
High-Low-Close

	95	96	97	98	99	2000*
High	2.89	4.44	5.71	40	95.81	83.38
Low	0.77	1.4	1.98	5.16	11.31	48.19
Close	2.34	2.08	5.66	38.78	75.38	60.25

*2000 price as of March 15

INTERNET BUSINESS
SERVICES

15
Exodus Communications

2821 Mission College Boulevard
Santa Clara, CA 95054
408-346-2200
Nasdaq: EXDS
www.exodus.net

Chairman: K.B. Chandrasekhar
President and CEO: Ellen M. Hancock

Earnings Progression	★
Revenue Growth	★ ★ ★ ★
Stock Growth	★ ★ ★
Consistency	★ ★ ★
Stability/Vulnerability	★ ★ ★ ★
Total Points	**15 points**

Operating a world-class Web site can drive a business to distraction. That's why giants like Yahoo! and eBay don't even run their own sites—they farm the job out to Exodus Communications, the leading provider of large-scale Internet server hosting.

Exodus pioneered the concept of building data centers expressly to handle the demands of high-volume Web site operations. Their customers don't have to worry about such things as security, maintenance, facilities, or staffing—Exodus handles everything.

The company's business model differs from most Web hosting services. Instead of renting time on computers it owns, Exodus houses customer-owned computers in locked cages and operates them according to the customer's instructions. Exodus has earned a sterling reputation for its expertise in keeping large sites up and running fast.

Exodus operates 16 Internet data centers connected by a private high-speed data network. Although its Internet data centers are impressive, Exodus's real value is its expertise. Internet computing is so new and different from traditional corporate data processing that few companies have the skills needed to manage the unpredictability of a major Web site. Exodus does.

The company has posted eye-popping annual growth rates and has compiled an impressive list of more than 800 customers. The outlook seems bright for Exodus. Internet research firm Forrester Research forecasts the hosting market will grow from $2 billion in 1999 to nearly $15 billion by 2003.

Founded in 1995, Exodus went public with its initial stock offering in 1998. It has about 500 employees and a market capitalization of about $14 billion.

EARNINGS PER SHARE PROGRESSION ★

The company has had a string of losses—but they have declined since 1997.

REVENUE GROWTH ★ ★ ★ ★

Past 4 years: 17,157 percent (263 percent per year)

STOCK GROWTH ★ ★ ★

Past year: 1,006 percent
Dollar growth: $10,000 over 1 year would have grown to $110,600.

CONSISTENCY ★ ★ ★

Positive earnings progression: None
Increased revenue: 4 consecutive years

STABILITY/VULNERABILITY ★ ★ ★ ★

The big guys are moving in with deep pockets and solid brand names, but Exodus is in a solid position.

EXODUS COMMUNICATIONS AT A GLANCE

Fiscal year ended: Dec. 31
Revenue in $ millions

	1995	1996	1997	1998	1999	4-Year Growth Avg. Annual (%)	4-Year Growth Total (%)
Revenue ($)	1.4	3.1	12.4	52.7	241.6	263	17,157
Earnings/share ($)	−0.12	−0.27	−1.73	−0.48	−0.73	NA	NA
PE ratio range	NA	NA	NA	NA	NA		

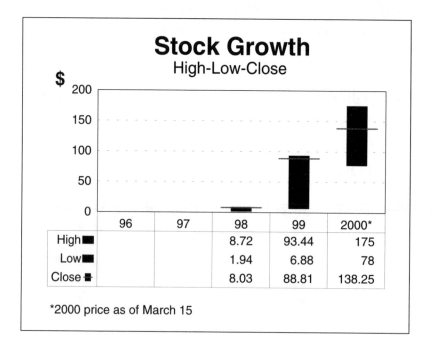

Stock Growth
High-Low-Close

	96	97	98	99	2000*
High■			8.72	93.44	175
Low■			1.94	6.88	78
Close ■			8.03	88.81	138.25

*2000 price as of March 15

DoubleClick, Inc.

INTERNET BUSINESS
SERVICES

41 Madison Avenue, 32nd Floor
New York, NY 10010
212-683-0001
Nasdaq: DCLK
www.doubleclick.com

Chairman and CEO: K.J. O'Connor
President: K.P. Ryan

Earnings Progression	★
Revenue Growth	★ ★ ★ ★
Stock Growth	★ ★ ★
Consistency	★ ★ ★
Stability/Vulnerability	★ ★ ★ ★
Total Points	**15 points**

DoubleClick has quickly established itself as the kingpin of online advertising, helping Web publishers large and small attract advertisers to their sites. In the process, the Madison Avenue operation siphons off a whopping 30 to 50 percent of the ad revenue it collects before passing the balance on to the sites that run the ads.

The company serves well over 1,000 Web publishers, delivering more than 20 billion ad hits per month for its advertising clients. DoubleClick has created a network of more than 90 large Web sites, such as AltaVista and *U.S. News & World Report,* that pay a fee to place their ads on small and medium-sized Web sites. In all, the firm handles ads from about 3,600 advertisers on about 10,000 different Web sites.

The company developed its own technology called Dynamic Advertising, Reporting, and Targeting (DART), which tracks ad results and uses those results to identify the best targets for those specific ads. The company also can handle planning and execution of online media campaigns for its customers.

DoubleClick recently acquired Abacus Direct, which seems like an ideal fit, because Abacus manages the nation's largest database of consumer buying behavior information used for target marketing on the Internet and through direct mail.

DoubleClick is not involved in the creative end of the advertising market. "We try to stay out of the creative world," explains CEO Kevin O'Connor. "Instead, we are creating an infrastructure that can deliver bytes."

Online advertising is projected to grow from $3 billion in billings in 1999 to $20 billion to $50 billion by 2005, so the upside could be enormous. And, DoubleClick is the clear leader in the market.

The Madison Avenue operation went public with its initial stock offering in 1998. DoubleClick has about 500 employees and a market capitalization of about $10 billion.

EARNINGS PER SHARE PROGRESSION   ★

The company has had a string of small losses.

REVENUE GROWTH   ★ ★ ★ ★

Past 3 years: 3,867 percent (226 percent per year)

STOCK GROWTH   ★ ★ ★

Past year: 1,037 percent
Dollar growth: $10,000 over 1 year would have grown to $113,700.

CONSISTENCY   ★ ★ ★

Positive earnings progression: None
Increased revenue: 3 consecutive years

STABILITY/VULNERABILITY   ★ ★ ★ ★

As the leader in the exploding online advertising market, DoubleClick should be solid for years to come.

DOUBLECLICK AT A GLANCE

Fiscal year ended: Dec. 31
Revenue in $ millions

	1995	1996	1997	1998	1999	3-Year Growth Avg. Annual (%)	Total (%)
Revenue ($)	—	6.51	30.6	80.2	258.3	226	3,867
Earnings/share ($)	—	–0.07	–0.19	–0.30	–0.42	NA	NA
PE ratio range	—	NA	NA	NA	NA		

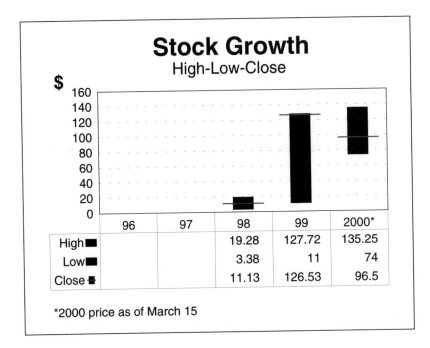

Stock Growth
High-Low-Close

	96	97	98	99	2000*
High ■			19.28	127.72	135.25
Low ■			3.38	11	74
Close ■			11.13	126.53	96.5

*2000 price as of March 15

17

Verio, Inc.

8005 S. Chester Street, Suite 200
Englewood, CO 80112
303-645-1900
Nasdaq: VRIO
www.verio.com

Chairman: Steven C. Halstedt
CEO: Justin Jaschke

Earnings Progression	★ ★ ★
Revenue Growth	★ ★ ★ ★
Stock Growth	★ ★
Consistency	★ ★ ★
Stability/Vulnerability	★ ★ ★
Total Points	**15 points**

If Verio has its way, it will be host to the world—the Internet world, that is. The Englewood, Colorado operation is the nation's largest host for business Web sites. More than a quarter million companies outsource the operation of their e-commerce sites to Verio.

Founded in 1996, Verio was the first Internet service provider (ISP) to recognize the opportunity to provide businesses specialized services in addition to Internet connections. The company targets the small and medium-sized business niche.

Verio offers a host of related services, including:

- **Dedicated Web site hosting.** Many of the nearly 300,000 Web sites Verio operates are run on a computer that is dedicated exclusively to a single company.

- **Network security.** Verio offers round-the-clock monitoring of each customer's Web site, much like a security firm that protects buildings.
- **Virtual Private Network (VPN).** Verio offers customers the ability to run private wide area internal networks over the Internet, saving up to 60 percent compared to using private leased lines.

Verio operates its own high-speed national network, which helps guarantee customers fast, reliable service. The company is global in scope, with customers in 170 countries.

Already the world's largest Web site host, Verio could experience exponential growth over the next five to ten years. The dedicated server market is expected to grow from about $150 million in 1998 to over $5 billion in 2003, according to Forrester Research, a Stamford, Connecticut research firm. And the bulk of that will come from smaller businesses that lack the resources to run their own sites.

Verio was founded in 1996 by a team of telephone industry veterans and went public with its initial stock offering in 1998. It has about 1,400 employees and a market capitalization of about $5 billion.

EARNINGS PER SHARE PROGRESSION ★ ★ ★
Large losses have become small losses the past two years.

REVENUE GROWTH ★ ★ ★ ★
Past 3 years: 10,849 percent (378 percent per year)

STOCK GROWTH ★ ★
Past year: 313 percent
Dollar growth: $10,000 over 1 year would have grown to $41,300.

CONSISTENCY ★ ★ ★
Positive earnings progression: 2 years
Increased revenue: 3 consecutive years

STABILITY/VULNERABILITY ★ ★ ★
The company's strength comes from its physical infrastructure and broad customer base.

VERIO AT A GLANCE

Fiscal year ended: Dec. 31
Revenue in $ millions

	1995	1996	1997	1998	1999	3-Year Growth Avg. Annual (%)	3-Year Growth Total (%)
Revenue ($)	—	2.36	35.7	120.6	258.4	378	10,849
Earnings/share ($)	—	-2.64	-19.93	-8.97	-2.55	NA	NA
PE ratio range	—	NA	NA	NA	NA		

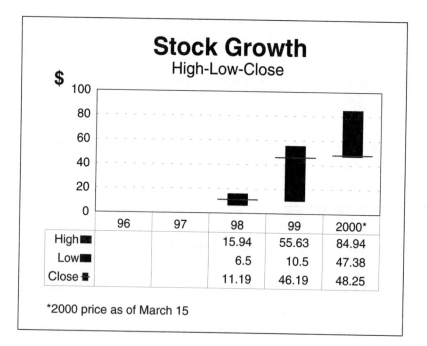

Stock Growth
High-Low-Close

$	96	97	98	99	2000*
High			15.94	55.63	84.94
Low			6.5	10.5	47.38
Close			11.19	46.19	48.25

*2000 price as of March 15

18

JDS Uniphase

163 Baypointe Parkway
San Jose, CA 95134
408-434-1800
Nasdaq: JDSU
www.jdsunph.com

CEO and Co-Chairman: Kevin N. Kalkhoven
President, COO, and Co-Chairman: Jozef Straus

Earnings Progression	
Revenue Growth	★ ★ ★ ★
Stock Growth	★ ★ ★ ★
Consistency	★ ★ ★
Stability/Vulnerability	★ ★ ★ ★
Total Points	**15 points**

With data traffic doubling every 100 days, experts are warning of a possible Internet "brownout." But recent technology advances may cause Internet speeds to accelerate rather than slow, making it possible for fiber-optic networks to move in a *minute* what it now takes a *day* to handle.

At the forefront of this technology is JDS Uniphase, the world's largest manufacturer of advanced fiber-optic components. The company's hardware can be inserted into existing fiber-optic networks to make them run much faster.

Started in the proverbial Silicon Valley garage in 1979, Uniphase went public in 1993 and set off on an impressive string of acquisitions:

- **Uniphase Telecommunications.** Acquired in 1995, this division makes the devices needed to control telecom and cable TV networks.

- **Fiberoptics Division.** This division, bought in 1996, makes special computer boards that connect fiber-optic links.
- **Uniphase Fiber Components.** Acquired in 1997, this division makes equipment that packs 80 signals into a fiber cable instead of just one.
- **Uniphase Laser Enterprise.** This division, bought in 1997, makes specialized semiconductors that pump signals into fiber links.
- **Uniphase Netherlands.** Acquired in 1998, this division makes various advanced components for operating fiber-optic networks.

Together, these mergers and acquisitions make JDS Uniphase the industry's primary source for advanced fiber-optic components.

JDS Uniphase has about 8,000 employees and a market capitalization of about $50 billion.

EARNINGS PER SHARE PROGRESSION

The company has gone from small gains to moderate losses.

REVENUE GROWTH   ★ ★ ★ ★

Past 4 years: 508 percent (57 percent per year)

STOCK GROWTH   ★ ★ ★ ★

Past 4 years: 7,134 percent (192 percent per year)
Dollar growth: $10,000 over 4 years would have grown to $714,400.

CONSISTENCY   ★ ★ ★

Positive earnings progression: None
Increased sales: 4 consecutive years

STABILITY/VULNERABILITY   ★ ★ ★ ★

Competitors include giants Lucent, Nortel, and Alcatel, but the company's extensive manufacturing capacity, know-how, and patented technologies are substantial.

JDS UNIPHASE AT A GLANCE

Fiscal year ended: June 30
Revenue in $ millions

	1995	1996	1997	1998	1999	4-Year Growth Avg. Annual (%)	Total (%)
Revenue ($)	46.5	73.7	113.2	185.2	282.8	57	508
Earnings/share ($)	0.02	0.03	–0.14	–0.14	–1.06	NA	NA
PE ratio range	88-265	71-290	NA	NA	NA		

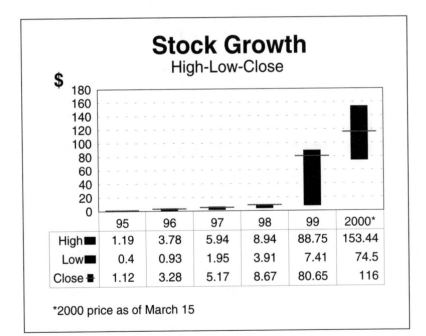

Stock Growth
High-Low-Close

$	95	96	97	98	99	2000*
High ■	1.19	3.78	5.94	8.94	88.75	153.44
Low ■	0.4	0.93	1.95	3.91	7.41	74.5
Close ■	1.12	3.28	5.17	8.67	80.65	116

*2000 price as of March 15

19

eBay, Inc.

2125 Hamilton Avenue
San Jose, CA 95125
408-558-7400
Nasdaq: EBAY
www.ebay.com

Chairman: Pierre M. Omidyar
President and CEO: Margaret C. Whitman

Earnings Progression	★ ★ ★
Revenue Growth	★ ★ ★ ★
Stock Growth	★ ★
Consistency	★ ★ ★
Stability/Vulnerability	★ ★ ★
Total Points	**15 points**

Welcome to eBay, flea market to the world. eBay was founded in 1995 with the idea of moving one of humanity's most primordial urges—bargain hunting—off the fairgrounds parking lot and onto the Web. A great deal for buyer and seller alike, eBay's online auction gives people access to the world's biggest bazaar without having to hop into the minivan and drive all over town.

It's easy to like the eBay business model. It has built-in margins, big growth potential, even natural barriers to would-be competitors. But that's not all—it has no inventory to carry, no warehouse to operate, no order fulfillment to worry about, and it can even rely, in large part, on word-of-mouth advertising. And, the company has natural staying power given that its constituency is best served by having a single place to meet and trade. Having dozens of venue options would only dilute the action.

The company's SafeHarbor program goes to great lengths to make its Web auction as fraud-proof as possible. Measures include independent verification of user identities, a Feedback Forum to check on reputations, an escrow money transfer service, and even free insurance up to $200.

It charges a nominal item listing fee and collects a 5 percent commission on most sales (somewhat less on high ticket items).

eBay's approach is working. Its site is second only to Amazon.com in visitors, and in a recent 12-month period, it auctioned about 35 million items to about 8 million registered users. The company is steadily adding new goods categories, such as its recently launched used car auction.

eBay went public with its initial stock offering in 1998. The company has about 150 employees and has a market capitalization of about $18 billion.

EARNINGS PER SHARE PROGRESSION ★ ★ ★
Past 2 years: 800 percent (200 percent per year)

REVENUE GROWTH ★ ★ ★ ★
Past 3 years: 60,303 percent (746 percent per year)

STOCK GROWTH ★ ★
Past year: 56 percent
Dollar growth: $10,000 over 1 year would have grown to $15,600.

CONSISTENCY ★ ★ ★
Increased earnings per share: 2 consecutive years
Increased revenue: 3 consecutive years

STABILITY/VULNERABILITY ★ ★ ★
The online auction business is so attractive that everybody wants in, including Yahoo!, Amazon.com, and even Microsoft. But eBay has earned the shopping junky's trust—and traffic.

EBAY AT A GLANCE

Fiscal year ended: Dec. 31
Revenue in $ millions

	1995	1996	1997	1998	1999	3-Year Growth Avg. Annual (%)	Total (%)
Revenue ($)	—	.372	5.74	47.7	224.7	746	60,303
Earnings/share ($)	—	0.00	0.01	0.05	0.09	200*	800*
PE ratio range	—	NA	NA	400-4940	NA		

*Earnings per share figures reflect 2-year growth.

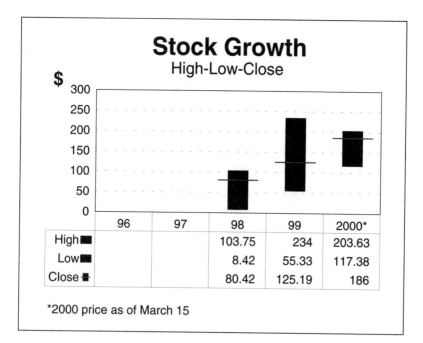

Stock Growth

High-Low-Close

	96	97	98	99	2000*
High			103.75	234	203.63
Low			8.42	55.33	117.38
Close			80.42	125.19	186

*2000 price as of March 15

20
Concentric Networks Corporation

1400 Parkmoor Avenue
San Jose, CA 95126
408-817-2800
Nasdaq: CNCX
www.concentric.net

President and CEO: Henry R. Nothaft

Earnings Progression	★ ★
Revenue Growth	★ ★ ★ ★
Stock Growth	★ ★ ★ ★
Consistency	★ ★ ★
Stability/Vulnerability	★ ★
Total Points	**15 points**

Internet cynics say that "www" actually stands for World Wide *Wait,* given how slow the Internet can be. To fight this problem, companies are buying reliable performance from Internet service providers (ISPs) such as Concentric Networks that offer their own high-speed networks.

Concentric's network covers North America with 19 major computer centers and about 150 access points in smaller markets. It provides high-speed connections between customer sites and the network and offers a variety of services designed to meet the needs of its business clientele, including:

- **ConcentricHost.** The world's second largest Web site host, ConcentricHost is a service in which businesses run their sites from a computer in a host's computer room.

- **Concentric Enterprise VPN.** The firm offers customized internal wide area networks (WANs) to companies under the Enterprise Virtual Private Network (VPN) brand.
- **Concentric Peak Protection.** Concentric's Peak Protection service shares work across its nine computer centers and also can work with computers operated by customers and even other ISPs.

Concentric has solid customer credentials. It operates Microsoft's WebTV network and provides services to Intuit, AT&T, Bloomberg, and others. Microsoft has invested in the company, as has SBC Communications, the country's largest local telephone company.

The San Jose, California operation went public with its initial stock offering in 1997. The company has about 500 employees and a market capitalization of about $2 billion.

EARNINGS PER SHARE PROGRESSION   ★ ★

The company's losses have declined somewhat over the past 3 years.

REVENUE GROWTH   ★ ★ ★ ★

Past 4 years: 5,831 percent (178 percent per year)

STOCK GROWTH   ★ ★ ★ ★

Past 2 years: 594 percent (163 percent per year)
Dollar growth: $10,000 over 2 years would have grown to $69,400.

CONSISTENCY   ★ ★ ★

Positive earnings progression: 2 of the past 3 years
Increased revenue: 4 consecutive years

STABILITY/VULNERABILITY   ★ ★

Concentric's tailored services should help blunt damage from a potential Internet backbone bandwidth glut.

CONCENTRIC NETWORKS AT A GLANCE

Fiscal year ended: Dec. 31
Revenue in $ millions

	1995	1996	1997	1998	1999	4-Year Growth Avg. Annual (%)	Total (%)
Revenue ($)	2.48	15.6	45.4	82.8	147.1	178	5,831
Earnings/share ($)	—	−5.94	−3.11	−3.33	−2.78	NA	NA
PE ratio range	—	NA	NA	NA	NA		

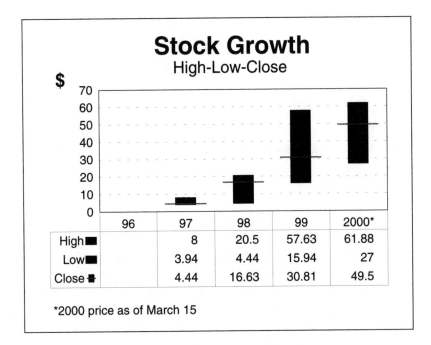

Stock Growth
High-Low-Close

	96	97	98	99	2000*
High		8	20.5	57.63	61.88
Low		3.94	4.44	15.94	27
Close		4.44	16.63	30.81	49.5

*2000 price as of March 15

INTERNET BUSINESS
SERVICES

21
ISS Group, Inc.

6600 Peachtree-Dunwoody Road
300 Embassy Row, Suite 500
Atlanta, GA 30328
678-443-6000
Nasdaq: ISSX
www.iss.net

Chairman, President, and CEO: Thomas A. Noonan

Earnings Progression	★ ★
Revenue Growth	★ ★ ★ ★
Stock Growth	★ ★
Consistency	★ ★ ★ ★
Stability/Vulnerability	★ ★ ★
Total Points	**15 points**

In a world in which highly sophisticated hackers can wreak havoc in an organization's computer network, information system security has become an absolute necessity. ISS Group specializes in protecting large corporate and government computer systems from outside intruders.

ISS designs and manufactures network security monitoring, detection, and response software that protects the security and integrity of computer databases and networks. The ISS system not only repels hackers, it also detects and monitors each attempt. Explains one ISS software user, "We see people rattling our doorknobs, but they're not getting in."

ISS has attracted an impressive list of customers, including 21 of the 25 largest U.S. banks, 9 of the top 10 telecommunications companies, 34 of the Fortune 50 companies, and more than 35 government agencies worldwide.

The Atlanta company's core product is the SAFEsuite software package, which incorporates several key components, including:

- **Internet Scanner.** Finds and fixes security holes through automated and comprehensive network security vulnerability detection and analysis.
- **System Scanner.** Serves as a security assessment system, helping manage security risks through detection and analysis of operating system, application, and user-controlled security weaknesses.
- **RealSecure.** Provides an integrated network- and host-based intrusion dection and response system.

ISS Group went public with its initial stock offering in 1998. It has about 350 employees and a market capitalization of about $3 billion.

EARNINGS PER SHARE PROGRESSION ★ ★

ISS had its first earnings in 1999 after a string of small losses.

REVENUE GROWTH ★ ★ ★ ★

Past 4 years: 45,231 percent (361 percent per year)

STOCK GROWTH ★ ★

Past year: 159 percent
Dollar growth: $10,000 over 1 year would have grown to $25,900.

CONSISTENCY ★ ★ ★ ★

Positive earnings progression: 2 consecutive years
Increased revenue: 4 consecutive years

STABILITY/VULNERABILITY ★ ★ ★

Small but growing, ISS Group has already attracted an impressive client base—and it is already profitable.

ISS GROUP AT A GLANCE

Fiscal year ended: Dec. 31
Revenue in $ millions

	1995	1996	1997	1998	1999	4-Year Growth Avg. Annual (%)	Total (%)
Revenue ($)	.257	4.46	13.4	49.2	116.5	361	45,231
Earnings/share ($)	–0.01	–0.04	–0.15	–0.14	0.18	NA	NA
PE ratio range	NA	NA	NA	NA	NA		

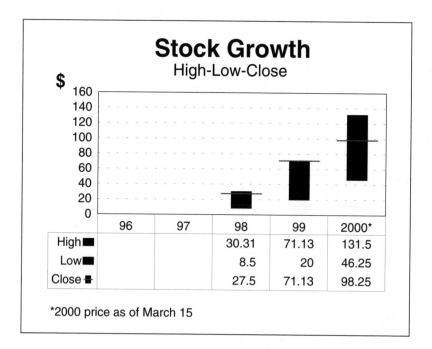

Stock Growth
High-Low-Close

$	96	97	98	99	2000*
High			30.31	71.13	131.5
Low			8.5	20	46.25
Close			27.5	71.13	98.25

*2000 price as of March 15

SOFTWARE

22
RealNetworks, Inc.

2601 Elliot Avenue, Suite 1000
Seattle, WA 98121
206-674-2700
Nasdaq: RNWK
www.real.com

Chairman and CEO: Robert Glaser

Earnings Progression	★ ★
Revenue Growth	★ ★ ★ ★
Stock Growth	★ ★ ★
Consistency	★ ★ ★
Stability/Vulnerability	★ ★ ★
Total Points	**15 points**

RealNetworks has brought real motion video to millions of home computers. It develops and markets software products designed to enable personal computers and other electronic devices to send and receive audio, video, and other multimedia services on both the Internet and corporate intranets.

The Seattle operation is the dominant player in the online streaming multimedia arena. More than 85 percent of all Web pages that use streaming media use RealNetworks technology. More than 400,000 hours of live streaming media programming is broadcast each week through RealNetworks.

In all, there are more than 100 million unique users of the company's RealPlayer technology. About a quarter of all Fortune 500 companies use RealNetworks to create streaming media presentations for their internal and external communications.

Through a recent agreement with GeoCities, RealNetworks has been able to expand its offerings to small business owners and consumers who can now create their own multimedia content with the help of the company's RealSystem G2 production tools and Web multimedia hosting services.

In addition to its RealVideo software, the company also offers Real-Audio, RealPix, RealJukebox, and RealText software—all of which can be downloaded through the Internet at <www.real.com>.

One of the company's newest offerings, made possible through a strategic alliance with Sony Corp., allows Internet users to download and transfer music through RealJukebox to Sony's portable audio players.

RealJukebox is one of the company's most popular features, with 22 million registered users. They use the technology to listen to music, record CD collections to PC hard drives, and load music from the Internet.

In 1999, the company launched the Real.com Network, which allows Internet visitors to download software and media content from more than 100 leading broadcast and Internet media companies.

Founded in 1994, RealNetworks went public with its initial stock offering in 1997. The company has about 450 employees and a market capitalization of about $11 billion.

EARNINGS PER SHARE PROGRESSION ★★
The company had its first year of earnings in 1999.

REVENUE GROWTH ★★★★
Past 4 years: 7,149 percent (192 percent per year)

STOCK GROWTH ★★★
Past 2 years: 1,634 percent (317 percent per year)
Dollar growth: $10,000 over 2 years would have grown to $173,400.

CONSISTENCY ★★★
Positive earnings progression: 1 year
Increased sales: 4 consecutive years

STABILITY/VULNERABILITY ★★★
The dominant player in this exciting, future-oriented technology, Real-Networks turned a profit for the first time in 1999.

REALNETWORKS AT A GLANCE

Fiscal year ended: Dec. 31
Revenue in $ millions

	1995	1996	1997	1998	1999	4-Year Growth Avg. Annual (%)	Total (%)
Revenue ($)	1.81	14.0	32.7	65.8	131.2	192	7,149
Earnings/share ($)	—	–0.03	–0.10	–0.15	0.04	NA	NA
PE ratio range	NA	NA	NA	NA	NA		

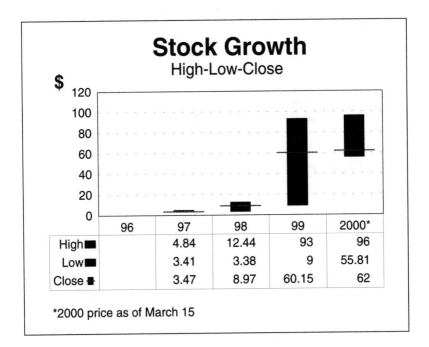

Stock Growth
High-Low-Close

	96	97	98	99	2000*
High		4.84	12.44	93	96
Low		3.41	3.38	9	55.81
Close		3.47	8.97	60.15	62

*2000 price as of March 15

ONLINE FINANCIAL
SERVICES

Ameritrade Holding
Corporation

4211 South 102nd Street
Omaha, NE 68127
402-331-7856
Nasdaq: AMTD
www.ameritrade.com

Chairman and Co-CEO: J. Joe Ricketts
Co-CEO: Thomas Lewis Jr.

Earnings Progression	★ ★
Revenue Growth	★ ★ ★ ★
Stock Growth	★ ★ ★ ★
Consistency	★ ★ ★
Stability/Vulnerability	★ ★
Total Points	**15 points**

A pioneer in the online brokerage business, Ameritrade has helped change the way Americans buy and sell stocks. But while its online trading concept is relatively new, Ameritrade founder Joe Ricketts has been breaking new ground in the brokerage industry for more than a quarter century.

Ricketts opened his first discount brokerage company in 1975. The firm, First Omaha Securities, was one of the first companies to offer discount commissions. Its $25 fee for trading 100 shares of stock helped attract a new generation of investors to the stock market.

In 1988, the company, which had changed its name to Accutrade, became the first brokerage firm to offer trading by Touch-Tone phone. In 1995, Ricketts purchased K. Aufhauser & Company and its WealthWeb service, which had been the first firm to offer securities trading over the

Internet in 1994. In 1996, Ricketts established eBroker, an Internet-only discount brokerage.

Ameritrade, which was officially launched in 1997, has attracted a growing customer base thanks to its flat rate commission of just $8 per trade. Ameritrade Holding consolidates all of the services of Ricketts's companies, including Accutrade; Ameritrade; AmeriVest, which offers discount services to banks, savings and loans, and credit unions; Advanced Clearing, a securities clearing and financial services firm; and the investment portal OnMoney.

Ameritrade has more than 700,000 customers for its online trading service, a figure that is growing quickly. The company has been adding about 100,000 new customers each quarter. Although Ameritrade has had profitable years, its emphasis recently has been on building its brand through aggressive marketing. The firm has spent millions of dollars on television and Internet advertising to attract new customers, a strategy company officials believe will pay off handsomely for the long term.

The Omaha-based operation went public with its initial stock offering in 1998. It has about 2,500 employees and a market capitalization of about $3 billion.

EARNINGS PER SHARE PROGRESSION ★ ★
Past 4 years: 40 percent (9 percent per year)

REVENUE GROWTH ★ ★ ★ ★
Past 4 years: 526 percent (59 percent per year)

STOCK GROWTH ★ ★ ★ ★
Past 2 years: 789 percent (198 percent per year)
Dollar growth: $10,000 over 2 years would have grown to $88,900.

CONSISTENCY ★ ★ ★
Increased earnings per share: 3 of the past 4 years
Increased revenue: 4 consecutive years

STABILITY/VULNERABILITY ★ ★
Through its aggressive marketing campaign, Ameritrade has become a leader in online stock trading. But the industry is still young, and the competition remains fierce.

AMERITRADE HOLDING AT A GLANCE

Fiscal year ended: Sept. 30
Revenue in $ millions

	1995	1996	1997	1998	1999	4-Year Growth Avg. Annual (%)	4-Year Growth Total (%)
Revenue ($)	42.9	65.3	95.7	164.2	268.3	59	526
Earnings/share ($)	0.05	0.07	0.08	0.00	0.07	9	40
PE ratio range	—	—	11-39	1859-6500	76-951		

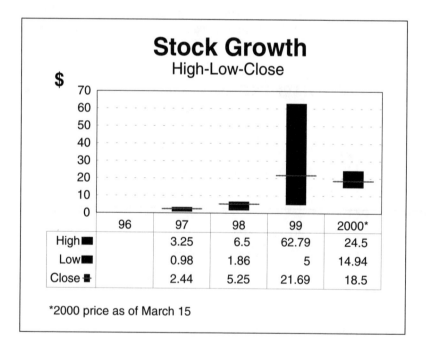

Stock Growth
High-Low-Close

$	96	97	98	99	2000*
High ■		3.25	6.5	62.79	24.5
Low ■		0.98	1.86	5	14.94
Close ■		2.44	5.25	21.69	18.5

*2000 price as of March 15

24
Lycos, Inc.

400-2 Totten Pond Road
Waltham, MA 02451
781-370-2700
Nasdaq: LCOS
www.lycos.com

President and CEO: Robert J. Davis

Earnings Progression	★
Revenue Growth	★ ★ ★ ★
Stock Growth	★ ★ ★ ★
Consistency	★ ★ ★
Stability/Vulnerability	★ ★ ★
Total Points	**15 points**

Web surfers have traditionally relied on portals, such as Yahoo! and Lycos, for links and search engines to navigate from site to site across the Net. But lately portals have been adding a variety of other services, such as free e-mail, personalized stock tickers, news, and shopping to attract users and crank up advertising revenue.

Lycos takes the concept a step further. Instead of just beefing up its original portal, the Waltham, Massachusetts operation has assembled an entire universe of interconnected Web sites dubbed the "Lycos Network." This diverse association of sites includes:

- **Online communities.** Tripod and Angelfire are two of the premier places on the Web for online recreational activities.
- **Online services and content.** Lycos offers free universal e-mail, the LYCOSShop automated online shopping tool, and online magazines such as *Wired* and *WebMonkey*.

- **Financial services.** Lycos acquired the financial information site Quote.com and teamed with Fidelity Investments to roll out the Powerstreet online personal financial service.
- **Navigation services.** The HotBot and Lycos search engines and WhoWhere Internet directory service give the company the deepest lineup of navigation tools on the Web.

Lycos seems to have realized the pre-eminent value of content earlier than its competitors. And owning its own media properties allows the company to integrate them into a cohesive whole—an advantage Yahoo! and other major portals don't have.

Founded in 1995, the company went public less than a year later and achieved profitability in 1997. Since then Lycos has enjoyed steady growth in the number of advertisers and in the average length and amount of ad contracts.

President and CEO Robert Davis worked in technology sales and marketing prior to founding Lycos. Lycos has about 800 employees and a market capitalization of about $8 billion.

EARNINGS PER SHARE PROGRESSION ★
Losses declined from 1998 to 1999.

REVENUE GROWTH ★ ★ ★ ★
Past 3 years: 2,476 percent (195 percent per year)

STOCK GROWTH ★ ★ ★ ★
Past 3 years: 2,925 percent (210 percent per year)
Dollar growth: $10,000 over 3 years would have grown to $303,500.

CONSISTENCY ★ ★ ★
Positive earnings progression: 1 year
Increased revenue: 3 consecutive years

STABILITY/VULNERABILITY ★ ★ ★
Lycos looks solid, thanks to a portfolio of leading brands, straight-line financial growth, aggressive marketing, and technology savvy unusual for a portal.

LYCOS AT A GLANCE

Fiscal year ended: July 31
Revenue in $ millions

	1995	1996	1997	1998	1999	3-Year Growth Avg. Annual (%)	3-Year Growth Total (%)
Revenue ($)	—	5.26	22.3	56.1	135.5	195	2,476
Earnings/share ($)	—	–0.10	–0.12	–1.57	–0.68	NA	NA
PE ratio range	—	NA	NA	NA	NA		

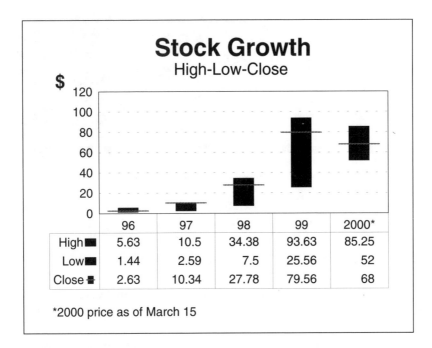

Stock Growth
High-Low-Close

$	96	97	98	99	2000*
High ■	5.63	10.5	34.38	93.63	85.25
Low ■	1.44	2.59	7.5	25.56	52
Close ■	2.63	10.34	27.78	79.56	68

*2000 price as of March 15

ONLINE FINANCIAL
SERVICES

25

CheckFree Holdings Corp.

4411 East Jones Bridge Road
Norcross, GA 30092
678-375-3387
Nasdaq: CKFR
www.checkfree.com

Chairman and CEO: Peter J. Knight
President: Peter F. Sinisgalli

Earnings Progression	★ ★ ★
Revenue Growth	★ ★
Stock Growth	★ ★ ★ ★
Consistency	★ ★ ★ ★
Stability/Vulnerability	★ ★
Total Points	**15 points**

Some day you may pay all your monthly bills with a few clicks of the mouse. CheckFree Holdings has developed the technology to make that happen.

The Georgia-based operation is the leading provider of financial electronic commerce services, software, and related products. Its products enable consumers to make electronic payments and collections, automate paper-based recurring financial transactions, and conduct secure Internet transactions.

CheckFree provides electronic transaction services for more than three million consumers through more than 350 financial institutions, Internet financial sites, and personal financial management software such as Quicken. It handles more than 125 million transactions annually.

CheckFree has developed relationships with well over 1,000 merchants nationwide that will enable the company to remit more than 50 percent of all its bill payments electronically. It also has been working with Yahoo!, WingspanBank.com, Excite@Home, and other Web sites and portals to put its bill-paying services at consumers' fingertips.

The firm believes consumers will be attracted to the electronic bill-paying concept for a variety of reasons. The technology will allow consumers to receive electronic bills through the Internet, pay any bill—electronic or paper—to anyone, and perform all the customary banking transactions (such as balance inquiries and transfers between accounts) at any time, 24 hours a day, seven days a week.

CheckFree introduced its "E-bill" technology in 1997, enabling merchants to deliver billings and marketing materials interactively to their customers over the Internet. Since then, the firm has signed contracts for E-bill services with more than 60 of the nation's largest billers (representing more than 500 million bills each month).

The company is also the leading provider of institutional portfolio management and information services and financial application software. It provides electronic commerce and financial applications software and services for businesses and financial institutions.

CheckFree has about 2,000 employees and a market capitalization of about $5 billion.

EARNINGS PER SHARE PROGRESSION ★ ★ ★
During the past 4 years, steadily dwindling losses turned to an 18-cent gain in 1999.

REVENUE GROWTH ★ ★
Past 4 years: 407 percent (50 percent per year)—but only 6 percent the past year.

STOCK GROWTH ★ ★ ★ ★
Past 4 years: 386 percent (48 percent per year)
Dollar growth: $10,000 over 4 years would have grown to $48,600.

CONSISTENCY ★ ★ ★ ★
Positive earnings progression: 3 consecutive years
Increased revenue: 4 consecutive years

STABILITY/VULNERABILITY ★ ★
As the leader in a niche that seems destined for strong future growth, CheckFree would seem to be a fairly solid bet.

CHECKFREE AT A GLANCE

Fiscal year ended: June 30
Revenue in $ millions

	1995	1996	1997	1998	1999	4-Year Growth Avg. Annual (%)	Total (%)
Revenue ($)	49.3	51	176.4	233.9	250.1	50	407
Earnings/share ($)	–0.01	–3.70	–3.44	–0.07	0.18	NA	NA
PE ratio range	NA	NA	NA	NA	111-581		

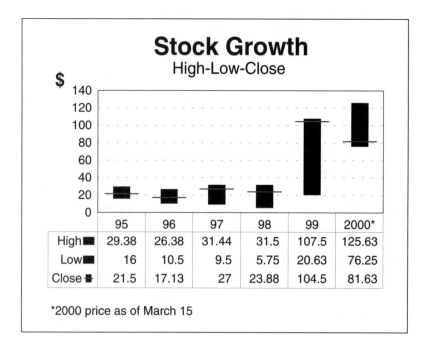

Stock Growth
High-Low-Close

$	95	96	97	98	99	2000*
High	29.38	26.38	31.44	31.5	107.5	125.63
Low	16	10.5	9.5	5.75	20.63	76.25
Close	21.5	17.13	27	23.88	104.5	81.63

*2000 price as of March 15

E-COMMERCE

S1 Corporation

3390 Peachtree Road, Suite 1700
Atlanta, GA 30326
404-812-6200
Nasdaq: SONE
www.s1.com

Chairman, President, and CEO: James S. Mahan III

Earnings Progression	★
Revenue Growth	★ ★ ★ ★
Stock Growth	★ ★
Consistency	★ ★ ★
Stability/Vulnerability	★ ★ ★ ★
Total Points	**14 points**

S1 Corporation helps banks and other financial companies around the world take their services to the Net.

Formerly known as Security First Technologies, S1 has been a pioneer in the Internet banking software business. More than 800 financial services companies have used S1 products and services to establish their own Web presence, including 33 of the top 100 financial institutions in the United States and nearly half of the world's top 100. Among its leading customers are Bank of America, Chase Manhattan, Deutsche Bank, Fleet-Boston, JP Morgan, and NetB@nk.

S1 makes software applications for online consumer, retail, corporate, and small business banking, and financial reporting.

The company's Virtual Financial Manager software suite is used by banks to build a customized Web portal, integrating banking, investment, loan, and credit card accounts at an institution with content such as news, weather, and sports. S1's software products cover a range of specialized Internet services, including;

- **Retail banking.** Used by small and mid-sized financial institutions, S1's retail banking software enables customers to perform a variety of tasks online, including bill payment, funds transfer, transaction reporting, account statement review, and e-mail correspondence.
- **Business suite.** For banks gearing their services to small and medium-sized companies, this application offers cash management, information reporting, payments and collections, transfers, bank mail, alerts and reminders, payroll services, and other features.
- **Corporate suite.** This application helps banks target larger corporate customers with such online services as transaction initiation, balance and transaction reporting, customer messaging, and custody and trade finance.

The Atlanta-based operation has 19 offices on five continents.

S1 Corporation went public with its initial stock offering in 1998. It has 1,700 employees and a market capitalization of about $5 billion.

EARNINGS PER SHARE PROGRESSION   ★
The company has had a string of large losses, although some are related to acquisitions.

REVENUE GROWTH   ★ ★ ★ ★
Past 3 years: 7,046 percent (315 percent per year)

STOCK GROWTH   ★ ★
The company had impressive growth after its 1998 IPO.

CONSISTENCY   ★ ★ ★
Positive earnings progression: None
Increased sales: 3 consecutive years

STABILITY/VULNERABILITY   ★ ★ ★ ★
Online banking will grow exponentially in coming years, and S1 is well positioned to capitalize on that growth.

S1 CORPORATION AT A GLANCE

Fiscal year ended: Dec. 31
Revenue in $ millions

	1995	1996	1997	1998	1999	3-Year Growth Avg. Annual (%)	Total (%)
Revenue ($)	—	1.3	10.8	24.2	92.9	315	7,046
Earnings/share ($)	—	−1.36	−1.52	−1.31	−3.36	NA	NA
PE ratio range	—	NA	NA	NA	NA		

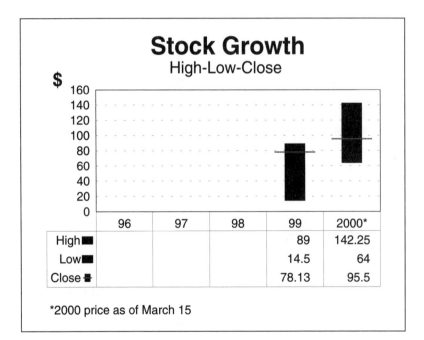

Stock Growth
High-Low-Close

	96	97	98	99	2000*
High				89	142.25
Low				14.5	64
Close				78.13	95.5

*2000 price as of March 15

27
Amazon.com, Inc.

1516 Second Avenue
Seattle, WA 98101
206-622-2335
Nasdaq: AMZN
www.amazon.com

Chairman, President, and CEO: Jeffrey P. Bezos

Earnings Progression	
Revenue Growth	★ ★ ★ ★
Stock Growth	★ ★ ★ ★
Consistency	★ ★ ★
Stability/Vulnerability	★ ★ ★
Total Points	**14 points**

What a system! With Amazon.com, founder Jeff Bezos has not only helped usher e-tailing into the American mainstream, he also spawned a corporate business model that would turn Wall Street on its head.

The company's revolutionary business model brings to mind the old joke: "We lose money on every sale, but we make it up in volume."

Launched in 1995, the online bookseller has never been profitable. In fact, its losses seem to grow exponentially year to year. The Seattle operation has spent hundreds of millions of dollars advertising its site, selling products at deep discounts, and building its order fulfillment infrastructure.

But despite the mounting losses, Bezos offers no apologies, nor does he wager any predictions of when the company may finally turn a profit.

So, how has Wall Street responded to this "Old Faithful" of red ink? By propelling its stock price into the stratosphere. Never has a company that has lost so much seen its stock price grow so fast.

But Bezos continues to stand by his strategy, which is to spend whatever it takes to capture the hearts of the American consumer—and hope that they remain loyal to Amazon.

The company, which began as an online retailer of books, has steadily added new products to the mix. It is the leading Internet seller of books, music, and videos. In all, it lists about 20 million unique items at its site, including toys, electronics, software, games, and home improvement products. It also recently reached an agreement with Drugstore.com to sell its products through the Amazon site.

Amazon claims more than 16 million customers and operates retailing Web sites in England and Germany as well.

Amazon.com went public with its initial stock offering in 1997. It has about 2,100 employees and a market capitalization of about $20 billion.

EARNINGS PER SHARE PROGRESSION

The company has no earnings, and losses have increased each of the past 4 years.

REVENUE GROWTH   ★ ★ ★ ★

Past 4 years: 320,839 percent (652 percent per year)

STOCK GROWTH   ★ ★ ★ ★

Past 2 years: 1,416 percent (291 percent per year)
Dollar growth: $10,000 over 2 years would have grown to $151,600.

CONSISTENCY   ★ ★ ★

Increased earnings per share: None
Increased revenue: 4 consecutive years

STABILITY/VULNERABILITY   ★ ★ ★

Amazon.com is the Internet's leading retailer, but will it ever turn a profit?

AMAZON.COM AT A GLANCE

Fiscal year ended: Dec. 31
Revenue in $ millions

	1995	1996	1997	1998	1999	4-Year Growth Avg. Annual (%)	Total (%)
Revenue ($)	.511	15.74	147.8	610	1,640	652	320,839
Earnings/share ($)	0.00	–0.02	–0.10	–0.42	–2.17	NA	NA
PE ratio range	—	—	NA	NA	NA		

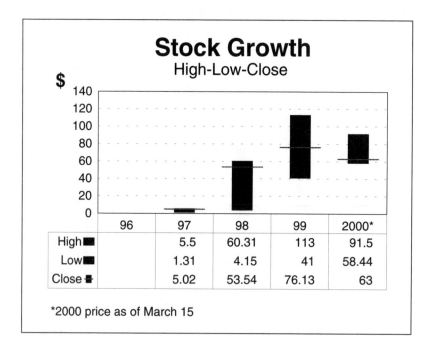

Stock Growth
High-Low-Close

$	96	97	98	99	2000*
High		5.5	60.31	113	91.5
Low		1.31	4.15	41	58.44
Close		5.02	53.54	76.13	63

*2000 price as of March 15

SOFTWARE

28

Entrust Technologies, Inc.

4975 Preston Park Boulevard, Suite 400
Plano, TX 75093
972-943-7300
Nasdaq: ENTU
www.entrust.com

Chairman: F. William Conner
President and CEO: John F. Ryan

Earnings Progression	★ ★ ★
Revenue Growth	★ ★ ★ ★
Stock Growth	★ ★
Consistency	★ ★ ★
Stability/Vulnerability	★ ★
Total Points	**14 points**

Trust is hard to come by on the Internet, but it can be arranged. Increasingly, companies are using a new technology called public key infrastructure (PKI) for secure e-commerce. Entrust Technologies is the leading supplier of PKI software.

Complex passwords called "keys" are used to make messages unreadable to all but the sender and intended receiver. Even if a hacker intercepts a message, it's indecipherable without the keys. Also, unique "digital certificates" are attached to messages as electronic IDs that confirm a sender's identity, rendering the security virtually unbreakable.

Most use a third-party PKI service, but big companies prefer to buy the software and set up security on their own. Entrust sells a suite of products offering PKI security, including:

- **EntrustFile Toolkit.** This tool enables programmers to add PKI security to their software applications.

133

- **Entrust/PKI.** The company's foundation product, this "certificate authority" software is used in the company's computer room to issue, revoke, and look up digital certificates.
- **Entrust/Entelligence.** This software allows individuals to use applications such as e-mail and Web browsers that have been secured with PKI.

These and other Entrust software products make it possible for a corporation to secure their internal systems and external e-commerce transactions. In addition, the company has made its products compatible with e-mail packages and browsers from Microsoft, Netscape, and Novell.

Demand for certification authority software has been growing at 100 percent per year, and analysts forecast the market to exceed $1 billion by 2001. Entrust has more than 800 customers, mostly large operations such as Federal Express, Citibank, and the U.S. Postal Service. It competes with VeriSign, IBM, and several other companies.

Spun off from network equipment giant Nortel in 1996, the company went public with its initial stock offering in 1998. It has about 450 employees and has a market capitalization of about $2 billion.

EARNINGS PER SHARE PROGRESSION   ★ ★ ★
Earnings growth past 2 years: 300 percent (100 percent per year)

REVENUE GROWTH   ★ ★ ★ ★
Past 4 years: 2,046 percent (115 percent per year)

STOCK GROWTH   ★ ★
Past year: 151 percent
Dollar growth: $10,000 over 1 year would have grown to $25,100.

CONSISTENCY   ★ ★ ★
Positive earnings progression: 1 year
Increased revenue: 4 consecutive years

STABILITY/VULNERABILITY   ★ ★
Competitors like VeriSign and IBM are formidable, but the market for PKI software could be huge.

ENTRUST TECHNOLOGIES AT A GLANCE

Fiscal year ended: Dec. 31
Revenue in $ millions

	1995	1996	1997	1998	1999	4-Year Growth Avg. Annual (%)	Total (%)
Revenue ($)	3.97	12.8	25	48.9	85.2	115	2,046
Earnings/share ($)	—	—	0.03	–0.76	0.12	100*	300*
PE ratio range	NA	NA	NA	NA	NA		

*Earnings per share data reflect 2-year growth.

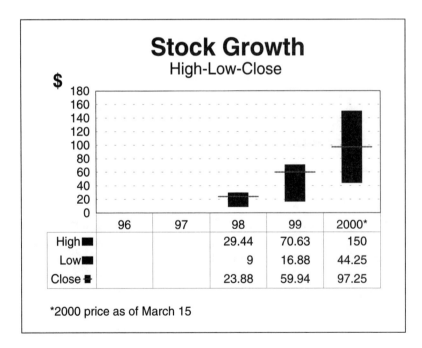

Stock Growth
High-Low-Close

	96	97	98	99	2000*
High■			29.44	70.63	150
Low■			9	16.88	44.25
Close ■			23.88	59.94	97.25

*2000 price as of March 15

ONLINE FINANCIAL
SERVICES

29

E*Trade Group, Inc.

4500 Bohannon Drive
Menlo Park, CA 94025
650-331-6000
Nasdaq: EGRP
www.etrade.com

Chairman and CEO: Christos M. Cotsakos
President: Kathy Levinson

Earnings Progression	
Revenue Growth	★ ★ ★ ★
Stock Growth	★ ★ ★ ★
Consistency	★ ★ ★
Stability/Vulnerability	★ ★ ★
Total Points	**14 points**

"It's time for E*Trade." No phrase in the vernacular is more representative of the Internet era. The very concept of cheap brokerage commissions and do-it-yourself online trading has captured the hearts, minds, and pocketbooks of independent investors everywhere.

E*Trade wasn't the first company to offer online brokerage services, but it has certainly put itself at the forefront of this exciting new industry through a rigorous and relentless advertising campaign. And with good reason. The stakes are enormous. Online trading has shaken the brokerage business to the bone.

And while the full-service broker has not yet gone the way of the dinosaur—and let's face it, there will always be investors who want and need brokers—the online trading industry has forced the big brokerage companies to change their ways. In fact, many of the major full-service brokers have grudgingly begun to offer their own online trading services.

E*Trade offers discounted brokerage trades at its Internet site, as well as through a telephone trading service. The E*Trade Web site also offers portfolio tracking, charting, and related information.

The company is growing rapidly—with new customer sign-ups soaring more than 100 percent per year. E*Trade had more than 1.5 million customers entering year 2000, after adding more than 1 million new customers in 1999. It handles about 100,000 transactions per day.

E*Trade plans to offer branded Web sites in the top 20 financial markets worldwide. The Menlo Park, California operation began offering electronic investing in 1992 and Internet investing in 1996. It went public with its initial stock offering in 1996. E*Trade has a market capitalization of $8.72 billion.

EARNINGS PER SHARE PROGRESSION

None

REVENUE GROWTH ★ ★ ★ ★

Past 4 years: 2,058 percent (115 percent per year)

STOCK GROWTH ★ ★ ★ ★

Past 3 years: 807 percent (109 percent per year)
Dollar growth: $10,000 over 3 years would have grown to $90,700.

CONSISTENCY ★ ★ ★

Positive earnings progression: None
Increased revenue: 4 consecutive years

STABILITY/VULNERABILITY ★ ★ ★

E*Trade is here to stay, but the competition is fierce, and the major Wall Street brokerage houses are just now wading into the online business.

E*TRADE GROUP AT A GLANCE

Fiscal year ended: Sept. 30
Revenue in $ millions

	1995	1996	1997	1998	1999	4-Year Growth Avg. Annual (%)	4-Year Growth Total (%)
Revenue ($)	28.8	62.5	156.4	245.3	621.4	115	2,058
Earnings/share ($)	—	0.01	0.10	0.02	–0 .23	NA	NA
PE ratio range	—	206-347	21-93	277-1805	NA		

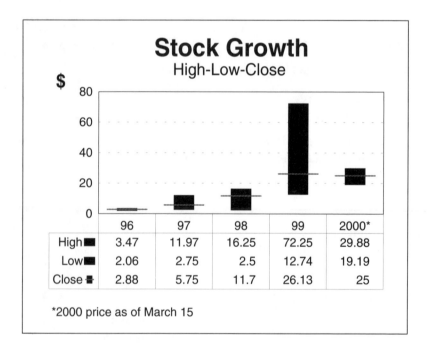

Stock Growth
High-Low-Close

$	96	97	98	99	2000*
High ■	3.47	11.97	16.25	72.25	29.88
Low ■	2.06	2.75	2.5	12.74	19.19
Close ■	2.88	5.75	11.7	26.13	25

*2000 price as of March 15

E-COMMERCE

30

Commerce One, Inc.

1600 Riviera Drive, Suite 200
Walnut Creek, CA 94596
925-941-6000
Nasdaq: CMRC
www.commerceone.com

Chairman, President, and CEO: Mark B. Hoffman

Earnings Progression	★ ★
Revenue Growth	★ ★ ★
Stock Growth	★ ★
Consistency	★ ★
Stability/Vulnerability	★ ★ ★ ★
Total Points	**13 points**

Through innovative technology and relentless marketing, Commerce One has managed to position itself squarely at center stage of the business-to-business e-commerce market.

And that's a mouthful, because business-to-business e-commerce (B2B) turns over ten times more dollars than the e-tailing industry. Trading partners use B2B software platforms to set up online marketplaces that handle corporate procurement over the Internet instead of via phone, fax, or direct computer file transfer.

The Silicon Valley operation has two lines of business. It sells B2B software products, and it also operates digital marketplaces of its own, collecting a small commission on each sale made. The company's products and services include:

- **Global Trading Web.** This worldwide trading community comprises many vertical marketplaces and is operated by Commerce One using its own software. It also provides services such as content management, order availability information, status tracking, and transaction support.

- **MarketSite.** Aspiring Internet market makers buy this software package to set up digital marketplaces of their own. Customers can buy the software and run it themselves or let Commerce One host it for a fee—an option favored by small and medium-sized companies.
- **BuySite.** This software package has modules to hook up the digital marketplace with internal corporate systems. There are two versions—one for large companies to operate on their own and the other for market-making firms that host digital marketplaces for companies too small to do it themselves.

Commerce One is in a fierce battle with Ariba to get the jump on as many top accounts as possible. Notable Commerce One customers include General Motors, Schlumberger, British Telecom, and Royal Dutch/Shell.

Commerce One went public with its initial stock offering in 1999. The company has about 250 employees and a market capitalization of about $13 billion.

EARNINGS PER SHARE PROGRESSION   ★ ★
Losses have declined the past year.

REVENUE GROWTH   ★ ★ ★
Past year: 1,208 percent

STOCK GROWTH   ★ ★
Commerce One went public in 1999 and experienced exceptional growth after the IPO.

CONSISTENCY   ★ ★
Positive earnings progression: 1 year
Increased revenue: 1 year

STABILITY/VULNERABILITY   ★ ★ ★ ★
The company's aggressive marketing has worked well so far, but it must keep the pressure on to maintain its edge.

COMMERCE ONE AT A GLANCE

Fiscal year ended: Dec. 31
Revenue in $ millions

	1995	1996	1997	1998	1999	1-Year Growth Avg. Annual (%)	1-Year Growth Total (%)
Revenue ($)	—	—	—	2.56	33.5	1,208	1,208
Earnings/share ($)	—	—	—	–2.76	–2.17	NA	NA
PE ratio range	—	—	—	NA	NA		

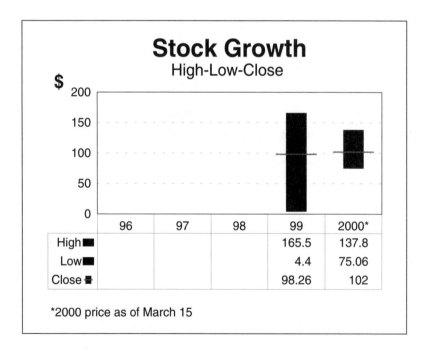

Stock Growth
High-Low-Close

$	96	97	98	99	2000*
High				165.5	137.8
Low				4.4	75.06
Close				98.26	102

*2000 price as of March 15

INFRASTRUCTURE

31
Harmonic, Inc.

549 Baltic Way
Sunnyvale, CA 94089
408-542-2500
Nasdaq: HLIT
www.harmonicinc.com

Chairman, President, and CEO: Anthony Ley

Earnings Progression	★ ★
Revenue Growth	★ ★ ★ ★
Stock Growth	★ ★ ★
Consistency	★ ★
Stability/Vulnerability	★ ★
Total Points	**13 points**

Running fiber-optic trunks between cities is only one step in the continuing quest for greater bandwidth. Broadband infrastructure also must be installed locally to route high-speed traffic as it comes hurtling in from the backbones.

Harmonic makes broadband hardware systems designed to handle that final leg. The Sunnyvale, California operation makes such transmission equipment as fiber-optic transmitters, receivers, and delivery devices used by digital cable, satellite, and wireless networks.

The company broke into the business of selling equipment to the cable television industry, which has fiber trunk lines feeding into slower coaxial cable plants running between cable TV offices and homes.

Today, Harmonic makes a full line of fiber-optic products for a variety of broadband delivery systems to send and receive video, audio, and data. Its product line includes:

- **METROLink.** This is a complete hardware package for such band-width-hungry network applications as video-on-demand, Internet telephone service, and high definition TV.
- **CyberStream.** Enables network operators to offer broadband Internet access. It includes such devices as home satellite modems and specialized corporate receiver/routers.
- **TRANsend.** Aptly named, this product line provides digital gateways that help cable TV networks make a smooth introduction of digital Internet services over their hybrid fiber/coaxial networks.

Harmonic went public with its initial stock offering in 1995. The company has about 300 employees and a market capitalization of about $3 billion.

EARNINGS PER SHARE PROGRESSION   ★ ★

Earnings growth past 4 years: 270 percent (39 percent per year). No real growth until 1999.

REVENUE GROWTH   ★ ★ ★ ★

Past 4 years: 370 percent (47 percent per year)

STOCK GROWTH   ★ ★ ★

Past 4 years: 1,626 percent (104 percent per year). Most growth came in 1999.
Dollar growth: $10,000 over 4 years would have grown to $173,000.

CONSISTENCY   ★ ★

Increased earnings per share: 2 of the past 4 years
Increased sales: 3 of the past 4 years

STABILITY/VULNERABILITY   ★ ★

Harmonic has stiff competition from Philips Electronics, Motorola, and others, but the media convergence business is booming.

HARMONIC AT A GLANCE

Fiscal year ended: Dec. 31
Revenue in $ millions

	1995	1996	1997	1998	1999	4-Year Growth Avg. Annual (%)	Total (%)
Revenue ($)	39.2	60.9	17.3	83.9	184.1	47	370
Earnings/share ($)	0.20	0.26	0.22	–0.93	0.74	39	270
PE ratio range	19-51	16-51	24-59	NA	10-137		

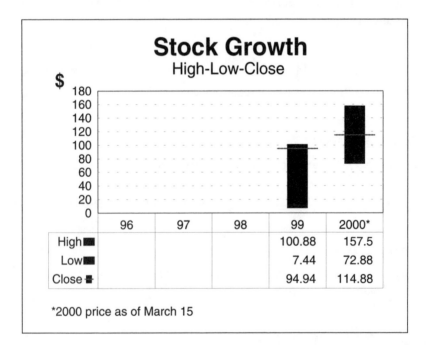

Stock Growth
High-Low-Close

$	96	97	98	99	2000*
High				100.88	157.5
Low				7.44	72.88
Close				94.94	114.88

*2000 price as of March 15

E-COMMERCE

32
VerticalNet, Inc.

700 Dresher Road
Horsham, PA 19044
215-328-6100
Nasdaq: VERT
www.verticalnet.com

Chairman: Douglas A. Alexander
President and CEO: Mark L. Walsh

Earnings Progression	★
Revenue Growth	★ ★ ★ ★
Stock Growth	★ ★
Consistency	★ ★ ★
Stability/Vulnerability	★ ★ ★
Total Points	**13 points**

It has been straight-up growth for VerticalNet, which is out to become the world's foremost business-to-business e-commerce market maker.

The company operates what it calls "vertical trading communities" for industries ranging from food processing to semiconductor manufacturing. It runs a separate Web site for each target audience designed to serve as a one-stop source for that market's needs: industry news, commentary, discussion groups, directories, online training, classifieds, product information, e-stores, and online trading.

The Horsham, Pennsylvania operation manages a portfolio of more than 50 Web sites, some started from scratch and others obtained by acquisition. These sites aren't glamorous places—examples include <pulpand paperonline.com>, <adhesivesealantsonline.com>, and <frozeningredients online.com>—but they've begun to attract a following among professionals in those fields.

VerticalNet attracts traffic to its Web sites with newspaperlike content and online services, such as discussion groups and directories. It then starts an online auction for products specific to the industry each site serves. This creates three revenue streams: (1) fees from banner advertisements, (2) margins on products sold from its e-stores, and (3) commissions collected on sales made at the online auctions.

VerticalNet has separate editorial staffs for each industry to help ensure quality content. Its business model resembles trade magazine publishing, but as a Web publisher, VerticalNet also can make money on e-store sales and commissions from each site's online auction.

Founded in 1997, VerticalNet has a market capitalization of about $3 billion. Company CEO and President Mark Walsh came to VerticalNet after a stint at America Online, where he founded and managed AOL Enterprise, the business-to-business division of AOL.

EARNINGS PER SHARE PROGRESSION ★

The company's long string of losses declined in 1999.

REVENUE GROWTH ★ ★ ★ ★

Past 4 years: 12,838 percent (235 percent per year)

STOCK GROWTH ★ ★

VerticalNet had outstanding growth after its 1999 IPO.

CONSISTENCY ★ ★ ★

Positive earnings progression: 1 year
Increased revenue: 4 consecutive years

STABILITY/VULNERABILITY ★ ★ ★

Still deep in the red, VerticalNet is a small player in a highly competitive business. But its early start and sharp execution show great promise.

VERTICALNET AT A GLANCE

Fiscal year ended: Dec. 31
Revenue in $ millions

	1995	1996	1997	1998	1999	4-Year Growth Avg. Annual (%)	4-Year Growth Total (%)
Revenue ($)	0.16	.285	.792	3.13	20.7	235	12,838
Earnings/share ($)	–0.09	–0.14	–0.95	–2.63	–1.51	NA	NA
PE ratio range	NA	NA	NA	NA	NA		

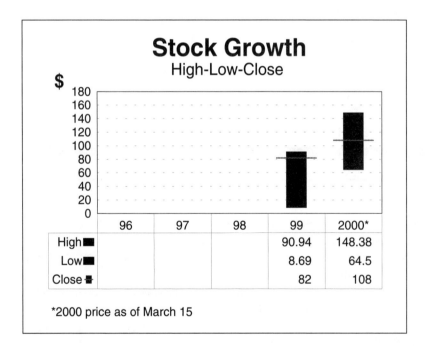

Stock Growth
High-Low-Close

$	96	97	98	99	2000*
High■				90.94	148.38
Low■				8.69	64.5
Close ■				82	108

*2000 price as of March 15

INFRASTRUCTURE

33
Brocade Communications

1901 Guadalupe Parkway
San Jose, CA 95131
408-487-8000
Nasdaq: BRCD
www.brocade.com

Chairman: Seth D. Neiman
President and CEO: Gregory L. Reyes

Earnings Progression	★ ★ ★
Revenue Growth	★ ★ ★
Stock Growth	★ ★
Consistency	★ ★ ★
Stability/Vulnerability	★ ★
Total Points	**13 points**

Internet traffic is so heavy and unpredictable that it has strained traditional data storage systems to the breaking point. But a new disk control technology promises to solve the problem, and Brocade Communications is leading the rescue team.

The technology, dubbed "storage area networks" (SANs), connects "disk farms" directly to the network instead of through a dedicated computer server. Brocade has emerged at the head of a pack of companies that make the specialized hardware and software needed to run SAN storage configurations.

The benefits of SANs are substantial, including faster service, better reliability, more room for growth, and lower operating costs. Large Web sites are expected to flock to the SAN technology over the next few years.

Brocade's strong product line helps differentiate the company from the competition. Its leading products include:

- **SilkWorm Fiber Channel Switches.** The company's controller devices have been rated the best performing and easiest to manage in product comparison studies.
- **Fabric OS.** This software is used to configure and operate interconnected switch "fabrics" containing thousands of disks.
- **Brocade SES.** Allows Brocade switches to be managed in computer rooms that are based on non-SAN disk technology.

The company is on a roll, with its products designed into disk solutions marketed by IBM, Dell, Compaq, StorageTek, Hitachi, and others.

The company, which has about 120 employees, made its initial public stock offering in 1999. It has a market capitalization of about $8 billion.

EARNINGS PER SHARE PROGRESSION ★ ★ ★

Brocade has reduced its losses the past 2 years.

REVENUE GROWTH ★ ★ ★

Past 2 years: 710 percent (185 percent per year)

STOCK GROWTH ★ ★

Brocade went public in 1999 and experienced a strong, steady run-up after the IPO.

CONSISTENCY ★ ★ ★

Declining losses: 2 consecutive years
Increased revenue: 2 consecutive years

STABILITY/VULNERABILITY ★ ★

Brocade Communications is off to a great start in a desirable niche, but competition is fierce.

BROCADE COMMUNICATIONS AT A GLANCE

Fiscal year ended: Oct. 31
Revenue in $ millions

	1995	1996	1997	1998	1999	2-Year Growth Avg. Annual (%)	Total (%)
Revenue ($)	—	—	8.48	24.2	68.7	185	710
Earnings/share ($)	—	—	–2.41	–2.36	–0.20	NA	NA
PE ratio range	—	—	NA	NA	NA		

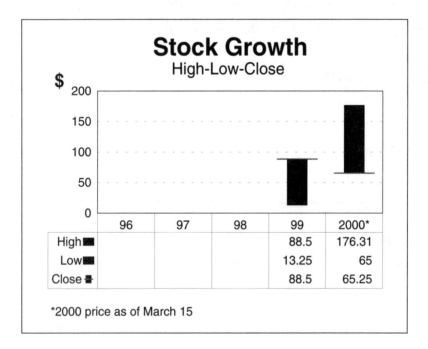

Stock Growth
High-Low-Close

$	96	97	98	99	2000*
High				88.5	176.31
Low				13.25	65
Close				88.5	65.25

*2000 price as of March 15

Bottomline Technologies, Inc.

E-COMMERCE

155 Fleet Street
Portsmouth, NH 03801
603-436-0700
Nasdaq: EPAY
www.bottomline.com

Chairman, President, and CEO: Daniel M. McGurl

Earnings Progression	★ ★ ★ ★
Revenue Growth	★ ★ ★
Stock Growth	★
Consistency	★ ★ ★
Stability/Vulnerability	★ ★
Total Points	**13 points**

As e-commerce between businesses grows, so will the need to conduct another business function online: paying bills. Bottomline Technologies is a software company that makes products for Internet billing and payment by companies.

The billing and payment niche is expected to boom along with e-commerce, and Bottomline certainly has the pedigree to become a blue chip player. After all, the company developed the Federal Reserve System's FedEDI electronic data interchange (EDI) software.

Bottomline was founded in 1989, just as major companies were beginning to switch their billing systems from paper to EDI transactions carried over private networks. Since then, it has expanded its products and converted them to run over the Internet. Its leading services include:

- **PayBase.** Capable of handling electronic payments across an entire enterprise, PayBase gives workers the ability to make payments

151

from their desktop while the company maintains centralized control. PayBase even has a module for laser check printing.
- **NeTransact.** A new product designed to complement PayBase, NeTransact covers the other side of the invoice-remittance cycle.
- **Services.** Although most company revenues come from software licensing, about one-third of Bottomline's income is derived from software maintenance and professional services.

The market for Bottomline's services continues to grow because of the many benefits of online billing, including lower transaction costs, fewer mistakes, automatic fraud control, and better cash management. In the not too distant future, nearly all corporate bills and payments will be handled electronically.

Bottomline has over 2,500 customers, including such names as Dell Computer, Banker's Trust, Aetna, Microsoft, Amazon.com, and Charles Schwab. Long-term growth potential appears promising because U.S. corporations issue about 25 *billion* paper checks each year.

Bottomline has about 280 employees and a market capitalization of about $500 million.

EARNINGS PER SHARE PROGRESSION ★ ★ ★ ★
Past 4 years: 330 percent (39 percent per year)

REVENUE GROWTH ★ ★ ★
Past 4 years: 160 percent (27 percent per year)

STOCK GROWTH ★
Bottomline went public in 1999 and experienced rocky growth after the IPO.

CONSISTENCY ★ ★ ★
Increased earnings per share: 3 of 4 years
Increased revenue: 5 consecutive years

STABILITY/VULNERABILITY ★ ★
Bottomline faces intense competition from both EDI and enterprise software companies, but their installed customer base puts them on sound footing.

BOTTOMLINE AT A GLANCE

Fiscal year ended: June 30
Revenue in $ millions

	1995	1996	1997	1998	1999	4-Year Growth Avg. Annual (%)	Total (%)
Revenue ($)	15.1	18.1	22.1	29.0	39.3	27	160
Earnings/share ($)	0.10	0.11	–0.23	0.20	0.43	39	330
PE ratio range	NA	NA	NA	NA	29-226		

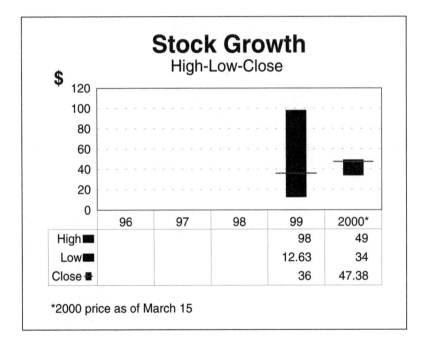

Stock Growth
High-Low-Close

$	96	97	98	99	2000*
High ■				98	49
Low ■				12.63	34
Close ■				36	47.38

*2000 price as of March 15

35

Redback Networks, Inc.

1389 Moffet Park Drive
Sunnyvale, CA 94089
408-548-3500
Nasdaq: RBAK
www.redback.com

Chairman: Pierre R. Lamond
President and CEO: Dennis L. Barsema

Earnings Progression	★ ★ ★
Revenue Growth	★ ★ ★
Stock Growth	★ ★
Consistency	★ ★ ★
Stability/Vulnerability	★ ★
Total Points	**13 points**

The Telecommunications Act of 1996 let loose a torrent of upstart network operators. Hundreds of companies—phone carriers, Internet service providers, and cable TV operators—jumped into the business with both feet. But in their mad rush to bring blazing bandwidth to the customer's door, few thought about how to manage all these new subscribers.

Enter Redback Networks, the leading independent provider of network subscriber management systems. The company makes sophisticated data switches designed specifically to manage subscriber traffic over high-speed data networks.

The Sunnyvale, California operation manufactures the SMS 1000 for large-scale carrier-class networks and the SMS 500, which is aimed at the mid-tier market. These products are big, expensive hardware devices that establish and terminate communications circuits for customers and keep track of their use.

Redback switches bridge the operational gap between the access devices connecting customers to networks and the Internet backbone. It's a hot market area, because the new "last mile" technologies such as Digital Subscriber Line and cable modems are rendering old-style subscriber management systems obsolete.

Although Redback competes directly with the likes of Cisco, business is booming, because of its well-engineered products.

The company's customer list includes regional Bell operating companies such as Ameritech, Bell Atlantic, and Southwestern Bell, and leading Internet backbone providers such as Qwest, MCI WorldCom's UUNET, Verio, EarthLink, and GTE.

Redback Networks went public with its initial stock offering in 1999. It has about 150 employees and a market capitalization of about $7 billion.

EARNINGS PER SHARE PROGRESSION ★ ★ ★

Losses have declined the past 2 years.

REVENUE GROWTH ★ ★ ★

Past 2 years: 133,858 percent (3,540 percent per year)

STOCK GROWTH ★ ★

Redback went public in 1999 and had very strong growth after its IPO.

CONSISTENCY ★ ★ ★

Positive earnings progression: 2 consecutive years
Increased revenue: 2 consecutive years

STABILITY/VULNERABILITY ★ ★

Redback Networks must continue building superior products to flourish in the face of giants such as Cisco Systems and Nortel Networks.

REDBACK NETWORKS AT A GLANCE

Fiscal year ended: Dec. 31
Revenue in $ millions

	1995	1996	1997	1998	1999	2-Year Growth Avg. Annual (%)	Total (%)
Revenue ($)	—	—	.048	9.21	64.3	3,540	133,858
Earnings/share ($)	—	–0.11	–2.05	–0.39	–0.32	NA	NA
PE ratio range	—	NA	NA	NA	NA		

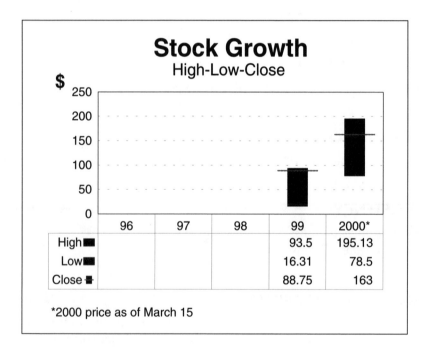

Stock Growth
High-Low-Close

	96	97	98	99	2000*
High				93.5	195.13
Low				16.31	78.5
Close				88.75	163

*2000 price as of March 15

SOFTWARE

36

WebTrends Corporation

851 SW Sixth Avenue, Suite 1200
Portland, OR 97204
503-294-7025
Nasdaq: WEBT
www.webtrends.com

Chairman and CEO: Elijahu Shapira
President: Glen Boyd

Earnings Progression	★ ★ ★
Revenue Growth	★ ★ ★
Stock Growth	★ ★
Consistency	★ ★
Stability/Vulnerability	★ ★ ★
Total Points	**13 points**

Corporations pour millions of dollars into the construction and maintenance of their Web sites. But how can they be sure all the money and resources are really paying off?

WebTrends makes software that helps thousands of organizations track their Web site traffic, user trends, Internet advertising effectiveness, and e-commerce activities at their sites.

The Portland operation's suite of Web analysis software is used by many of the largest Internet service providers (ISPs) and more than a third of all Fortune 500 companies, including AT&T, IBM, and Microsoft. International sales account for about 25 percent of total revenue.

WebTrends introduced its first product, a Web site traffic analysis software package called WebTrends Log Analyzer, in 1996 and has added a broad range of related software products since then, including:

- **Enterprise Suite.** This software enables users to manage complex server configurations and to integrate Web site traffic analysis data with existing databases to provide advanced analysis.
- **Professional Suite.** This application package integrates Web site traffic analysis with other content management and traffic analysis features, along with monitoring, alerting, and recovery.
- **Firewall Suite.** This software manages, monitors, and reports firewall activity. (Firewalls are used to help keep Web sites secure.)
- **Security Analyzer.** Secures Internet servers and other devices.

Founded in 1993, WebTrends went public with its initial stock offering in 1999. It has about 80 employees and a market capitalization of about $1 billion.

EARNINGS PER SHARE PROGRESSION   ★ ★ ★
Past 2 years: 400 percent (123 percent per year)

REVENUE GROWTH   ★ ★ ★
Past 2 years: 386 percent (120 percent per year)

STOCK GROWTH   ★ ★
WebTrends had strong growth after its 1999 IPO.

CONSISTENCY   ★ ★
Increased earnings per share: 1 year
Increased revenue: 2 consecutive years

STABILITY/VULNERABILITY   ★ ★ ★
This is a quickly growing company with a strong share of a vital Internet niche. And best of all, WebTrends is already making money.

WEBTRENDS AT A GLANCE

Fiscal year ended: Dec. 31
Revenue in $ millions

	1995	1996	1997	1998	1999	2-Year Growth Avg. Annual (%)	2-Year Growth Total (%)
Revenue ($)	—	—	4.05	8.01	19.7	120	386
Earnings/share ($)	—	—	0.04	0.03	0.20	123	400
PE ratio range	—	—	NA	NA	110-500		

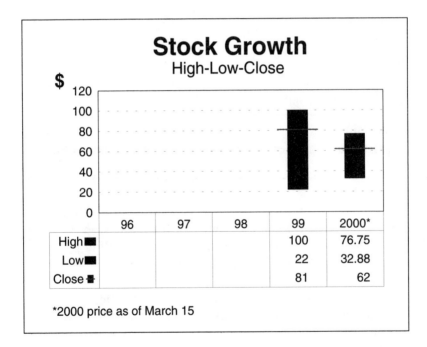

Stock Growth
High-Low-Close

$	96	97	98	99	2000*
High ■				100	76.75
Low ■				22	32.88
Close ■				81	62

*2000 price as of March 15

SOFTWARE

37

Open Market, Inc.

One Wayside Road
Burlington, MA 01803
781-359-3000
Nasdaq: OMKT
www.openmarket.com

Chairman: Shikhar Ghosh
President and CEO: Gary B. Eichhorn

Earnings Progression	★ ★
Revenue Growth	★ ★ ★
Stock Growth	★ ★ ★
Consistency	★ ★ ★ ★
Stability/Vulnerability	★
Total Points	**13 points**

Open Market is aptly named, because it literally opened the Web site software market. Founded in 1994—a month earlier than Netscape Communications—the company pioneered the concept of selling packaged software to companies so they wouldn't have to program e-commerce sites themselves.

Open Market's products are used both for business-to-business trading and selling to consumers. The company's customer list includes America Online, Disney, and Time Warner but is mainly made up of smaller corporations. Open Market's broad product line runs the gamut of what it takes to manage an e-commerce site, including:

- **Transact.** The company's flagship product, Transact is a high-end package that handles order entry, fulfillment, and customer service.
- **LiveCommerce.** This product enables companies to make large catalogs available to their customers over the Web.

- **ShopSite.** This low-end software product makes it easy for small businesses with little technical expertise to create their own e-commerce Web sites.
- **Internet Publishing System.** This package is used to help automate publishing Web pages and personalize them for individual customers.

Open Market has been criticized for losing focus and branching off into too many product areas. Some of these projects came through acquisition, and others were generated in-house—and were ill-fated.

The company's management team realized the errors and has been bringing products into line with the competition. Open Market is still a formidable competitor and is enjoying market-leading status with an installed base of about 12,000 licenses. Its recent acquisition of content management software maker FutureTense should put its streamlined product line on a par with BroadVision in the important area of automatic content personalization to fit site visitor profiles.

Before joining Open Market in 1995, CEO Gary Eichhorn did stints as a vice president at Hewlett-Packard and Digital Equipment. Open Market has about 400 employees and a market capitalization of about $2 billion.

EARNINGS PER SHARE PROGRESSION ★★
Losses have declined the past 2 years.

REVENUE GROWTH ★★★
Past 4 years: 4,084 percent (154 percent per year)

STOCK GROWTH ★★★
Past 3 years: 234 percent (50 percent per year)
Dollar growth: $10,000 over 3 years would have grown to $33,400.

CONSISTENCY ★★★★
Positive earnings progression: 2 consecutive years
Increased revenue: 4 consecutive years

STABILITY/VULNERABILITY ★
The red hot e-commerce software market has attracted intense competition, but Open Market's large installed customer base is an asset.

OPEN MARKET AT A GLANCE

Fiscal year ended: Dec. 31
Revenue in $ millions

	1995	1996	1997	1998	1999	4-Year Growth Avg. Annual (%)	Total (%)
Revenue ($)	1.85	22.5	61.4	62.1	77.4	154	4,084
Earnings/share ($)	−0.53	−0.96	−1.87	−0.92	−0.36	NA	NA
PE ratio range	NA	NA	NA	NA	NA		

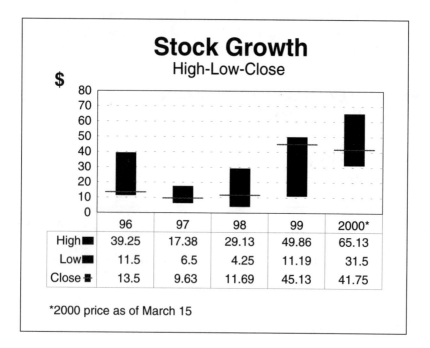

Stock Growth
High-Low-Close

	96	97	98	99	2000*
High	39.25	17.38	29.13	49.86	65.13
Low	11.5	6.5	4.25	11.19	31.5
Close	13.5	9.63	11.69	45.13	41.75

*2000 price as of March 15

INTERNET BUSINESS
SERVICES

24/7 Media, Inc.

1250 Broadway
New York, NY 10001
212-231-7100
Nasdaq: TFSM
www.247media.com

Chairman: Jacob I. Friesel
President and CEO: David J. Moore

Earnings Progression	★ ★
Revenue Growth	★ ★ ★
Stock Growth	★ ★
Consistency	★ ★ ★
Stability/Vulnerability	★ ★
Total Points	**12 points**

The sun never sets on the Internet economy. The same goes for the online advertising business, where the worldwide barrage of banner ads proceeds without pause.

A new breed of ad agency has emerged to handle the special needs of online advertising, and New York–based 24/7 Media is at the forefront.

24/7 Media's business has two basic parts: (1) a network of online advertisers and Web sites, and (2) the technology to put the two together. The company not only places ads through its ad network, it also handles such tasks as billing, reporting, and performance analysis. The company's lineup of services includes:

- **24/7 Media Networks.** It places banner ads from about 700 advertisers into nearly 3,000 Web sites. The company's new "Adfinity" ad server technology chooses the best ad to insert into a Web page based on the demographic profile of the person viewing it.

- **24/7 Mail.** This division of 24/7 Media helps companies use e-mail to market directly to customers. It operates a database of more than 15 million e-mail users who have signed up to receive solicitations in certain market categories.
- **24/7 Profilz.** The company recently rolled out the industry's first online database of Web user profiles, which customers use for ad targeting and market research.

24/7 Media has emerged as one of the leading Internet advertising and direct marketing firms. It claims to reach over half of all American Web users and has set up advertising networks focused on e-commerce auction sites, small business, and health care as part of its focus on advertising within the business-to-business arena.

President and CEO David Moore spent most of his career developing media properties, including the Lifetime cable TV channel.

The company made its initial public stock offering in 1998. It has a market capitalization of about $1 billion.

EARNINGS PER SHARE PROGRESSION   ★ ★
Losses have declined the past 2 years.

REVENUE GROWTH   ★ ★ ★
Past 2 years: 2,757 percent (436 percent per year)

STOCK GROWTH   ★ ★
Past year: 100 percent
Dollar growth: $10,000 over 1 year would have grown to $20,000

CONSISTENCY   ★ ★ ★
Positive earnings progression: 2 consecutive years
Increased revenues: 2 consecutive years

STABILITY/VULNERABILITY   ★ ★
24/7 Media has plenty of competition in AdForce, DoubleClick, FlyCast, and others. But its fast start in a booming market should help the company on its way.

24/7 MEDIA AT A GLANCE

Fiscal year ended: Dec. 31
Revenue in $ millions

	1995	1996	1997	1998	1999	2-Year Growth Avg. Annual (%)	Total (%)
Revenue ($)	—	—	3.15	20.5	90.0	436	2,757
Earnings/share ($)	—	—	–2.45	–1.44	–1.25	NA	NA
PE ratio range	—	—	NA	NA	NA		

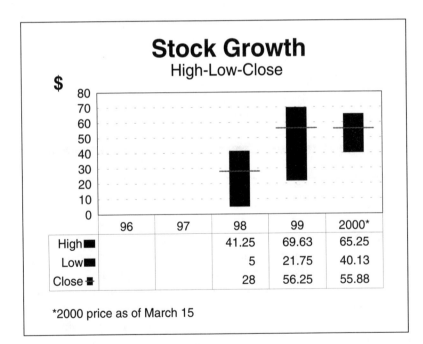

Stock Growth
High-Low-Close

$

	96	97	98	99	2000*
High■			41.25	69.63	65.25
Low■			5	21.75	40.13
Close▇			28	56.25	55.88

*2000 price as of March 15

39
China.com Corp.

20th Floor, Citicorp Centre
18 Whitfeld Road
Causeway Bay, Hong Kong
Nasdaq: CHINA
www.china.com

Chairman: Raymond Ch'ien
CEO: Peter Yip

Earnings Progression	
Revenue Growth	★ ★ ★ ★
Stock Growth	★ ★
Consistency	★ ★ ★
Stability/Vulnerability	★ ★ ★
Total Points	**12 points**

China.com is an Internet portal with growth potential the size of China—and beyond. Young and aggressive, China.com is quickly establishing itself as the America Online of Asia. If it succeeds—and early growth figures have been impressive—the returns could be staggering.

Of course, there are no sure things in the Internet economy, but some knowledgeable parties have taken more than a passing interest in China.com. In fact, America Online is one of the leading investors in China.com, which went public with its initial stock offering in 1999. Other companies with a stake in the Hong Kong–based portal include Mitsui, Sun Microsystems, Bay Networks, and 24/7 Media.

China.com offers news, sports, market information, horoscopes, message boards, online shopping options, e-mail, Web search, and other options similar to AOL. The company has Web sites in both English and

Chinese. Its other portals include <www.hongkong.com>, <www.taiwan.com>, and <www.cww.com>. All three are Chinese language sites. On the other hand, <www.china.com> is an English language site that focuses on Chinese and Asian issues.

The company also offers Internet advertising services and corporate Internet strategy and development services. Its advertising division, which includes the sale, economic delivery, and tracking of advertisements on a network of Web sites, has been developed in connection with U.S.–based 24/7 Media. Its advertising market base includes not just China and Taiwan, but Japan, South Korea, Singapore, India, Australia, Vietnam, Thailand, the Philippines, Malaysia, Laos, and Cambodia.

The company's early growth has been very rapid, soaring from 400,000 registered users to more than two million during the last six months of 1999. And in a market area with well over a billion Chinese consumers, there is still incredible room for growth.

China.com was incorporated in the Cayman Islands in 1997. It has a market capitalization of about $4 billion and more than 450 employees.

EARNINGS PER SHARE PROGRESSION

China.com has had a string of small losses.

REVENUE GROWTH   ★ ★ ★ ★

Past 3 years: 66,900 percent (775 percent per year)

STOCK GROWTH   ★ ★

China.com went public in 1999 and experienced strong gains after it's IPO.

CONSISTENCY   ★ ★ ★

Positive earnings progression: 1 year
Increased revenue: 3 consecutive years

STABILITY/VULNERABILITY   ★ ★ ★

China.com is on firm financial footing with such big-time investors as AOL and 24/7 Media, and its potential is obvious.

CHINA.COM AT A GLANCE

Fiscal year ended: Dec. 31
Revenue in $ millions

	1995	1996	1997	1998	1999	3-Year Growth Avg. Annual (%)	Total (%)
Revenue ($)	—	0.03	0.51	2.69	20.1	775	66,900
Earnings/share ($)	—	0.025	–0.18	–0.36	–0.35	NA	NA
PE ratio range	—	NA	NA	NA	NA		

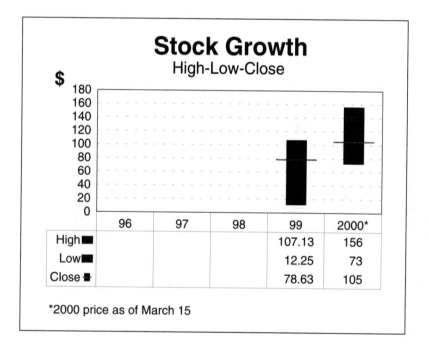

	96	97	98	99	2000*
High ■				107.13	156
Low ■				12.25	73
Close ■				78.63	105

*2000 price as of March 15

SOFTWARE

40

Inktomi Corp.

4100 East Third Avenue
Foster City, CA 94404
650-653-2800
Nasdaq: INKT
www.inktomi.com

Chairman, President, and CEO: David C. Peterschmidt

Earnings Progression	★
Revenue Growth	★ ★ ★ ★
Stock Growth	★ ★
Consistency	★ ★ ★
Stability/Vulnerability	★ ★
Total Points	**12 points**

In Lakota tribal legend, Inktomi was a clever spider—which is a pretty fair characterization of Inktomi's Internet software. The Foster City, California operation designs search engine software that helps millions of Internet surfers find their way around the Web.

The company's signature product, the Inktomi Universal Search Engine, is the most widely used search software on the Internet. It's built into many of the Web's leading portals to help direct Internet users to the sites they need. The best-known portals using Inktomi software are Yahoo!, LookSmart, Microsoft Network, and America Online.

Inktomi also offers several other related software products, including:

- **Directory Engine.** This software is used by portals and big Web sites to compile and manage direct links to other sites.
- **Shopping Engine.** Offered by e-commerce companies, this software enables shoppers to find and compare deals.

169

- **Traffic Server.** The Internet's leading "caching" software, Traffic Server stores frequently downloaded content closer to users to speed performance.
- **Content Delivery Suite.** This is a management tool Web site operators use to deploy and track content across their networks.

In addition to selling software, Inktomi partners with Web portals that use its search engine and collects about half a cent commission per Web page retrieved. It also splits the sales commissions collected by e-tail sites that use the Inktomi Shopping Engine.

Before founding Inktomi, CEO David Peterschmidt started Sybase, the database software company. Inktomi went public with its initial stock offering in 1998. The company has about 500 employees and a market capitalization of about $12 billion.

EARNINGS PER SHARE PROGRESSION   ★

Inktomi has had a string of small losses.

REVENUE GROWTH   ★ ★ ★ ★

Past 3 years: 13,334 percent (241 percent per year)

STOCK GROWTH   ★ ★

Past year: 174 percent
Dollar growth: $10,000 over 1 year would have grown to $27,400.

CONSISTENCY   ★ ★ ★

Positive earnings progression: 1 year
Increased revenue: 3 consecutive years

STABILITY/VULNERABILITY   ★ ★

Inktomi is a dominant player in the search engine software market, but software giants like Microsoft and Novell could challenge.

INKTOMI AT A GLANCE

Fiscal year ended: Sept. 30
Revenue in $ millions

	1995	1996	1997	1998	1999	3-Year Growth Avg. Annual (%)	Total (%)
Revenue ($)	—	.530	5.78	20.4	71.2	241	13,334
Earnings/share ($)	—	−0.51	−0.18	−0.31	−0.24	NA	NA
PE ratio range	—	NA	NA	NA	NA		

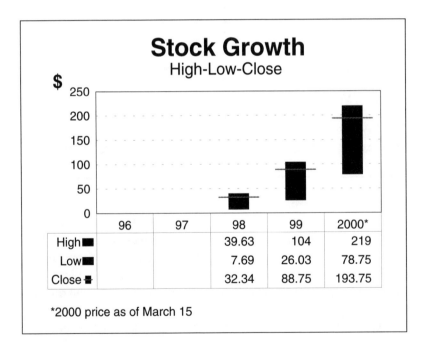

Stock Growth
High-Low-Close

	96	97	98	99	2000*
High			39.63	104	219
Low			7.69	26.03	78.75
Close			32.34	88.75	193.75

*2000 price as of March 15

SOFTWARE

41

Verity, Inc.

894 Ross Drive
Sunnyvale, CA 94089
408-541-1500
Nasdaq: VRTY
www.verity.com

Chairman and CEO: Gary J. Sbona
President: Anthony J. Bettencourt III

Earnings Progression	★ ★ ★
Revenue Growth	★ ★ ★
Stock Growth	★
Consistency	★ ★ ★
Stability/Vulnerability	★ ★
Total Points	**12 points**

Pinpointing pertinent information on the ever-expanding World Wide Web is no small task, with billions of pages of content already posted and millions more being added every week. Search engines can help, but Verity software picks up where other search engines leave off, ferreting out very specific information instantly on an unlimited range of topics.

Verity's software serves the role of an online librarian. It can quickly search, filter, display, and save information stored on corporate databases, intranets, CD-ROMs, and the Internet, using classification standards developed by librarians.

The speed of the search may be the most amazing aspect of Verity's K2 search engine. It can search hundreds of millions of documents in less than a second.

The Sunnyvale, California operation is the leading provider of knowledge retrieval software. Its software products are used by more than 1,300 corporations, e-commerce sites, government agencies, online service providers, Internet publishers, and software developers, including AT&T, CNET, Cisco, Compaq, Dow Jones, IBM, and Lotus.

Verity offers a family of software products, including:

- **Knowledge Organizer**—a program similar to the Yahoo! search engine
- **Document Navigator**—a program designed to help users search long articles in academic journals
- **Information Server**—a program that enables administrators to organize, build, and centrally maintain indices of documents stored on Web and file servers
- **Internet Spider**—a search tool used to index multiple domains
- **Agent Server**—a program that enables proactive notification and dissemination of specific information to users and work groups

The company also offers a variety of application development tools that allow customers to integrate Verity's search tools into their own applications, products, or services.

Founded in 1988, Verity went public with its initial stock offering in 1995. The company has about 300 employees and a market capitalization of about $1.5 billion.

EARNINGS PER SHARE PROGRESSION ★★★
The company had its first profit in 1999, reversing a string of losses.

REVENUE GROWTH ★★★
Past 4 years: 305 percent (42 percent per year)

STOCK GROWTH ★
Past 4 years: 92 percent (18 percent per year)
Dollar growth: $10,000 over 4 years would have grown to $19,200.

CONSISTENCY ★★★
Positive earnings progression: 2 consecutive years
Increased revenues: 3 of the past 4 years

STABILITY/VULNERABILITY ★★
The search engine market is becoming increasingly crowded, but Verity's software fills a unique niche—and the company is profitable.

VERITY AT A GLANCE

Fiscal year ended: May 31
Revenue in $ millions

	1995	1996	1997	1998	1999	4-Year Growth Avg. Annual (%)	Total (%)
Revenue ($)	15.9	30.7	42.7	38.9	64.4	42	305
Earnings/share ($)	−1.09	−0.06	−0.82	−0.74	0.44	NA	NA
PE ratio range	NA	NA	NA	NA	29-140		

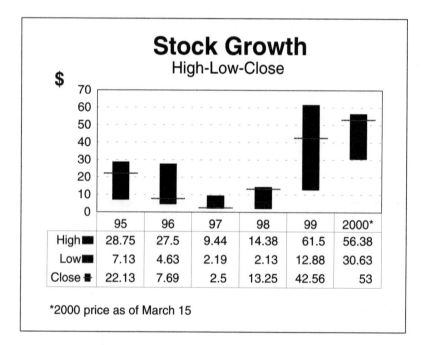

Stock Growth
High-Low-Close

$	95	96	97	98	99	2000*
High ■	28.75	27.5	9.44	14.38	61.5	56.38
Low ■	7.13	4.63	2.19	2.13	12.88	30.63
Close ✦	22.13	7.69	2.5	13.25	42.56	53

*2000 price as of March 15

42

Copper Mountain Networks, Inc.

2470 Embarcadero Way
Palo Alto, CA 02451
781-370-2700
Nasdaq: CMTN
www.coppermountain.com

Chairman: Joseph D. Markee
President and CEO: Richard S. Gilbert

Earnings Progression	★ ★
Revenue Growth	★ ★ ★
Stock Growth	★ ★
Consistency	★ ★ ★
Stability/Vulnerability	★ ★
Total Points	**12 points**

The battle raging between telephone and cable TV networks for control of the "last mile" of wire into homes and businesses is shaping up to be one of the great business donnybrooks of all time. If you're inclined to place your wager on the phone lines, Copper Mountain may be the best place to start.

The "copper" in the company's name alludes to the basic copper telephone lines still connecting virtually all homes and small businesses. Copper Mountain makes devices that move data dozens of times faster over normal phone lines by using Digital Subscriber Line (DSL) technology.

The Palo Alto, California operation offers three product lines:

1. **Customer premise equipment.** The CopperRocket series of modemlike devices is used in homes and businesses to become DSL compatible.
2. **Central office equipment.** The CopperEdge series of DSL concentrators is used in local telephone switching offices and Internet service provider computer rooms to receive DSL connections from users.
3. **DSL network management.** The company also makes a software product called CopperView for centrally configuring and managing DSL networks.

Copper Mountain offers solutions to wire office buildings and even whole campuses with high-speed DSL connections. That—and heavy investment in ensuring that its products can work alongside non-DSL equipment—has allowed Copper Mountain to take the lead in providing DSL to business.

Founded in 1996, Copper Mountain went public with its initial stock offering in 1999. The company has about 150 employees and a market capitalization of about $2 billion.

EARNINGS PER SHARE PROGRESSION   ★ ★
Copper Mountain went from a loss in 1998 to a gain in 1999.

REVENUE GROWTH   ★ ★ ★
Past 2 years: 53,312 percent (1,320 percent per year)

STOCK GROWTH   ★ ★
The company went public in 1999 and experienced strong gains after the IPO.

CONSISTENCY   ★ ★ ★
Positive earnings progression: 1 year
Increased revenue: 2 consecutive years

STABILITY/VULNERABILITY   ★ ★
The company's technology and niche focus should help in the booming DSL market.

COPPER MOUNTAIN AT A GLANCE

Fiscal year ended: Dec. 31
Revenue in $ millions

	1995	1996	1997	1998	1999	2-Year Growth Avg. Annual (%)	Total (%)
Revenue ($)	—	—	.211	21.8	112.7	1,320	53,312
Earnings/share ($)	—	—	—	−0.31	0.21	NA	NA
PE ratio range	—	—	NA	NA	NA		

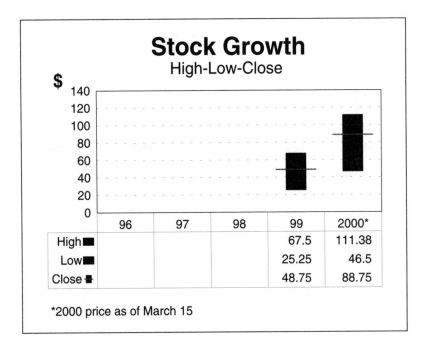

Stock Growth
High-Low-Close

	96	97	98	99	2000*
High■				67.5	111.38
Low■				25.25	46.5
Close ■				48.75	88.75

*2000 price as of March 15

43

PSINet, Inc.

510 Huntmar Park Drive
Herndon, VA 20170
703-904-4100
Nasdaq: PSIX
www.domain.com

Chairman and CEO: William L. Schrader
President and COO: Harold S. Wills

Earnings Progression	
Revenue Growth	★ ★ ★ ★
Stock Growth	★ ★
Consistency	★ ★ ★
Stability/Vulnerability	★ ★ ★
Total Points	**12 points**

Being first isn't everything, but in the Internet economy it has its advantages. Back in 1989—when most surfers were academics hoping to keep the Internet noncommercial—PSINet saw the vast potential and set up shop as the world's first Internet service provider (ISP).

From the beginning, the strategy of the Virginia-based operation has been to provide Internet access to businesses, not consumers. The strategy is a good one, because 65 percent of the $10 billion Internet access market comes from business customers.

PSINet spent the past decade building the world's largest IP-only network. It was the first company to connect Asia, North America, and Europe with dedicated Internet links, which is why PSINet is regarded as one of the Internet's primary backbones. Its services include:

- **PSINet Global Network.** The company has more than 600 points of presence in 22 countries, with high-speed backbone links between major cities.
- **Transaction Network Services.** This subsidiary gives PSINet the world's largest network for point-of-sale transactions. Customers include American Express and First Data.
- **Internet applications.** PSIVoice, the company's voice-over IP offering, was introduced in 1999. It also offers services for e-mail, Internet fax, and videocasting.
- **Web site hosting.** It has teamed with Hewlett-Packard to offer business customers its PSINet Dedicated Hosting service.

PSINet has over 70,000 customers. Heavy investments to expand its presence in Europe and Asia have set the table for continued growth.

The company went public with its initial stock offering in 1995. PSINet has about 1,900 employees and a market capitalization of about $4 billion.

EARNINGS PER SHARE PROGRESSION
PSINet has had a long string of losses.

REVENUE GROWTH ★ ★ ★ ★
Past 4 years: 1,333 percent (95 percent per year)

STOCK GROWTH ★ ★
Past 4 years: 170 percent (28 percent per year)
Dollar growth: $10,000 over 4 years would have grown to $27,000.

CONSISTENCY ★ ★ ★
Positive earnings progression: None
Increased sales: 4 consecutive years

STABILITY/VULNERABILITY ★ ★ ★
MCI WorldCom and other major telecoms are formidable competitors, but PSINet's worldwide network is a substantial asset.

PSINET AT A GLANCE

Fiscal year ended: Dec. 31
Revenue in $ millions

	1995	1996	1997	1998	1999	4-Year Growth Avg. Annual (%)	4-Year Growth Total (%)
Revenue ($)	38.7	89.8	121.9	259.6	554.7	95	1,333
Earnings/share ($)	−0.89	−0.70	−0.57	−2.61	−3.36	NA	NA
PE ratio range	NA	NA	NA	NA	NA		

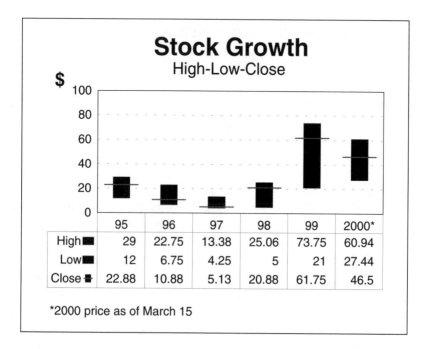

Stock Growth
High-Low-Close

	95	96	97	98	99	2000*
High	29	22.75	13.38	25.06	73.75	60.94
Low	12	6.75	4.25	5	21	27.44
Close	22.88	10.88	5.13	20.88	61.75	46.5

*2000 price as of March 15

ISPs AND PORTALS

44

Covad Communications Group

2330 Central Expressway
Santa Clara, CA 95050
408-844-7500
Nasdaq: COVD
www.covad.com

Chairman: Charles McMinn
President and CEO: Robert Knowling, Jr.

Earnings Progression	★ ★
Revenue Growth	★ ★ ★
Stock Growth	★ ★
Consistency	★ ★
Stability/Vulnerability	★ ★ ★
Total Points	**12 points**

Covad Communications is spreading high-speed Internet access service across America. The San Francisco–based operation is a leading broadband service provider, offering high-speed Internet access using Digital Subscriber Line (DSL) technology.

DSL technology is used to speed up transmission on traditional copper phone lines. It can deliver speeds up to 25 times faster than standard modem connections, and you can use DSL for phone calls even when logged onto the Internet.

Covad offers DSL services through Internet service providers to small and medium-sized businesses and home users. The company is adding quickly to its service network. By the end of the year 2000, Covad is expected to have DSL service available to Internet users in the nation's 100 largest metropolitan areas, covering about 40 percent of all homes and 45 percent of all businesses.

Covad claims to have the nation's largest DSL network, with about 1,000 operational central offices and well over 30,000 DSL-based high-speed access lines installed. It recently had orders from about 300 Internet service providers, enterprises, and telecommunications carriers, including AT&T, Oracle, Prodigy, PSINet, Qwest, Stanford University, Verio, and Sun Microsystems.

The company plans to continue to expand its service offerings, such as voice via DSL and e-commerce applications, through strategic alliances with broadband-related service providers.

Covad was founded in 1996 by two former Intel employees who used about $1 million in seed money from Intel to get the operation off the ground. The company later picked up another $7.5 million in seed money from venture capital firms.

The company went public with its initial stock offering in 1999. Covad has about 350 employees and a market capitalization of about $6 billion.

EARNINGS PER SHARE PROGRESSION ★ ★
Losses declined by about 50 percent in 1999.

REVENUE GROWTH ★ ★ ★
Past 2 years: 255,669 percent (4,800 percent per year)

STOCK GROWTH ★ ★
Covad went public in 1999 and had strong but rocky growth after the IPO.

CONSISTENCY ★ ★
Positive earnings progression: 1 year
Increased revenue: 2 consecutive years

STABILITY/VULNERABILITY ★ ★ ★
Covad Communications is a young company with strong potential and very rapid growth.

COVAD COMMUNICATIONS AT A GLANCE

Fiscal year ended: Dec. 31
Revenue in $ millions

	1995	1996	1997	1998	1999	2-Year Growth Avg. Annual (%)	Total (%)
Revenue ($)	—	—	.026	5.33	66.5	4,800	255,669
Earnings/share ($)	—	—	−0.47	−5.31	−2.67	NA	NA
PE ratio range	—	—	NA	NA	NA		

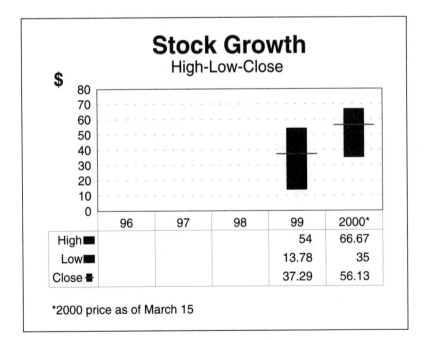

Stock Growth
High-Low-Close

$	96	97	98	99	2000*
High				54	66.67
Low				13.78	35
Close				37.29	56.13

*2000 price as of March 15

45

Netscout Systems, Inc.

4 Technology Park Drive
Westford, MA 01886
978-614-4000
Nasdaq: NTCT
www.netscout.com

Chairman and CEO: Anil K. Singhal
President: Narenda Popat

Earnings Progression	★ ★ ★ ★
Revenue Growth	★ ★ ★ ★
Stock Growth	
Consistency	★ ★ ★
Stability/Vulnerability	★
Total Points	**12 points**

NetScout Systems is riding into the network management market on the broad shoulders of Cisco Systems.

The Westford, Massachusetts operation makes software that helps companies direct, monitor, and analyze their computer traffic across both their corporate intranets and the Internet. Its biggest customer is Cisco Systems, which integrates NetScout's software into its network management products.

The two companies have had a strategic alliance since 1994. Cisco Systems works with NetScout to synchronize product development, then integrates the specially designed NetScout software into its networking systems.

Sales through Cisco account for about 50 percent of NetScout's total annual revenue.

NetScout's flagship product is its Application Flow Management system, which tracks and analyzes traffic by software applications, such as e-mail and order entry, across the network. Specific benefits include:

- Measuring response times for network-based software applications
- Monitoring and troubleshooting network usage to prevent malfunctions and pinpoint problems
- Capacity planning to measure and identify trends in network usage
- Policy enforcement to ensure adherence to corporate guidelines
- Accounting and chargeback function, which breaks down usage by user, department, or application, in order to charge for network use

Formerly known as Frontier Software, the company was incorporated in 1984 and changed its name to NetScout in 1997. It went public with its initial stock offering in 1999. NetScout Systems has about 250 employees and a market capitalization of about $900 million.

EARNINGS PER SHARE PROGRESSION ★ ★ ★ ★

Earnings growth past 4 years: 1,333 percent (95 percent per year)

REVENUE GROWTH ★ ★ ★ ★

Past 4 years: 1,046 percent (84 percent per year)

STOCK GROWTH

NetScout went public in 1999 and had a rocky performance after its IPO.

CONSISTENCY ★ ★ ★

Increased earnings: 3 of the last 4 years
Increased revenue: 4 consecutive years

STABILITY/VULNERABILITY ★

Staying a step ahead of the pack is always a challenge in the software business, and the company must compete with Hewlett-Packard, IBM, and Computer Associates. NetScout is heavily reliant on Cisco as its primary distribution channel, but the alliance has been very lucrative to date.

NETSCOUT SYSTEMS AT A GLANCE

Fiscal year ended: March 31
Revenue in $ millions

	1995	1996	1997	1998	1999	4-Year Growth Avg. Annual (%)	Total (%)
Revenue ($)	5.9	15.7	30.6	42.8	67.6	84	1,046
Earnings/share ($)	0.03	0.09	0.26	0.23	0.43	95	1,333
PE ratio range	NA	NA	NA	NA	NA		

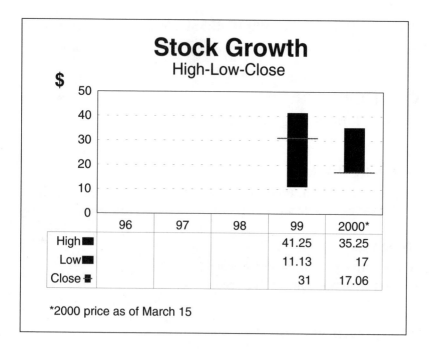

Stock Growth
High-Low-Close

$	96	97	98	99	2000*
High ■				41.25	35.25
Low ■				11.13	17
Close ■				31	17.06

*2000 price as of March 15

SOFTWARE

46

Vignette Corporation

901 South Mopac Expressway
Austin, TX 78746
512-306-4300
Nasdaq: VIGN
www.vignette.com

Chairman: Ross B Garber
President and CEO: Gregory A. Peters

Earnings Progression	
Revenue Growth	★ ★ ★
Stock Growth	★ ★ ★
Consistency	★ ★
Stability/Vulnerability	★ ★ ★
Total Points	**11 points**

When a major banking operation decided to offer some of its services online, it used Vignette application software to build a Web site that gave its customers the ability to apply for loans and insurance online, manage their investment portfolios, and scan through timely news and research.

The Austin, Texas software maker has helped hundreds of companies develop and manage their e-commerce operations. Vignette is a leading supplier of e-business software applications for building online businesses.

Vignette's software applications make it easy for customers to conduct business online by automating the ordering process. More than 500 major businesses have used Vignette software to build their Web-based operations, including AT&T, BMW, CBS Broadcasting, and FedEx.

Vignette sells three software products that can be used stand-alone or as an integrated suite:

1. **StoryServer.** Used to build e-stores and Internet portal sites. Story-Server manages all Web site content and builds Web pages on the fly to fit the individual visitor's profile.
2. **Syndication Server.** Used to deliver content throughout an e-commerce company's network of affiliated Web sites. Syndication Server automatically exchanges information with affiliated sites for the purpose of attracting quality traffic.
3. **Multi-Channel Server.** This product lets e-commerce companies reach beyond the Web to coordinate all forms of customer contact, including e-mail, cellular phones, and other media.

Vignette's product line also includes tools to operate and maintain Web sites and to exchange information with internal computer databases. Its "lifestyle personalization" functions help companies adjust their Web site offerings to conform to the interests of their visitors.

Founded in 1995, Vignette went public with its initial stock offering in 1999. The firm has about 310 employees and a market capitalization of about $12 billion.

EARNINGS PER SHARE PROGRESSION
None

REVENUE GROWTH   ★ ★ ★
Past 2 years: 2,854 percent (445 percent per year)

STOCK GROWTH   ★ ★ ★
Vignette had exceptional growth after its 1999 IPO.

CONSISTENCY   ★ ★
Positive earnings progression: None
Increased revenue: 2 consecutive years

STABILITY/VULNERABILITY   ★ ★ ★
Vignette is the market leader in this high-demand sector.

VIGNETTE AT A GLANCE

Fiscal year ended: Dec. 31
Revenue in $ millions

	1995	1996	1997	1998	1999	2-Year Growth Avg. Annual (%)	Total (%)
Revenue ($)	—	—	3.02	16.2	89.2	445	2,854
Earnings/share ($)	—	—	−0.21	−0.73	−0.98	NA	NA
PE ratio range	—	—	NA	NA	NA		

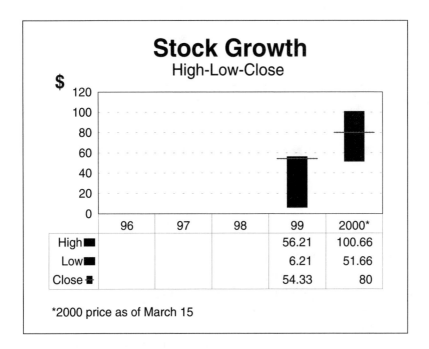

Stock Growth
High-Low-Close

$	96	97	98	99	2000*
High ■				56.21	100.66
Low ■				6.21	51.66
Close ■				54.33	80

*2000 price as of March 15

47
Excite@Home Corp.

450 Broadway Street
Redwood City, CA 94063
650-569-5000
Nasdaq: ATHM
www.excite.com

Chairman: Thomas Jermoluk
President and CEO: George Bell

Earnings Progression	
Revenue Growth	★ ★ ★ ★
Stock Growth	★ ★ ★
Consistency	★ ★
Stability/Vulnerability	★ ★
Total Points	**11 points**

Did the growing presence of Excite@Home scare America Online (AOL) into its megamerger with Time Warner?

Excite is an Internet service provider (ISP) that connects homes to the Web over wires strung by cable TV operators. The scary part for AOL is that cable modems can download Internet data dozens of times faster than typical PC modems hooked up through the standard telephone lines most AOL subscribers use.

That superior broadband performance has helped Excite@Home cut into AOL's subscriber base. In fact, AOL Chairman Steve Case was so concerned about the disparity, he went to Congress to try to persuade them that cable hook-ups should be opened to *all* ISPs.

Excite has exclusive cable Internet access agreements with more than 20 cable companies through the next three to five years and is actively seeking to sign more.

The company's Web portal, Excite.com, is one of the five busiest sites on the Internet. It has more than a million subscribers and receives more than 100 million page views per day. It features news, weather, sports, stock quotes, 18 programmed channels of content, a Web search engine, e-mail, PAL instant messaging, chat, and online shopping.

The company also offers a small business Internet service called @Work, which uses high-speed phone lines instead of cable.

The Redwood City, California operation got its name from the 1998 merger of the portal Excite with @Home, an ISP. @Home was formed by a consortium of most of the biggest cable TV networks, including Comcast, Cox Communications, Cablevision, and AT&T (which entered the cable TV business with its acquisition of Tele-Communications, Inc.).

Founded in 1994, Excite@Home went public with its initial stock offering in 1996. The company has about 2,500 employees and a market capitalization of about $15 billion.

EARNINGS PER SHARE PROGRESSION
None

REVENUE GROWTH ★ ★ ★ ★
Past 3 years: 49,737 percent (693 percent per year)

STOCK GROWTH ★ ★ ★
Past 2 years: 241 percent (85 percent per year)
Dollar growth: $10,000 over 2 years would have grown to $34,100.

CONSISTENCY ★ ★
Positive earnings progression: None
Increased revenue: 3 consecutive years

STABILITY/VULNERABILITY ★ ★
AOL is certainly the dominant player in this niche, but there's plenty of room in the emerging "broadband-to-the-curb" Internet access market, and Excite@Home has backers with deep pockets.

EXCITE@HOME AT A GLANCE

Fiscal year ended: Dec. 31
Revenue in $ millions

	1995	1996	1997	1998	1999	3-Year Growth Avg. Annual (%)	Total (%)
Revenue ($)	—	.676	7.44	48.0	336.9	693	49,737
Earnings/share ($)	—	−0.13	−1.07	−0.47	−4.14	NA	NA
PE ratio range	—	NA	NA	NA	NA		

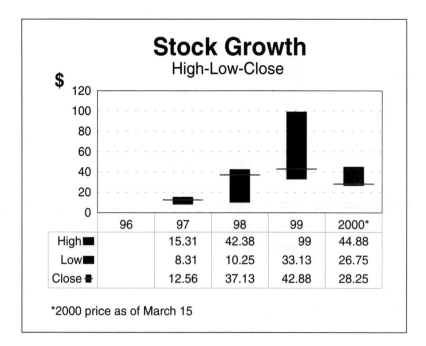

Stock Growth
High-Low-Close

$	96	97	98	99	2000*
High ■		15.31	42.38	99	44.88
Low ■		8.31	10.25	33.13	26.75
Close ■		12.56	37.13	42.88	28.25

*2000 price as of March 15

INFRASTRUCTURE

Ariba, Inc.

1314 Chesapeake Terrace
Sunnyvale, CA 94089
408-543-3800
Nasdaq: ARBA
www.ariba.com

Chairman: Keith J. Krach
President and CEO: Larry Mueller

Earnings Progression	★ ★
Revenue Growth	★ ★
Stock Growth	★ ★
Consistency	★ ★
Stability/Vulnerability	★ ★ ★
Total Points	**11 points**

You want growth potential? How about a clear shot at supplying half the software to facilitate more than $1 trillion in online purchases a year?

That's the opportunity Ariba is chasing. The Sunnyvale, California operation's new breed of e-commerce software is used by businesses to trade with other businesses over the Internet.

Ariba is in a race with its arch rival, Commerce One, to lock in as many big corporate customers as possible. The battleground is intense because large corporations often use hundreds of suppliers who also need e-commerce software, and those companies tend to use the same software as their big corporate customers.

Ariba's software automates corporate procurement processes previously handled manually by purchasing agents. Its secret to success is that it automatically makes "apples-to-apples" comparisons between otherwise incompatible product catalogs of various trading partners. Its lineup of market-making products includes:

- **Ariba Auction.** Used by a single seller to offer goods or services to multiple buyers.
- **Ariba Exchange.** Creates an open market in which many buyers and sellers participate using a bid/ask system.
- **Ariba ReverseAuction.** A single buyer solicits bids from multiple vendors.

The company also sells a variety of products used within companies to manage such internal purchasing processes as purchase authorization and order tracking.

Ariba went public with its initial stock offering in 1999. The company has about 400 employees and a market capitalization of about $17 billion.

EARNINGS PER SHARE PROGRESSION ★ ★

Ariba's losses declined from 1998 to 1999.

REVENUE GROWTH ★ ★

Past year: 443 percent

STOCK GROWTH ★ ★

Ariba went public in 1999 and experienced strong gains following its IPO.

CONSISTENCY ★ ★

Declining losses per share: 1 year
Increased revenue: 1 year

STABILITY/VULNERABILITY ★ ★ ★

Ariba faces competition from both Commerce One and such established corporate application vendors as SAP, Oracle, and PeopleSoft. But its head start in this lucrative sector should give Ariba an important edge.

ARIBA AT A GLANCE

Fiscal year ended: Sept. 30
Revenue in $ millions

	1995	1996	1997	1998	1999	1-Year Growth Avg. Annual (%)	Total (%)
Revenue ($)	—	—	—	8.36	45.4	443	443
Earnings/share ($)	—	—	—	–0.95	–0.48	NA	NA
PE ratio range	—	—	—	NA	NA		

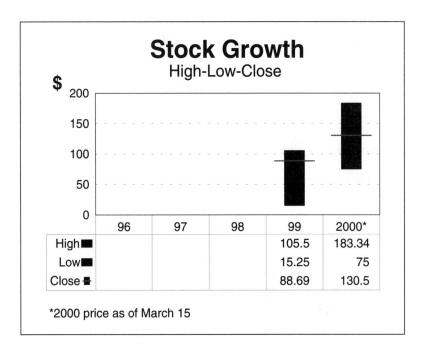

Stock Growth
High-Low-Close

	96	97	98	99	2000*
High ■				105.5	183.34
Low ■				15.25	75
Close ■				88.69	130.5

*2000 price as of March 15

49
InfoSpace.com, Inc.

15375 N.E. 90th Street
Redmond, WA 98052
425-882-1602
Nasdaq: INSP
www.infospace.com

Chairman and CEO: Naveen Jain
President: Bernee D.L. Strom

Earnings Progression	★
Revenue Growth	★ ★ ★
Stock Growth	★ ★ ★
Consistency	★ ★
Stability/Vulnerability	★ ★
Total Points	**11 points**

You're on the road in another city, looking for a good Chinese restaurant. Thanks to InfoSpace.com, you'll soon be able to find your way to the closest one with a few clicks on your cell phone.

InfoSpace offers systems and services that give cellular phone users the ability to call up localized content, buy goods online with a single click, send instant messages, read e-mails, and access their address books and calendars.

The Redmond, Washington operation offers a range of Internet information infrastructure systems and services for consumers, merchants, and wireless companies, including:

- **Consumer services.** InfoSpace supplies a broad range of online content to Web sites, including maps, white pages and yellow pages directories, news, message boards, e-mail, and online shopping.

InfoSpace has an affiliate network of more than 2,000 Web site operators such as America Online, Lycos, go2net, *The Wall Street Journal,* and ABC LocalNet.

- **Wireless services.** InfoSpace provides content, online shopping, and other Internet services for wireless devices, such as PCs, cellular phones, pagers, laptop computers, screen telephones, and television set-top boxes. The company has strategic alliances with AT&T Wireless, GTE Wireless, Sprint, and Lucent.
- **Merchant services.** Merchants can promote and sell their products online through the InfoSpace network, including food, apparel, flowers, insurance, movies, music, toys, electronics, and office supplies.

Founded in 1996, InfoSpace.com went public with its initial stock offering in 1998. It has about 100 employees and a market capitalization of about $10 billion.

EARNINGS PER SHARE PROGRESSION ★

Losses declined from 1998 to 1999.

REVENUE GROWTH ★ ★ ★

Past 2 years: 2,067 percent (365 percent per year)

STOCK GROWTH ★ ★ ★

Past year: 1,023 percent
Dollar growth: $10,000 over 1 year would have grown to $112,300.

CONSISTENCY ★ ★

Positive earnings progression: 1 year
Increased sales: 2 consecutive years

STABILITY/VULNERABILITY ★ ★

The company has a network of affiliates, merchants, and wireless partners, and it has seen a rapid rise in revenues—but still no profit.

INFOSPACE.COM AT A GLANCE

Fiscal year ended: Dec. 31
Revenue in $ millions

	1995	1996	1997	1998	1999	2-Year Growth Avg. Annual (%)	Total (%)
Revenue ($)	—	—	1.68	9.41	36.4	365	2,067
Earnings/share ($)	—	—	–0.01	–0.15	–0.08	NA	NA
PE ratio range	—	—	NA	NA	NA		

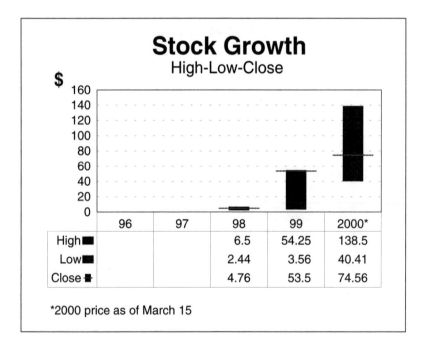

Stock Growth
High-Low-Close

$	96	97	98	99	2000*
High ■			6.5	54.25	138.5
Low ■			2.44	3.56	40.41
Close ■			4.76	53.5	74.56

*2000 price as of March 15

SOFTWARE

50

Allaire, Inc.

One Alewife Center
Cambridge, MA 02140
617-761-2000
Nasdaq: ALLR
www.allaire.com

Chairman: J.J. Allaire
President and CEO: David Orfao

Earnings Progression	★ ★
Revenue Growth	★ ★ ★
Stock Growth	★ ★
Consistency	★ ★
Stability/Vulnerability	★ ★
Total Points	**11 points**

There was a period in the mid-1990s when Microsoft had a virtual lock on the market for low-end software programming tools. But its tools were geared to PCs and local networks—not Web sites. As a result, the Web has opened up the programming game to a whole new wave of software tool companies, such as Allaire, that focus exclusively on the Internet.

Allaire makes a suite of Web development products used by computer programmers to build Web sites.

The Cambridge, Massachusetts operation has developed its products for a broad range of applications by working with about 1,800 business partners, including system integrators, consultants, Internet service providers, and software developers. Its leading products include:

- **ColdFusion Studio.** Allaire's flagship product, ColdFusion, is one of the most popular application servers in the industry. It's used to develop and operate Web sites.
- **Jrun.** This development tool is used for programming in Java.
- **Allaire Spectra.** Spectra is used to personalize the content Web site visitors see, based on a profile containing individual preferences and previous visits. It also automates the management of site content, such as product sheets, pictures, copy, and other features.

Founder and Chairman J.J. Allaire started the company with just $18,000 of his own money. Allaire went public with its initial stock offering in 1999. It has about 165 employees and a market capitalization of about $2 billion.

EARNINGS PER SHARE PROGRESSION ★ ★

Allaire has no earnings, but losses have declined the past 2 years.

REVENUE GROWTH ★ ★ ★

Past 2 years: 621 percent (167 percent per year)

STOCK GROWTH ★ ★

The stock did not begin trading until 1999, but it had very impressive gains that year.

CONSISTENCY ★ ★

Increased earnings per share: None
Increased revenue: 2 consecutive years

STABILITY/VULNERABILITY ★ ★

Allaire is off to a good start in a competitive market, and its giant customer base will be hard to budge.

ALLAIRE AT A GLANCE

Fiscal year ended: Dec. 31
Revenue in $ millions'

	1995	1996	1997	1998	1999	2-Year Growth	
						Avg. Annual (%)	Total (%)
Revenue ($)	—	—	7.65	21	55.2	167	621
Earnings/share ($)	—	—	−4.58	−4.54	−0.53	NA	NA
PE ratio range	—	—	NA	NA	NA		

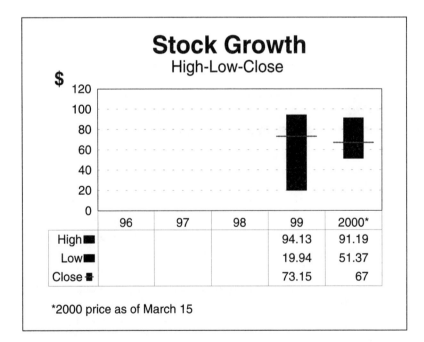

Stock Growth
High-Low-Close

$	96	97	98	99	2000*
High■				94.13	91.19
Low■				19.94	51.37
Close ■				73.15	67

*2000 price as of March 15

51
Net Perceptions

7901 Flying Cloud Drive
Eden Prairie, MN 55344
612-903-9424
Nasdaq: NETP
www.netperceptions.com

President and CEO: Steven J. Snyder

Earnings Progression	
Revenue Growth	★ ★ ★ ★
Stock Growth	★ ★
Consistency	★ ★ ★
Stability/Vulnerability	★ ★
Total Points	**11 points**

"May I show you anything of interest?" That's the question all good e-tailers want to ask online shoppers as they browse their sites.

To help them answer that question, Net Perceptions offers e-tailers "collaborative filtering" software that tracks individual shopping habits and tailors the online shopping experience accordingly. Personal preferences are constantly updated and expanded according to an entire demographic group, making it both accurate and inexpensive to maintain.

The Minneapolis-based operation is the premier provider of products and services based on collaborative filtering technology. Among the company's leading products are:

- **Net Perceptions Recommendation Engine.** Predicts an individual's interests and tastes and instantly makes product recommendations most likely to get a response.

- **Net Perceptions for Ad Targeting.** Automatically targets banner ads presented on Web pages according to each visitor's profile.
- **Net Perceptions for Marketing Campaigns.** Targets e-mail marketing campaigns at the individual recipient level based on up-to-date profile information.

In addition to products for e-tailers, the firm offers two products for internal use. Net Perceptions for Call Centers provides personal profiles that sales reps use when talking to prospects during telephone calls, and Net Perceptions Knowledge Management helps employees search corporate databases with personalized search filters.

Company founder and CEO Steven Snyder worked for Microsoft prior to starting Net Perceptions in 1996. The company went public with its initial stock offering in 1999. Net Perceptions has about 100 employees and a market capitalization of about $1 billion.

EARNINGS PER SHARE PROGRESSION
Losses have increased the past 3 years.

REVENUE GROWTH   ★ ★ ★ ★
Past 3 years: 377,400 percent (1,455 percent per year)

STOCK GROWTH   ★ ★
Net Perceptions went public in 1999 and had strong gains after the IPO.

CONSISTENCY   ★ ★ ★
Positive earnings progression: None
Increased revenue: 3 consecutive years

STABILITY/VULNERABILITY   ★ ★
Competition is getting fierce in the profiling software business, and Microsoft is moving in. But once a customer hooks up a product, getting them to change is no small challenge.

NET PERCEPTIONS AT A GLANCE

Fiscal year ended: Dec. 31
Revenue in $ millions

	1995	1996	1997	1998	1999	3-Year Growth Avg. Annual (%)	Total (%)
Revenue ($)	—	.004	.317	4.48	15.1	1,455	377,400
Earnings/share ($)	—	–0.13	–0.34	–0.35	–0.68	NA	NA
PE ratio range	—	NA	NA	NA	NA		

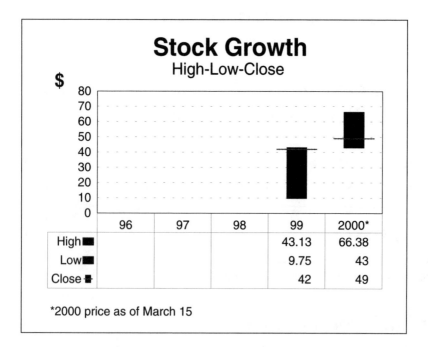

Stock Growth
High-Low-Close

$	96	97	98	99	2000*
High■				43.13	66.38
Low■				9.75	43
Close ■				42	49

*2000 price as of March 15

INTERNET BUSINESS
SERVICES

52

Critical Path, Inc.

320 1st Street
San Francisco, CA 94105
415-808-8800
Nasdaq: CPTH
www.cp.net

Chairman: David Hayden
President and CEO: Douglas Hickey

Earnings Progression	★
Revenue Growth	★ ★ ★
Stock Growth	★ ★
Consistency	★ ★ ★
Stability/Vulnerability	★ ★
Total Points	**11 points**

With nearly a half-billion electronic mailboxes worldwide, the e-mail business is exploding across cyberspace. Nearly a half-trillion e-mail messages were sent in 1999—a figure that seems to be doubling every two or three years.

Critical Path is grabbing an increasing share of that e-mail market by expanding its electronic messaging services and acquiring other companies in the business.

The San Francisco–based e-mail hosting operation provides messaging services for Internet service providers, Web hosting companies, Web portals, and corporations. It hosts e-mail systems for Compuserv, E*Trade, Network Solutions, Sprint, AOL Latin America, Asiamail, British Telecom, and several hundred other organizations.

By using an outside e-mail hosting service such as Critical Path, corporations and Web companies can reduce costs associated with acquiring and maintaining hardware and software and recruiting and retaining systems engineering and administrative personnel. Critical Path also offers clients a flexible system architecture designed to support global service over millions of mailboxes across millions of Web domains. Other advantages include:

- Faster access to advanced technologies
- Maintenance of network and system security
- Control over their own brand and functionality through customized Web-based e-mail interfaces. Critical Path works completely behind the scenes.

Founded in 1997, Critical Path went public with its initial stock offering in 1999. It has about 250 employees and a market capitalization of about $3 billion.

EARNINGS PER SHARE PROGRESSION   ★

Losses declined from 1998 to 1999.

REVENUE GROWTH   ★ ★ ★

Past 2 years: 179,900 percent (3,240 percent per year)

STOCK GROWTH   ★ ★

Critical Path went public in 1999 and had solid gains after the IPO.

CONSISTENCY   ★ ★ ★

Positive earnings progression: 1 year
Increased revenue: 2 consecutive years

STABILITY/VULNERABILITY   ★ ★

Small but growing, Critical Path has yet to turn a profit. However, it is a strong competitor in a fast-growing sector.

CRITICAL PATH AT A GLANCE

Fiscal year ended: Dec. 31
Revenue in $ millions

	1995	1996	1997	1998	1999	2-Year Growth Avg. Annual (%)	Total (%)
Revenue ($)	—	—	.009	.897	16.2	3,240	179,900
Earnings/share ($)	—	—	−0.04	−2.17	−0.99	NA	NA
PE ratio range	—	—	NA	NA	NA		

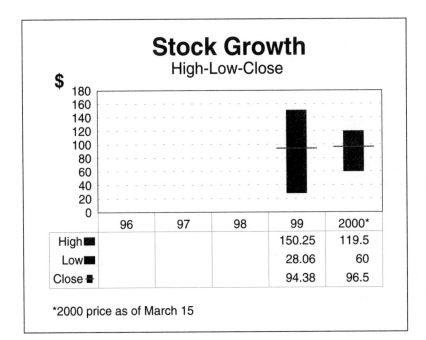

	96	97	98	99	2000*
High				150.25	119.5
Low				28.06	60
Close				94.38	96.5

*2000 price as of March 15

53

Optibase Ltd.

3031 Tisch Way
Plaza West, Suite 1
San Jose, CA 95128
408-260-6760
Nasdaq: OBAS
www.optibase.com

Chairman: Mordechai Gorfung
President: Amir Aharoni
CEO: Ran Eisenberg

Earnings Progression	★ ★
Revenue Growth	★ ★
Stock Growth	★ ★
Consistency	★ ★ ★
Stability/Vulnerability	★ ★
Total Points	**11 points**

If a picture is worth a thousand words, then video must be worth a million.

That's what Optibase is banking on. The Israel-based operation makes systems for handling digital video, the key component of the booming computer multimedia arena.

Because of infrastructure technology shortcomings, Internet videos tend to be short in length, suffer from poor resolution, and are painfully slow and unreliable. Optibase provides the "video infrastructure" needed to upgrade hardware in order to facilitate high-end multimedia applications. Its products include:

- **Video publishing tools.** These are full-blown environments used by professionals to produce digital videos. Optibase makes composing tools to create content in both the MPEG and DVD formats.

- **Digital video hardware.** Optibase manufactures special computer boards that are installed in computers and networking devices. Some products are used to create DVDs and CD-ROMs. Others are used for video projection, digital broadcasting over cable TV networks, and even to play back digital video at point-of-sale kiosks.
- **Digital video networking.** The company also makes hardware and software to deploy streaming video applications for such uses as videoconferencing, Internet news and entertainment videocasting, security video surveillance, and computer-based training.

Optibase is at the cutting edge of digital video. It has applied for several patents for proprietary technologies to make MPEG work better and has recently focused on creating video networking technology to make the Internet handle video faster and more reliably.

The company sells mainly through distributors and systems integrators. Major customers include Time Warner, Bloomberg, and NEC.

Optibase went public with its initial stock offering in 1999. The company has about 100 employees and a market capitalization of about $350 million.

EARNINGS PER SHARE PROGRESSION ★ ★
Past year: 100 percent

REVENUE GROWTH ★ ★
Past 2 years: 81 percent (34 percent per year)

STOCK GROWTH ★ ★
Optibase went public in 1999 and experienced very strong gains after it's IPO.

CONSISTENCY ★ ★ ★
Positive earnings progression: 2 consecutive years
Increased revenue: 2 consecutive years

STABILITY/VULNERABILITY ★ ★
Optibase's products fill a need now, but will other technology advances down the road cut into its market?

OPTIBASE AT A GLANCE

Fiscal year ended: Dec. 31
Revenue in $ millions

	1995	1996	1997	1998	1999	2-Year Growth Avg. Annual (%)	2-Year Growth Total (%)
Revenue ($)	—	—	14.4	20.4	26.1	34	81
Earnings/share ($)	—	—	–0.01	0.27	0.54	100*	100*
PE ratio range	—	—	NA	NA	NA		

*Earnings per share growth figures reflect 1 year.

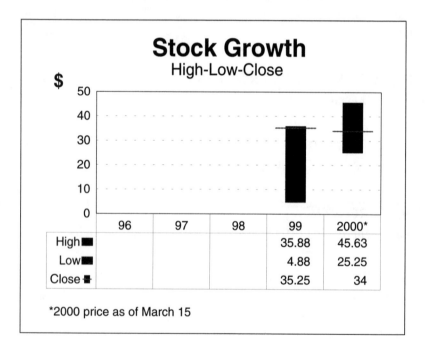

	96	97	98	99	2000*
High ■				35.88	45.63
Low ■				4.88	25.25
Close ■				35.25	34

*2000 price as of March 15

SOFTWARE

54
BackWeb Technologies Ltd.

2077 Gateway Place, #500
San Jose, CA 95110
408-933-1700
Nasdaq: BWEB
www.backweb.com

Chairman and CEO: Eli Barkat

Earnings Progression	★ ★
Revenue Growth	★ ★
Stock Growth	★ ★
Consistency	★ ★ ★
Stability/Vulnerability	★ ★
Total Points	**11 points**

In cyberspace, there are few things more distasteful than spam—not the canned variety, but the barrage of junk e-mail promoting everything from porno Web sites to get-rich-quick schemes. The spam epidemic has become a major problem for corporate Web users who sometimes miss important e-mail messages that get lost in the dozens of spams that land in their e-boxes each day.

BackWeb Technologies has helped companies solve the spam problem by developing a "push" technology that directs important Internet messages to the right people at the right time.

The Israel-based operation makes a suite of software products designed to improve communications within an organization and between businesses. Its signature software suite, BackWeb Foundation, features several key components, including:

- **BackWeb Server.** This software is able to receive digital data from various sources, such as the Internet, intranet sites, and databases, and automatically sends the information to the proper computer users.
- **BackWeb Client.** This application allows computer users to receive data communications from BackWeb servers while they are using other applications. The system displays information through "flashes" and other displays and user interfaces, so that important messages are conveyed quickly to the designated recipient.

BackWeb Technologies went public with its initial stock offering in 1999. It has about 150 employees and a market capitalization of about $1.5 billion.

EARNINGS PER SHARE PROGRESSION   ★ ★

Losses have declined since 1997.

REVENUE GROWTH   ★ ★

Past year: 70 percent

STOCK GROWTH   ★ ★

BackWeb was first issued in 1999 and has shown solid gains since its IPO.

CONSISTENCY   ★ ★ ★

Positive earnings progression: 2 consecutive years
Increased revenue: 2 consecutive years

STABILITY/VULNERABILITY   ★ ★

This innovative young company is off to a strong start in a vital niche.

BACKWEB TECHNOLOGIES AT A GLANCE

Fiscal year ended: Dec. 31
Revenue in $ millions

	1995	1996	1997	1998	1999	1-Year Growth Avg. Annual (%)	Total (%)
Revenue ($)	—	—	5.6	9.5	15.4*	70	70
Earnings/share ($)	—	—	–6.95	–6.16	–1.59*	NA	NA
PE ratio range	—	—	NA	NA	NA		

*Figures in the 1999 column reflect first three quarters only. One-year growth refers to 1997–1998.

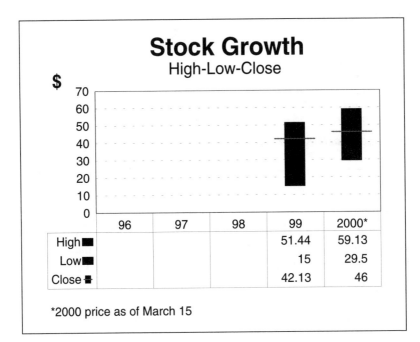

Stock Growth
High-Low-Close

	96	97	98	99	2000*
High ■				51.44	59.13
Low ■				15	29.5
Close ■				42.13	46

*2000 price as of March 15

INTERNET BUSINESS
SERVICES

55

The InterCept Group, Inc.

3150 Holcombe Bridge Road, Suite 200
Norcross, GA 30071
770-248-9600
Nasdaq: ICPT
www.intercept.net

Chairman and CEO: John W. Collins
President: Donny R. Jackson

Earnings Progression	★ ★
Revenue Growth	★ ★
Stock Growth	★ ★
Consistency	★ ★ ★
Stability/Vulnerability	★ ★
Total Points	**11 points**

InterCept Group offers small community banks access to the same type of electronic transaction services the big institutions use. The company provides electronic funds transfer services, data communication management, check imaging, Internet banking, and other processing services for about 700 community banks and savings institutions.

The Georgia-based operation is the largest third-party processor of automatic teller machine transactions in the southeastern United States. InterCept offers a wide range of services for savings institutions, including:

- **Electronic funds transfer.** The firm offers automatic funds transfer services for banks, including transactions for money machines, point of sale, debit card and scrip debit transactions, funds transfers, and remote banking transactions.

- **BancAccess Internet banking.** InterCept helps community banks establish an Internet presence, offering electronic banking functions that help small banks set up online banking services for their customers.
- **Data communications management.** Through its InterCept Network, the company is able to eliminate certain long distance charges for its customers.
- **Client/server enterprise software and services.** InterCept offers ledger and financial management, loan and deposit processing, financial accounting, and related services.

The InterCept Group went public with its initial stock offering in 1998. The company has about 230 employees and a market capitalization of about $250 million.

EARNINGS PER SHARE PROGRESSION ★ ★

Earnings growth past year: 230 percent

REVENUE GROWTH ★ ★

Past 2 years: 103 percent (43 percent per year)

STOCK GROWTH ★ ★

Past year: 309 percent
Dollar growth: $10,000 over 1 year would have grown to $40,900.

CONSISTENCY ★ ★ ★

Positive earnings progression 2 consecutive years
Increased revenue: 2 consecutive years

STABILITY/VULNERABILITY ★ ★

Small and growing, The InterCept Group has carved out a nice niche in a profitable sector.

THE INTERCEPT GROUP AT A GLANCE

Fiscal year ended: Dec. 31
Revenue in $ millions

	1995	1996	1997	1998	1999	2-Year Growth	
						Avg. Annual (%)	Total (%)
Revenue ($)	—	—	23.3	28.9	47.2	43	103
Earnings/share ($)	—	—	–0.06	0.30	0.96	230	NA
PE ratio range	—	—	NA	15-30	20-60		

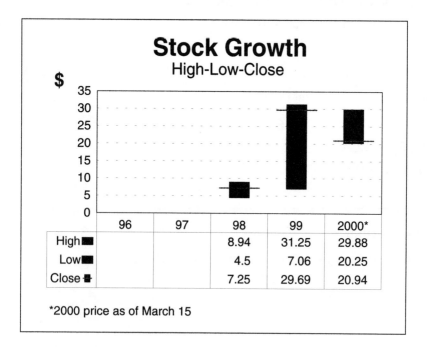

	96	97	98	99	2000*
High■			8.94	31.25	29.88
Low■			4.5	7.06	20.25
Close■			7.25	29.69	20.94

*2000 price as of March 15

56

TeleTech Holdings, Inc.

INTERNET BUSINESS
SERVICES

1700 Lincoln Street, Suite 1400
Denver, CO 80203
303-894-4000
Nasdaq: TTEC
www.teletech.com

Chairman: Kenneth D. Tuchman
President and CEO: Scott Thompson

Earnings Progression	★ ★
Revenue Growth	★ ★ ★ ★
Stock Growth	
Consistency	★ ★ ★
Stability/ Vulnerability	★ ★
Total Points	**11 points**

As the World Wide Web becomes increasingly interactive, the need also grows for customer services people to facilitate the interactive exchange of information. TeleTech hires thousands of customer service people to answer Internet e-mails on product information, technical problems, and other inquiries for its client companies.

Founded in 1982, the Denver-based operation has traditionally been involved in answering toll-free phone calls from customers of its client companies. But in the past three years, TeleTech also has ramped up its Internet customer service operation. For many of its newer customers, the company handles inquiries both from phone calls and e-mail.

TeleTech's client list includes Ford, the U.S. Postal Service, GTE Communications, American Express Membership Banking, Blockbuster.com, and Priceline Perfect YardSale, among others. The firm recently reached an agreement with Allstate Insurance to handle customer inquiries 24 hours a day through both toll-free calls and e-mails. That was a major adjustment for Allstate, where the only direct channel to customers had been through its agents.

TeleTech offers a variety of specialties, including presales product or service education, processing and fulfilling information requests for products or services, verifying sales and activating services, directing callers to product or service sources, receiving orders for and processing purchases of products or services, and providing initial post-sales support, including operating instructions for new products.

The company has operations around the world, with offices in New Zealand, Australia, Argentina, Mexico, England, Brazil, Singapore, and Canada.

The company has more than 16,000 customer services representatives. Its target market includes organizations involved in telecommunications, financial services, technology, government, and transportation industries.

TeleTech went public with its initial stock offering in 1996. It has a market capitalization of about $3 million.

EARNINGS PER SHARE PROGRESSION ★ ★
Past 4 years: 475 percent (54 percent per year)

REVENUE GROWTH ★ ★ ★ ★
Past 4 years: 908 percent (78 percent per year)

STOCK GROWTH
Past 3 years: 29 percent (9 percent per year)
Dollar growth: $10,000 over 3 years would have grown to $12,900.

CONSISTENCY ★ ★ ★
Increased earnings per share: 1 year
Increased revenue: 4 consecutive years

STABILITY/VULNERABILITY ★ ★
The company still does more business off the Internet than on, but its Internet-related revenue is growing rapidly—and it is a leader in this specialized niche.

TELETECH HOLDINGS AT A GLANCE

Fiscal year ended: Dec. 31
Revenue in $ millions

	1995	1996	1997	1998	1999	4-Year Growth Avg. Annual (%)	Total (%)
Revenue ($)	50.5	165.5	279.1	369	509.3	78	908
Earnings/share ($)	0.08	0.24	0.35	0.31	0.46	54	475
PE ratio range	NA	65-170	29-99	20-59	12-76		

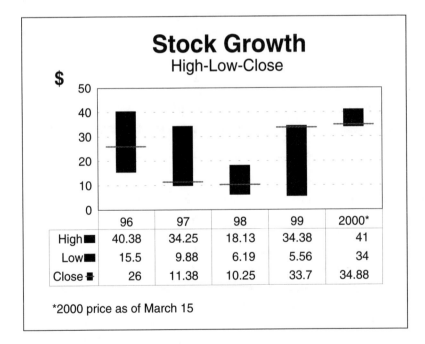

Stock Growth
High-Low-Close

	96	97	98	99	2000*
High■	40.38	34.25	18.13	34.38	41
Low■	15.5	9.88	6.19	5.56	34
Close ■	26	11.38	10.25	33.7	34.88

*2000 price as of March 15

SOFTWARE

Sagent Technology, Inc.

800 W. El Camino Real, Suite 300
Mountain View, CA 94040
650-815-3100
Nasdaq: SGNT
www.sagent.com

President and CEO: Kenneth C. Gardner

Earnings Progression	★
Revenue Growth	★ ★ ★ ★
Stock Growth	★ ★
Consistency	★ ★ ★
Stability/Vulnerability	★
Total Points	**11 points**

With Sagent Technology software, companies can gather and analyze volumes of information on customers and prospects that will help them keep those customers and attract new prospects.

Sagent's leading product is the Data Mart Solution (DMS), a suite of software products capable of gathering data from a variety of sources, including relational databases, mainframe databases, and the Internet. The software organizes data into a common structure known as the "data mart" that is used to focus on the needs of a specific group of users. Companies can analyze the data and provide access to it through personal computers, reports, and the Internet.

For instance, when CellStar Corp. wanted to find a way to help its sales force and key customers work more effectively with customers, it used Sagent's DMS software to gather customer information, monitor the sales process, perform customer rankings, and identify high margin products. It also used DMS software to post the information in a database that was accessible to its sales force and key customers around the world.

In all, Sagent has more than 1,000 customers across a wide range of industries. Among its leading corporate customers are Barnesandnoble .com, Bell South Cellular, J.P. Morgan, Jiffy Lube, and MCI WorldCom. The company markets its products worldwide.

The Mountain View, California operation claims that, in addition to helping businesses analyze the needs and patterns of their customers, its software also can help control costs, improve quality, and shorten cycle times.

The key competitive advantages of the company's DMS software is that it combines several functions in a single product and is able to handle a very large number of users and a large amount of data.

Founded in 1995, Sagent Technology went public with its initial stock offering in 1999. Sagent has about 150 employees and a market capitalization of about $600 million.

EARNINGS PER SHARE PROGRESSION   ★
The company's losses declined in 1999.

REVENUE GROWTH   ★ ★ ★ ★
Past 3 years: 16,692 percent (453 percent per year)

STOCK GROWTH   ★ ★
Sagent had impressive growth after its 1999 IPO.

CONSISTENCY   ★ ★ ★
Positive earnings progression: 1 year
Increased sales: 3 consecutive years

STABILITY/VULNERABILITY   ★
Like all young software companies, Sagent Technology is vulnerable to heavy competition from established software firms and other upstart operations.

SAGENT TECHNOLOGY AT A GLANCE

Fiscal year ended: Dec. 31
Revenue in $ millions

	1995	1996	1997	1998	1999	3-Year Growth Avg. Annual (%)	Total (%)
Revenue ($)	—	.240	7.08	17	40.3	453	16,692
Earnings/share ($)	—	–2.67	–2.41	–3.52	–0.45	NA	NA
PE ratio range	—	NA	NA	NA	NA		

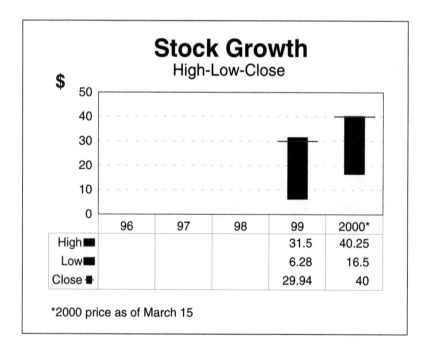

Stock Growth
High-Low-Close

$	96	97	98	99	2000*
High■				31.5	40.25
Low■				6.28	16.5
Close■				29.94	40

*2000 price as of March 15

Terayon Communications Systems

INFRASTRUCTURE

2952 Bunker Hill Lane
Santa Clara, CA 95054
408-727-4400
Nasdaq: TERN
www.terayon.com

Chairman and President: Shlomo Rakib
CEO: Zaki Rakib

Earnings Progression	★
Revenue Growth	★ ★ ★
Stock Growth	★ ★
Consistency	★ ★
Stability/Vulnerability	★ ★
Total Points	**10 points**

A battle for the "last mile" separating your home from the Internet is raging between the local phone company and your cable TV operator. The cable guy wants you to bypass the phone system on your way to the Web, and Terayon is arming him for the battle.

Terayon makes equipment that carries Internet traffic over cable TV networks. Installing it turns your local cable company into an Internet service provider (ISP). The company's product lineup includes:

- **Cable modems.** These are boxes that sit atop your television set or next to your home PC and handle data at rates up to about 25 times faster than the typical 56K phone modem.

- **Headend equipment.** Terayon's CherryPicker system sits in the cable company office and "grooms" feeds from the Internet, local broadcast TV, and satellites. It also can be used to insert local advertising programs and offer other services.
- **Network management systems.** The company's TeraView Element Management software lets operators centrally configure and monitor their networks.

Adding Internet traffic to cable TV networks is no small task, however, because Web traffic is two-way and comes in unpredictable bursts.

Terayon has come up with one of the best technologies for the problem, which has helped it land such big customers as Cablevision Systems and Japan's leading cable company, Jupiter Communications.

The Silicon Valley operation went public with its initial stock offering in 1999. Terayon Communications has about 150 employees and a market capitalization of about $3 billion.

EARNINGS PER SHARE PROGRESSION   ★

Losses decreased from 1998 to 1999.

REVENUE GROWTH   ★ ★ ★

Past 2 years: 4,497 percent (578 percent per year)

STOCK GROWTH   ★ ★

Past year: 70 percent
Dollar growth: $10,000 invested over 1 year would have grown to $17,000.

CONSISTENCY   ★ ★

Positive earnings progression: 1 year
Increased sales: 2 consecutive years

STABILITY/VULNERABILITY   ★ ★

Competitors like Sony, Motorola, and Samsung are formidable, but excellent technology makes this upstart company a success.

TERAYON COMMUNICATIONS AT A GLANCE

Fiscal year ended: Dec. 31
Revenue in $ millions

	1995	1996	1997	1998	1999	2-Year Growth Avg. Annual (%)	2-Year Growth Total (%)
Revenue ($)	—	—	2.11	31.7	97.0	578	4,497
Earnings/share ($)	—	—	–5.27	–8.53	–3.04	NA	NA
PE ratio range	—	—	NA	NA	NA		

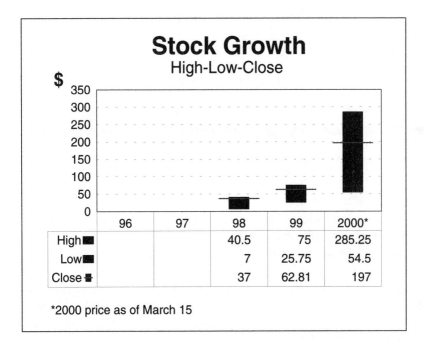

Stock Growth
High-Low-Close

$	96	97	98	99	2000*
High			40.5	75	285.25
Low			7	25.75	54.5
Close			37	62.81	197

*2000 price as of March 15

59

Juniper Networks, Inc.

385 Ravendale Drive
Mountain View, CA 94043
650-526-8000
Nasdaq: JNPR
www.junipernetworks.com

Chairman, President, and CEO: Scott Kriens

Earnings Progression	★
Revenue Growth	★ ★ ★
Stock Growth	★ ★
Consistency	★ ★
Stability/Vulnerability	★ ★
Total Points	**10 points**

If you decided to take on Cisco Systems in the router business—a market it thoroughly dominates—what would your plan be? Juniper Networks has an answer: hire the top engineers in the industry and encourage them to create innovative new products that customers can't resist.

The Mountain View, California operation has only been in business since 1995, but it has already made major inroads into the Internet technology arena. Juniper specializes in high-speed routers that direct traffic over Internet backbone links. It focuses on products used by Internet service providers (ISPs).

Juniper's products have earned a reputation as the best backbone routers in the business, no small feat going up against a company like Cisco. Its leading products include:

- **M40 Internet backbone router.** Perhaps the fastest backbone router in existence, the M40 combines raw hardware performance with software-enabled routing intelligence, enabling ISPs to not only move data packets faster, but to engineer how traffic is handled.

- **M20 Internet backbone router.** This router is designed for use by ISPs at major network entry points to efficiently gather incoming traffic and distribute it into Internet backbone links.
- **Physical interface cards.** Juniper makes optional boards that plug into its routers to let them work with different networking protocols or to provide specialized network services.

All of the company's products work with its flagship JUNOS operating system, which has been the key to Juniper's early success. Juniper's customer base includes some of the leading names in the communications industry, including MCI WorldCom, Williams Communications, PSINet, Ericsson, Qwest, and Verio.

Juniper Networks went public with its initial stock offering in 1999. It has about 200 employees and a market capitalization of about $23 billion.

EARNINGS PER SHARE PROGRESSION ★
Losses declined from 1998 to 1999.

REVENUE GROWTH ★ ★ ★
Past year: 2,593 percent

STOCK GROWTH ★ ★
Juniper went public in 1999 and had very strong growth following the IPO.

CONSISTENCY ★ ★
Positive earnings progression: 1 year
Increased sales: 1 year

STABILITY/VULNERABILITY ★ ★
Tiny Juniper Networks must be substantially better to win orders against Cisco Systems, Lucent, and Nortel Networks, but the company's technology prowess is a great asset on which to build.

JUNIPER NETWORKS AT A GLANCE

Fiscal year ended: Dec. 31
Revenue in $ millions

	1995	1996	1997	1998	1999	1-Year Growth Avg. Annual (%)	Total (%)
Revenue ($)	—	—	—	3.81	102.6	2,593	2,593
Earnings/share ($)	—	—	—	–0.73	–0.22	NA	NA
PE ratio range	—	—	—	NA	NA		

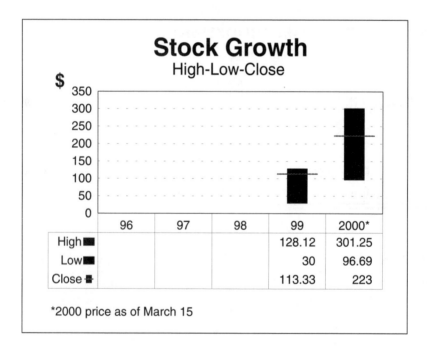

Stock Growth
High-Low-Close

$	96	97	98	99	2000*
High■				128.12	301.25
Low■				30	96.69
Close ■				113.33	223

*2000 price as of March 15

INFRASTRUCTURE

60

Extreme Networks, Inc.

3585 Monroe Street
Santa Clara, CA 95051
408-579-2800
Nasdaq: EXTR
www.extremenetworks.com

Chairman, President, and CEO: Gordon Stitt

Earnings Progression	★ ★
Revenue Growth	★ ★
Stock Growth	★ ★
Consistency	★ ★
Stability/Vulnerability	★ ★
Total Points	**10 points**

The battle between data switches and routers resembles the conflict between jocks and nerds. Switches are dumber, but faster; routers are intelligent, but are more complicated and costly.

Chalk up another win for the jocks. Switches are winning the hardware battle for connecting local area networks (LANs) to Internet backbones, and Extreme Networks is a leader in this critical market niche.

The company manufactures Layer 3 switches, which combine some Internet protocol routing intelligence with the lightning-fast speed of switching. The combination delivers a lot more bandwidth in a simpler, less-expensive package.

Network managers are struggling to keep things moving as more users and bandwidth-hungry multimedia applications come online. They're converting to switches in droves to keep up with the increasing demand for bandwidth.

Extreme leads the industry with nearly 25 percent of the global market for Layer 3 switch devices. Its product line includes:

- **Summit access switches.** These switches connect personal computers, servers, and printers to LANs.
- **Summit LAN switches.** These connect LANs together at ten times the typical network speed, allowing companies to create "local" area networks across entire metropolitan areas.
- **BlackDiamond core switches.** These switches serve as the internal backbone that weaves together traffic from many LANs and act as a gateway to the Internet.
- **ExtremeWare.** This is networking software used by companies to configure and manage their internal networks.

Extreme Networks sells direct, but a big part of its sales are made to large manufacturers, such as 3Com and Compaq, who resell Extreme products under private labels. Customers include the likes of PSINet, British Telecom, and Excite@Home.

The company made its initial public stock offering in 1999. It has a market capitalization of about $4 billion.

EARNINGS PER SHARE PROGRESSION   ★ ★
Losses declined dramatically from 1998 to 1999.

REVENUE GROWTH   ★ ★
Past year: 315 percent

STOCK GROWTH   ★ ★
Extreme went public in 1999 and experienced strong gains after its IPO.

CONSISTENCY   ★ ★
Positive earnings progression: 1 year
Increased revenue: 1 year

STABILITY/VULNERABILITY   ★ ★
Extreme Networks has succeeded thus far dancing around the feet of network equipment giants Cisco and Nortel Networks, but it must stay on its toes to keep things going.

EXTREME NETWORKS AT A GLANCE

Fiscal year ended: June 30
Revenue in $ millions

	1995	1996	1997	1998	1999	1-Year Growth	
						Avg. Annual (%)	Total (%)
Revenue ($)	—	—	—	23.6	98	315	315
Earnings/share ($)	—	—	—	–0.44	–0.06	NA	NA
PE ratio range	—	—	—	NA	NA		

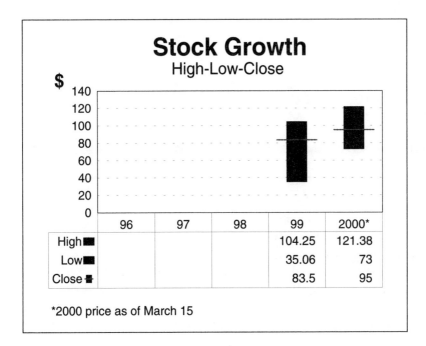

Stock Growth
High-Low-Close

$	96	97	98	99	2000*
High ■				104.25	121.38
Low ■				35.06	73
Close ■				83.5	95

*2000 price as of March 15

ISPs AND PORTALS

61
EarthLink Network, Inc.

3100 New York Drive
Pasadena, CA 91107
626-296-2400
Nasdaq: ELNK
www.earthlink.net

Chairman: Sky D. Dayton
President and CEO: C. Gary Betty

Earnings Progression	
Revenue Growth	★ ★ ★ ★
Stock Growth	★ ★
Consistency	★ ★
Stability/Vulnerability	★ ★
Total Points	**10 points**

Almost everybody knows that America Online (AOL) is the biggest Internet service provider (ISP), but few know who number two is. It's Earth-Link Network, a six-year-old company out of Pasadena, California.

EarthLink has earned a reputation as one of the best ISPs because of its infrequent busy signals, speedy network performance, and an uncluttered portal that puts nothing extraneous between its subscribers and the Web. EarthLink has consistently placed at or near the top of ISP user satisfaction rankings.

But the company's young management team understands that being hip isn't enough. EarthLink's relentless growth strategy has given its dial-up network a presence in virtually every local market in North America.

Mergers and acquisitions have given the company more than 3 million subscribers and a revenue stream approaching $700 million, surpassing such well-known names as Prodigy and Microsoft Network. That's small potatoes compared to AOL's subscriber base of about 20 million, but EarthLink has a plan:

- **Establish the brand.** The company has launched a massive marketing campaign to burn the EarthLink brand into mass consumer consciousness.
- **Play "Pepsi" to AOL's "Coca Cola."** Position the company as the preferred alternative to millions of "sophomore" America Online customers who EarthLink's management team feels are becoming disaffected with AOL's service.
- **Focus on small business.** EarthLink is second only to Verio in hosting business Web sites and plans to woo more with a suite of new services.

EarthLink made its initial public stock offering in 1997. It has about 1,400 employees and has a market capitalization of about $1 billion.

EARNINGS PER SHARE PROGRESSION
EarthLink has had increasing losses much of the past 4years.

REVENUE GROWTH ★ ★ ★ ★
Past 4 years: 14,397 percent (247 percent per year)

STOCK GROWTH ★ ★
Past 2 years: 230 percent (82 percent per year)
Dollar growth: $10,000 over 2 years would have grown to $33,000.

CONSISTENCY ★ ★
Positive earnings progression: None
Increased revenue: 4 consecutive years

STABILITY/VULNERABILITY ★ ★
Cutthroat competition abounds on all fronts—AOL, MCI WorldCom, and cable TV companies included—but EarthLink's network, big customer base, and emerging brand help.

EARTHLINK NETWORK AT A GLANCE

Fiscal year ended: Dec. 31
Revenue in $ millions

	1995	1996	1997	1998	1999	4-Year Growth Avg. Annual (%)	Total (%)
Revenue ($)	3	32.5	80.9	175.9	434.9	247	14,397
Earnings/share ($)	−0.49	−2.57	−1.50	−2.48	−3.32	NA	NA
PE ratio range	—	NA	NA	NA	NA		

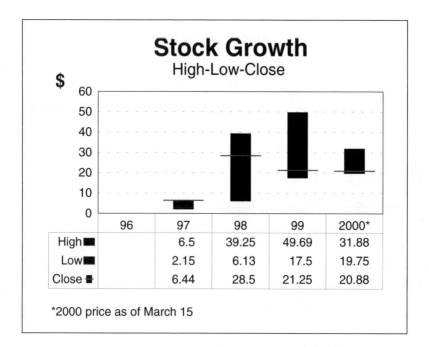

Stock Growth
High-Low-Close

$	96	97	98	99	2000*
High ■		6.5	39.25	49.69	31.88
Low ■		2.15	6.13	17.5	19.75
Close ■		6.44	28.5	21.25	20.88

*2000 price as of March 15

62

Liberate Technologies

2 Circle Star Way
San Carlos, CA 94070
650-701-4000
Nasdaq: LBRT
www.liberate.com

Chairman: David J. Roux
President and CEO: Mitchell E. Kertzman

Earnings Progression	★
Revenue Growth	★ ★ ★
Stock Growth	★ ★
Consistency	★ ★
Stability/Vulnerability	★ ★
Total Points	**10 points**

Liberate Technologies helps liberate Internet users from their computers. The company makes software designed to deliver Internet content to other information appliances, such as television set-top boxes, game consoles, smart phones, and handheld digital devices.

The San Carlos, California operation sells its products to telecommunications companies, cable and satellite television operators, Internet service providers, and information appliance manufacturers to incorporate in their systems. In all, Liberate has licensed its software to more than 30 operations, including America Online, Cable & Wireless, U.S. West, Fujitsu, General Instrument, Cox Communications, Nintendo, Sega, Sony, NEC, and Philips. The firm also has strategic alliances with leading technology companies, such as Cisco Systems, Inktomi, Lucent Technologies, and Sun Microsystems.

U.S. West is in the test phase of a program that uses Liberate software to enable consumers to watch television programs, surf the Web, make phone calls, and access caller identification functionality through a television set-top box equipped with a speaker phone.

Liberate's software is highly versatile, enabling network operators to send Internet data over many kinds of networks, including high-speed cable television and telecommunications networks, wireless networks, and standard phone lines. Its proprietary technology makes it possible to view Internet content on virtually any display device.

Liberate began operations in 1995 as a division of Oracle, which still holds about a 48 percent share of the company. Liberate began shipping its first products in 1997. Liberate President Mitchell E. Kertzman came to the company from Sybase, where he served as chairman, CEO, and president.

Liberate Technologies went public with its initial stock offering in 1999. The company has about 250 employees and a market capitalization of about $7 billion.

EARNINGS PER SHARE PROGRESSION ★
Losses declined from 1998 to 1999.

REVENUE GROWTH ★ ★ ★
Past 2 years: 6,191 percent (692 percent per year)

STOCK GROWTH ★ ★
Liberate went public in 1999 and experienced very strong gains after the IPO.

CONSISTENCY ★ ★
Positive earnings progression: 1 year
Increased revenue: 2 consecutive years

STABILITY/VULNERABILITY ★ ★
Liberate Technologies is a small, young company in an exploding sector. Its 48 percent ownership by Oracle gives it some stability, and its experienced management should help Liberate stand up to the competition.

LIBERATE TECHNOLOGIES AT A GLANCE

Fiscal year ended: May 31
Revenue in $ millions

	1995	1996	1997	1998	1999	2-Year Growth Avg. Annual (%)	Total (%)
Revenue ($)	—	—	.275	10.3	17.3	692	6,191
Earnings/share ($)	—	—	—	−1.67	−0.59	NA	NA
PE ratio range	—	—	—	NA	NA		

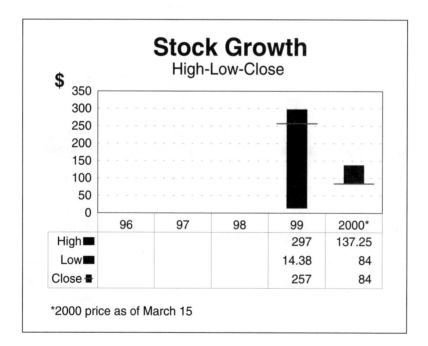

Stock Growth
High-Low-Close

$	96	97	98	99	2000*
High ■				297	137.25
Low ■				14.38	84
Close ■				257	84

*2000 price as of March 15

SOFTWARE

63

Phone.com, Inc.

800 Chesapeake Drive
Redwood City, CA 94063
650-562-0200
Nasdaq: PHCM
www.phone.com

Chairman and CEO: Alain Rossmann
President: Charles Parrish

Earnings Progression	
Revenue Growth	★ ★ ★
Stock Growth	★ ★ ★
Consistency	★ ★
Stability/Vulnerability	★ ★
Total Points	**10 points**

Who says you have to be at your PC or TV to hook up to the Internet? Not Phone.com, which is working hard to put the World Wide Web in your pocket.

One day soon nearly all cell phones will serve as terminals for e-mail, stock quotes, trading, and other Internet applications. But most cell phone infrastructures were designed only for voice and must be retrofitted to handle Internet traffic.

Phone.com is the leading provider of Internet-over-cellular technology. The company's product line includes these software development tools and data delivery platforms:

- **UP.Link Server Suite,** a soup-to-nuts collection of tools used to connect cell networks to the Internet
- **UP.Browser,** a Web browser and messaging system for cell phones

- **UP.SDK,** a software development kit used to make Internet content and other software applications cell phone compatible

The Redwood City, California operation markets to cell network operators, software companies, Internet content providers, and cell phone manufacturers.

The company has taken a lead role in its technology area. It helped establish a technical standards body called the Wireless Application Forum (WAP) with industry powerhouses Nokia, Motorola, and Ericsson. Significantly, much of the original WAP specification is based on Phone.com technology—giving the company an advantage.

Founded in 1994, Phone.com has a market capitalization of about $10 billion and a management team with a strong background in this niche. The company has about 250 employees.

EARNINGS PER SHARE PROGRESSION

Losses have increased in each of the past 4 years.

REVENUE GROWTH   ★ ★ ★

Past 2 years: 4,489 percent (580 percent per year)

STOCK GROWTH   ★ ★ ★

Phone.com went public in 1999 and experienced extremely strong gains after its IPO.

CONSISTENCY   ★ ★

Positive earnings progression: None
Increased revenue: 2 consecutive years

STABILITY/VULNERABILITY   ★ ★

Microsoft has announced the intention to compete with Phone.com head on, but many agile niche players have flourished in the same situation.

PHONE.COM AT A GLANCE

Fiscal year ended: June 30
Revenue in $ millions

	1995	1996	1997	1998	1999	2-Year Growth Avg. Annual (%)	2-Year Growth Total (%)
Revenue ($)	—	—	.292	2.205	13.4	580	4,489
Earnings/share ($)	−0.02	−0.53	−1.67	−2.03	−3.11	NA	NA
PE ratio range	NA	NA	NA	NA	NA		

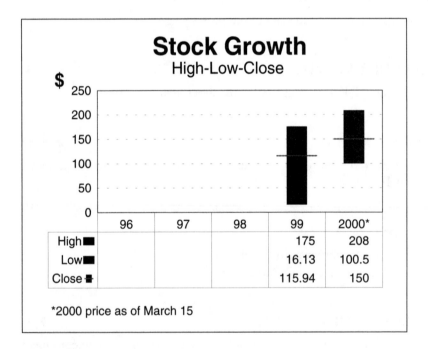

Stock Growth
High-Low-Close

	96	97	98	99	2000*
High				175	208
Low				16.13	100.5
Close				115.94	150

*2000 price as of March 15

E-COMMERCE

64

RoweCom, Inc.

725 Concord Avenue
Cambridge, MA 02138
617-497-5800
Nasdaq: ROWE
www.rowe.com

Chairman, President, and CEO: Richard Rowe

Earnings Progression	★
Revenue Growth	★ ★ ★ ★
Stock Growth	★
Consistency	★ ★ ★
Stability/Vulnerability	★
Total Points	**10 points**

It's no Amazon, but RoweCom ships a lot of literature. The company sells magazine subscriptions, newspapers, journals, and books to corporate customers through its e-commerce Web sites.

The Cambridge, Massachusetts operation is the leading business-to-business Internet supplier of periodicals, books, and other printed sources of commercial, scientific, and general information—referred to by the company as "knowledge resources." The firm offers corporate clients and their employees convenient access to one of the largest catalogs of knowledge resources on the Internet.

RoweCom targets companies and organizations in such knowledge-intensive industries as financial and professional services, technology, health care, and academic and nonprofit institutions. Among its more than 20,000 clients are PricewaterhouseCoopers, Arthur Andersen, Charles Schwab, Prudential, Hewlett-Packard, Johns Hopkins, and Dun & Bradstreet.

The company's flagship services, Knowledge Store (kStore) and Knowledge Library (kLibrary), offer 240,000 subscription titles, 4,000 market research reports online, and millions of discounted books. The kStore and kLibrary systems are designed to cut costs and facilitate decentralized purchasing of knowledge resources by businesses and their employees, while giving management the tools to monitor and control purchases. Managers can set guidelines for purchases and then receive detailed reports of all sales to their employees.

The company has operations throughout North America and Europe.

Founded in 1994, RoweCom went public with its initial stock offering in 1999. It has about 100 employees and a market capitalization of about $400 million.

EARNINGS PER SHARE PROGRESSION ★

Losses declined from 1998 to 1999.

REVENUE GROWTH ★ ★ ★ ★

Past 4 years: 94,838 percent (455 percent per year)

STOCK GROWTH ★

RoweCom went public in 1999 and had an up-and-down performance after its IPO.

CONSISTENCY ★ ★ ★

Positive earnings progression: 1 year
Increased sales: 4 consecutive years

STABILITY/VULNERABILITY ★

Although its revenue is growing impressively, RoweCom is a long way from profitability. However, it is the leader in its market segment.

ROWECOM AT A GLANCE

Fiscal year ended: Dec. 31
Revenue in $ millions

	1995	1996	1997	1998	1999	4-Year Growth Avg. Annual (%)	Total (%)
Revenue ($)	.324	3.116	12.89	19.05	307.6	455	94,838
Earnings/share ($)	—	—	−0.79	−1.87	−1.60	NA	NA
PE ratio range	NA	NA	NA	NA	NA		

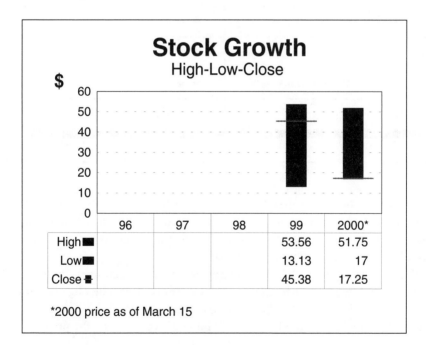

Stock Growth
High-Low-Close

	96	97	98	99	2000*
High				53.56	51.75
Low				13.13	17
Close				45.38	17.25

*2000 price as of March 15

INFRASTRUCTURE

65

Foundry Networks, Inc.

680 W. Maude Avenue, Suite 3
Sunnyvale, CA 94086
408-530-3300
Nasdaq: FDRY
www.foundrynet.com

Chairman, President, and CEO: Bobby Johnson, Jr.

Earnings Progression	★ ★
Revenue Growth	★ ★
Stock Growth	★ ★
Consistency	★ ★
Stability/Vulnerability	★ ★
Total Points	**10 points**

Computer hardware is called "iron" because physical equipment will always be needed to process data. Foundry Networks apparently had that in mind when it chose its name, because the company is going after the network hardware business with a vengeance.

The Sunnyvale, California operation makes specialized routers, switches, and Internet traffic management systems. Its product line is centered around the Gigabit Ethernet local area network (LAN) protocol, which is competing with other LAN technologies to become the predominant standard running beneath the Internet protocol.

Focusing on a single standard allows Foundry to offer high-performance products at a competitive price. In fact, Foundry's business model bears a strong resemblance to that used by Sun Microsystems. Sun made its mark pushing hot computers running the then-new Unix operating system at a low price and rode the Unix craze to the top. Foundry hopes to do the same with its high-speed Gigabit Ethernet network equipment. Its product lineup includes:

- **FastIron switches.** These switches are used to connect large numbers of users from slower Ethernet LANs into higher speed LANs and Internet backbones running Gigabit Ethernet.
- **BigIron switching routers.** These are used in big data centers to manage local traffic, such as within a corporate campus.
- **NetIron core routers.** These are used by ISPs to connect to major Internet backbone links.

Foundry products are installed in the world's largest ISPs, including America Online, EarthLink, AT&T WorldNet, MSN, and Cable & Wireless. Foundry products also are used by mid-sized and large companies across a broad range of industries, as well as portals, e-commerce sites, universities, and government organizations.

Foundry went public with its initial stock offering in 1999. It has about 150 employees and a market capitalization of about $15 billion.

EARNINGS PER SHARE PROGRESSION ★★
Foundry went from a loss to a gain from 1998 to 1999.

REVENUE GROWTH ★★
Past year: 683 percent

STOCK GROWTH ★★
Foundry went public in 1999 and had very strong gains after the IPO.

CONSISTENCY ★★
Positive earnings progression: 1 year
Increased revenue: 1 year

STABILITY/VULNERABILITY ★★
Foundry's Gigabit Ethernet bet has paid off so far, and the company understands the importance of price/performance leadership.

FOUNDRY NETWORKS AT A GLANCE

Fiscal year ended: Dec. 31
Revenue in $ millions

	1995	1996	1997	1998	1999	1-Year Growth Avg. Annual (%)	Total (%)
Revenue ($)	—	—	—	17.04	133.5	683	683
Earnings/share ($)	—	—	—	−0.36	0.19	NA	NA
PE ratio range	—	—	—	—	284-867		

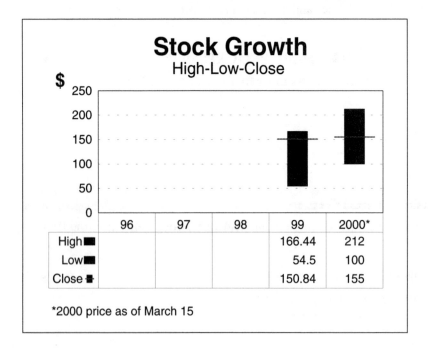

Stock Growth
High-Low-Close

	96	97	98	99	2000*
High ■				166.44	212
Low ■				54.5	100
Close ■				150.84	155

*2000 price as of March 15

66
Global Crossing Ltd.

45 Reid Street, Wessex House
Hamilton, HM 12
Bermuda
441-296-8600
Nasdaq: GBLX
www.globalcrossing.com

Chairman: Gary Winnick
CEO: Robert Annunziata
President: David L. Lee

Earnings Progression	★
Revenue Growth	★ ★
Stock Growth	★ ★
Consistency	★ ★
Stability/Vulnerability	★ ★
Total Points	**9 points**

Internet traffic must travel either via satellite or submarine cable to move between continents. Global Crossing is betting on the latter because, even underwater, fiber-optic cables are faster, more reliable, and less expensive.

The company is building the world's first global fiber-optic data/voice network running the Internet protocol. Its first link, between the United States and the United Kingdom, went into service in 1998. Links connecting Europe, the Far East, Latin America, and Africa are to be completed by the end of 2000.

International data traffic is growing over 100 percent a year, and such new bandwidth-hungry applications as video conferencing and Internet telephone service should increase demand for transoceanic links.

The company's offerings include:

- **Global Crossing network services.** Covering five continents and more than 200 major cities, the network directly reaches over 80 percent of all Internet traffic.
- **Global Center hosting services.** Global hosts Web sites for about 300 companies with big international audiences. Clients include Yahoo!, MP3.com, eToys, Ziff Davis, and multinational corporations that run worldwide intranets.
- **Vertical industry services.** Global offers service packages tailored to the needs of such industries as wholesale distribution, retailing, manufacturing, and financial services.

Global Crossing went public with its initial stock offering in 1998. The company has about 150 employees and a market capitalization of about $42 billion.

EARNINGS PER SHARE PROGRESSION   ★

Losses declined from 1998 to 1999.

REVENUE GROWTH   ★ ★

Past year: 294 percent

STOCK GROWTH   ★ ★

Past year: 122 percent
Dollar growth: $10,000 over 1 year would have grown to $22,100.

CONSISTENCY   ★ ★

Positive earnings progression: 1 year
Increased revenue: 1 year

STABILITY/VULNERABILITY   ★ ★

Global's undersea network and data centers are state-of-the-art, but the company must continue adding value with customer services.

GLOBAL CROSSING AT A GLANCE

Fiscal year ended: Dec. 31
Revenue in $ millions

	1995	1996	1997	1998	1999	Avg. Annual (%)	Total (%)
						1-Year Growth	
Revenue ($)	—	—	—	424.1	1,672	294	294
Earnings/share ($)	—	—	−0.04	−0.38	−0.27	NA	NA
PE ratio range	—	—	NA	NA	NA		

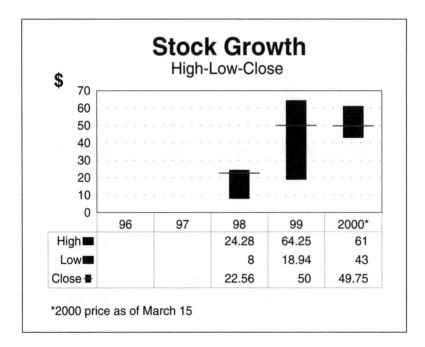

Stock Growth
High-Low-Close

	96	97	98	99	2000*
High			24.28	64.25	61
Low			8	18.94	43
Close			22.56	50	49.75

*2000 price as of March 15

67
Media Metrix, Inc.

250 Park Avenue South
New York, NY 10003
212-515-8700
Nasdaq: MMXI
www.mediametrix.com

Chairman and CEO: Tod Johnson
President: Mary Ann Packo

Earnings Progression	
Revenue Growth	★ ★ ★ ★
Stock Growth	★
Consistency	★ ★
Stability/Vulnerability	★ ★
Total Points	**9 points**

Traffic is everything in the Internet economy, which puts a premium on measuring and evaluating Web traffic. Audience measurement is important in any medium, and Media Metrix has emerged as the Internet ratings king.

The New York operation publishes a number of specialized reports, including *The Web Report,* which measures such things as unique visitors to a Web site and the demographic composition of visits. Its *Q-Metrix* report offers information linking Internet usage to other consumer patterns, such as products used, radio and TV habits, and lifestyle.

The company also offers about a dozen other products that report on such areas as traffic referral between sites, local market statistics, and the performance of ad networks such as DoubleClick.

Media Metrix compiles this information by continuously sampling a representative panel of about 50,000 Internet users. An important distinction is that hidden "spy programs" are not used. Rather, the company uses noninvasive techniques learned from measuring traditional media audiences.

Media Metrix syndicates its data to advertisers, ad agencies, Internet properties, and financial institutions. Its account roster includes many of the Web's biggest names, such as America Online, Amazon.com, IBM, Yahoo!, and Microsoft.

Two factors should help Media Metrix continue its strong growth. First is the growing importance of Internet market intelligence. Pressure is growing to make better use of precious advertising dollars, both on the Web and in traditional media. The second is the need for a common reference. Advertisers, agencies, and media properties need a standard currency in which to deal. Nielsen fills that role for TV; Arbitron is the standard for radio.

Media Metrix went public with its initial stock offering in 1999. The company has about 100 employees and a market capitalization of about $1 billion.

EARNINGS PER SHARE PROGRESSION
Losses have increased for the past 4 years.

REVENUE GROWTH   ★ ★ ★ ★
Past 3 years: 1,800 percent (171 percent per year)

STOCK GROWTH   ★
Media Metrix went public in 1999 and had modest gains since the IPO.

CONSISTENCY   ★ ★
Positive earnings progression: None
Increased revenue: 3 consecutive years

STABILITY/VULNERABILITY   ★ ★
Media Metrix has competition from Nielsen and others, but its head start and savvy management team should help it grow.

MEDIA METRIX AT A GLANCE

Fiscal year ended: Dec. 31
Revenue in $ millions

	1995	1996	1997	1998	1999	3-Year Growth Avg. Annual (%)	Total (%)
Revenue ($)	—	1.03	3.18	6.33	20.5	171	1,890
Earnings/share ($)	−0.03	−0.26	−0.38	−0.56	−1.25	NA	NA
PE ratio range	NA	NA	NA	NA	NA		

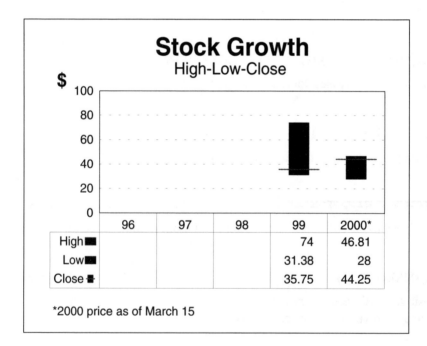

Stock Growth
High-Low-Close

	96	97	98	99	2000*
High ■				74	46.81
Low ■				31.38	28
Close ■				35.75	44.25

*2000 price as of March 15

SOFTWARE

68

SilverStream Software, Inc.

One Burlington Woods, Suite 200
Burlington, MA 01803
781-238-5400
Nasdaq: SSSW
www.silverstream.com

Chairman: David R. Skok
President and CEO: David A. Litwack

Earnings Progression	
Revenue Growth	★ ★ ★
Stock Growth	★ ★
Consistency	★ ★
Stability/Vulnerability	★ ★
Total Points	**9 points**

Companies need a lot more than just a pretty Web site to succeed in the e-commerce business. They also need to interact with customers. But Web browsers can't interpret information stored in most internal computer systems, so they rely on "application server" software to handle the movement of information and transactions between the two sides.

SilverStream Software is a leading maker of application server software. Founded in 1996, the company's software package welds traditional transaction processing with Web browser software.

The Burlington, Massachusetts operation's product line includes:

- **SilverStream Application Server.** This is the platform that connects Web browsers to internal computer systems. It handles database connections, business logic, and presentation of the Web page user interface.

- **SilverStream Designer.** This is a single graphical programming environment that works for programming a Web page, writing business logic, and connecting to internal databases.
- **Enterprise Data Connectors.** These "drivers" are used to connect the Web site to internal management software packages from SAP, PeopleSoft, and others.
- **Management Console.** This graphical command center is used to perform such Web site operations tasks as maintaining security and tuning performance.

Depending on how it's programmed, the SilverStream Application Server can handle such functions as content management, customer personalization, and automatically "pushing" new information out to customers.

SilverStream Software went public with its initial stock offering in 1999. The company has about 250 employees and a market capitalization of about $2 billion.

EARNINGS PER SHARE PROGRESSION
None

REVENUE GROWTH   ★ ★ ★
Past 2 years: 9,177 percent (870 percent per year)

STOCK GROWTH   ★ ★
SilverStream had outstanding growth after its 1999 IPO.

CONSISTENCY   ★ ★
Positive earnings progression: None
Increased sales: 2 consecutive years

STABILITY/VULNERABILITY   ★ ★
With at least two dozen other application server vendors, and more entering the market, SilverStream Software faces some stiff competition.

SILVERSTREAM SOFTWARE AT A GLANCE

Fiscal year ended: Dec. 31
Revenue in $ millions

	1995	1996	1997	1998	1999	2-Year Growth Avg. Annual (%)	Total (%)
Revenue ($)	—	—	0.249	6.81	23.1	870	9,177
Earnings/share ($)	—	—	−0.86	−1.33	−1.71	NA	NA
PE ratio range	—	—	NA	NA	NA		

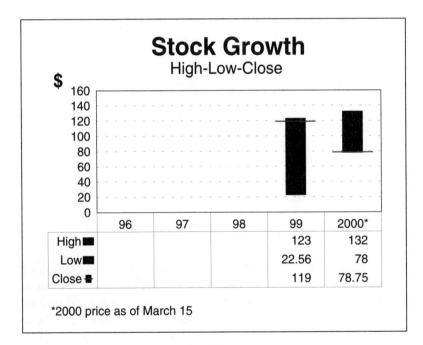

Stock Growth
High-Low-Close

$	96	97	98	99	2000*
High ■				123	132
Low ■				22.56	78
Close ■				119	78.75

*2000 price as of March 15

INTERNET BUSINESS
SERVICES

69

National Information Consortium, Inc.

12 Corporate Woods
10975 Benson Street, Suite 390
Overland Park, KS 66210
877-234-3468
Nasdaq: EGOV
www.nicusa.com

Chairman: Jeffrey S. Fraser
President and CEO: James B. Dodd

Earnings Progression	
Revenue Growth	★ ★ ★
Stock Growth	★ ★
Consistency	★ ★
Stability/Vulnerability	★ ★
Total Points	**9 points**

The National Information Consortium (NIC) is in the business of bringing big government to your home computer. The Kansas-based operation contracts with state and municipal government agencies to build and operate Internet portals and applications that allow businesses and citizens to access government information and to complete government-based transactions online.

For instance, NIC has set up Web sites for a number of states that enable such functions as driver's license record searches, professional license renewals, Internet tax filings, information requests, sales and use tax payments, and automobile registration renewals.

NIC has built and managed sites for a growing number of states, including Arkansas, Georgia, Indiana, Iowa, Kansas, Maine, Nebraska, Utah, and Virginia. It also has done projects for the City of Indianapolis and Marion County, Indiana.

The key elements of NIC's strategy include:

- A customer-focused, one-stop government portal that permits businesses and citizens to conduct transactions and process information 24 hours a day, seven days a week
- A cost-efficient financial model that minimizes the use of government resources
- Working relationships with governments to maximize their use of the Internet technology, while addressing such critical issues as privacy and security of citizens

Incorporated in 1998, NIC went public with its initial stock offering in 1999. It has about 100 employees and a market capitalization of about $2 billion.

EARNINGS PER SHARE PROGRESSION

Losses have increased the past 2 years.

REVENUE GROWTH ★ ★ ★

Past 2 years: 5,623 percent (658 percent per year)

STOCK GROWTH ★ ★

National Information Consortium went public in 1999 and had strong gains after the IPO.

CONSISTENCY ★ ★

Positive earnings progression: None
Increased revenue: 2 consecutive years

STABILITY/VULNERABILITY ★ ★

Good concept and plenty of room to grow, but NIC is still young.

NATIONAL INFORMATION CONSORTIUM AT A GLANCE

Fiscal year ended: Dec. 31
Revenue in $ millions

	1995	1996	1997	1998	1999	2-Year Growth Avg. Annual (%)	Total (%)
Revenue ($)	—	—	.996	28.6	57	658	5,623
Earnings/share ($)	—	—	−0.01	−0.21	−0.24	NA	NA
PE ratio range	—	—	NA	NA	NA		

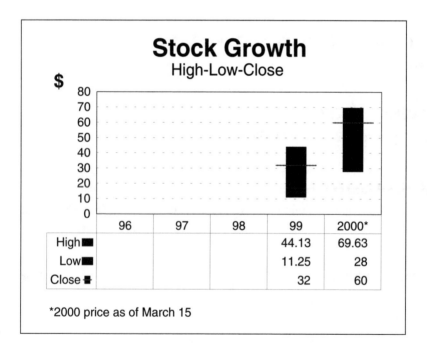

Stock Growth
High-Low-Close

$	96	97	98	99	2000*
High ■				44.13	69.63
Low ■				11.25	28
Close ▪				32	60

*2000 price as of March 15

Fatbrain.com, Inc.

E-TAILING

2550 Walsh Avenue
Santa Clara, CA 95051
408-845-0100
Nasdaq: FATB
www.fatbrain.com

Chairman, President, and CEO: Chris MacAskill

Earnings Progression	
Revenue Growth	★ ★ ★ ★
Stock Growth	★
Consistency	★ ★
Stability/Vulnerability	★ ★
Total Points	**9 points**

When you're ready to "fatten" your brain, think Fatbrain.com. The online retailer sells technical books, technology-based training courses, product manuals, research reports, and other information resources. In all, the company offers more than 300,000 information resource titles from more than 8,000 publishers, covering more than 800 technical and business categories. The Santa Clara, California e-tailer also operates two physical retail stores to complement its online sales.

Fatbrain.com promotes itself as much more than an online technical bookseller. Its online training and certification center offers a selection of more than 2,500 products, including CD courses, videos, Web-based training courseware, and printed materials.

The firm can customize its service for corporations to create intranet bookstores geared to employees of those corporations. More than 1.3 million employees of customer sites have access to their company's customized bookstore through their desktop computers. Customers can save up to 40 percent off the cover price of specialty books by ordering through Fatbrain.com.

The company also has developed a new concept in Internet publishing with its eMatter division. Through eMatter, authors, publishers, and corporations can publish and sell their works online, earning at least 50 percent royalties on every copy sold. It gives publishers a chance to sell work that might have been too short or too specialized to sell in book format. eMatter is the first secure digital publishing service on the Internet.

In all, Fatbrain.com claims a customer base of about 200,000 individuals and businesses.

Formerly known as Computer Literacy, Inc., Fatbrain.com was incorporated in 1994 and began selling books through its online store in 1996. One of the company's leading investors is Paul G. Allen, cofounder of Microsoft. The company, which went public with its initial stock offering in 1998, has about 150 employees and a market capitalization of about $300 million.

EARNINGS PER SHARE PROGRESSION
Losses have increased the past 4 years.

REVENUE GROWTH   ★ ★ ★ ★
Past 3 years: 19,511 percent (480 percent per year)

STOCK GROWTH   ★
Past year: 86 percent
Dollar growth: $10,000 over 1 year would have grown to $18,600.

CONSISTENCY   ★ ★
Positive earnings progression: None
Increased revenue: 3 consecutive years

STABILITY/VULNERABILITY   ★ ★
Like all online retailers, Fatbrain.com is vulnerable to competition, but it has established a specific niche and does have significant investment from Microsoft cofounder Paul Allen.

FATBRAIN.COM AT A GLANCE

Fiscal year ended: Jan. 31
Revenue in $ millions

	1995	1996	1997	1998	1999	3-Year Growth Avg. Annual (%)	Total (%)
Revenue ($)	—	0.18	10.9	19.8	35.3	480	19,511
Earnings/share ($)	−0.10	−0.38	−2.11	−2.87	−4.39	NA	NA
PE ratio range	NA	NA	NA	NA	NA		

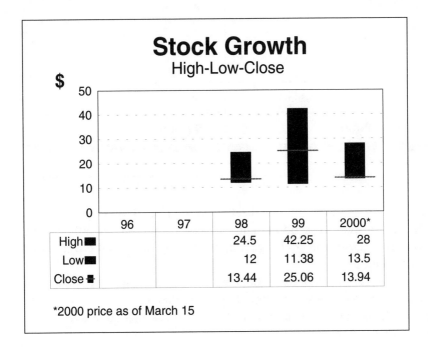

Stock Growth
High-Low-Close

	96	97	98	99	2000*
High			24.5	42.25	28
Low			12	11.38	13.5
Close			13.44	25.06	13.94

*2000 price as of March 15

E-TAILING

71

Barnesandnoble.com, Inc.

76 Ninth Avenue
New York, NY 10011
212-414-6000
Nasdaq: BNBN
www.barnesandnoble.com

Chairman: Leonard Riggio
CEO: Jonathon Bulkeley

Earnings Progression	★ ★
Revenue Growth	★ ★ ★
Stock Growth	
Consistency	★ ★
Stability/Vulnerability	★ ★
Total Points	**9 points**

Amazon.com isn't the only bookseller on the Net. Barnesandnoble.com (BN.com), a spin-off of Barnes and Noble, Inc., got into the online game well after Amazon.com, but it's beginning to make a run at the Web-based book behemoth.

Amazon.com still pulls in about ten times the revenue of BN.com, but BN.com already seems a lot closer to profitability. In a recent nine-month period, BN.com reported a loss of 9¢ per share compared to a $1.22 per share loss for Amazon.

Launched in 1997, BN.com became the fourth largest e-commerce site on the Web within its first two years of operation, according to Media Metrix. It sells more than eight million books, including the world's largest selection of new, out-of-print, and rare books. It has the largest standing inventory of any online bookseller. It has sold products to more than two million customers in more than 180 countries.

The site offers one-click ordering, extensive author chats, book synopses, and reader reviews. It has become the exclusive bookseller for America Online and AOL's 18 million subscribers. It also has affiliate agreements with more than 120,000 Web sites, and strategic alliances with Lycos and Microsoft Network.

Following Amazon's lead, BN.com also has been adding products other than books. In 1999, it added an online music store that offers a broad range of music, including 16 main categories and more than 1,000 subcategories (such as big band jazz, boogie woogie jazz, Brazilian jazz, etc.).

The New York–based retailer also added a prints and posters gallery and an electronic greeting card service in 1999. The e-mail greetings can be personalized and enhanced with animation and music.

BN.com went public with its initial stock offering in 1999. It has about 700 employees and a market capitalization of about $3 billion.

EARNINGS PER SHARE PROGRESSION ★ ★

Losses declined in 1999, with positive earnings projected for as early as 2001.

REVENUE GROWTH ★ ★ ★

Past 2 years: 1,602 percent (312 percent per year)

STOCK GROWTH

The stock dropped dramatically in the months following its 1999 IPO.

CONSISTENCY ★ ★

Declining losses per share: 1 year
Increased revenue: 2 consecutive years

STABILITY/VULNERABILITY ★ ★

Online retailing has not been particularly profitable for anyone, but BN.com is on stable footing and seems to be making major inroads into the consumer market.

BARNESANDNOBLE.COM AT A GLANCE

Fiscal year ended: Dec. 31
Revenue in $ billions

	1995	1996	1997	1998	1999	2-Year Growth Avg. Annual (%)	Total (%)
Revenue ($)	—	—	11.9	61.8	202.5	312	1,602
Earnings/share ($)	—	—	−0.09	−0.59	−0.36	NA	NA
PE ratio range	—	—	NA	NA	NA		

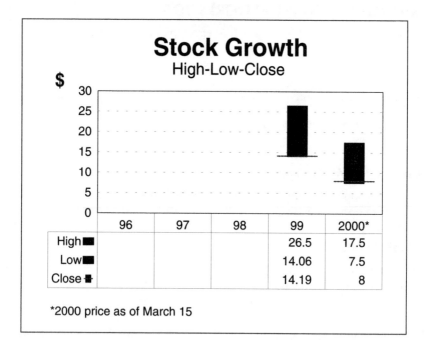

Stock Growth
High-Low-Close

$	96	97	98	99	2000*
High				26.5	17.5
Low				14.06	7.5
Close				14.19	8

*2000 price as of March 15

E-COMMERCE

72

Healtheon/WebMD

4600 Patrick Henry Drive
Santa Clara, CA 95054
408-876-5000
Nasdaq: HLTH
www.healtheon.com

Chairman: James H. Clark
President: W. Michael Long
CEO: Jack Dennison

Earnings Progression	
Revenue Growth	★ ★ ★ ★
Stock Growth	★
Consistency	★ ★
Stability/Vulnerability	★ ★
Total Points	**9 points**

Is the Internet good for your health? It can be, with a little help from Healtheon/WebMD. The company's Web site offers a vast library of information on health and fitness, including current news and information on health trends, a medical directory of herbs and drugs, an overview of conditions and diseases, a guide to finding a physician, and articles on life stages and nutrition.

Despite the volumes of consumer information available at its site, Healtheon/WebMD is primarily an e-commerce firm. It offers a comprehensive suite of transaction services to the various companies and organizations served by the U.S. health care industry. Its target market includes:

- **Health care providers.** The company helps physician groups, hospitals, and other caregivers determine patient eligibility, make referrals, and authorize treatments.

- **Payors.** HMOs, insurers, and third party administrators use Healtheon to check eligibility, order tests, and offer other services.
- **Medical suppliers.** Laboratories and pharmaceutical makers can exchange e-commerce transactions with care providers and payors through the Healtheon/WebMD system.
- **Health consumer entities**. Self-funded employers, smaller health plans, and plan brokers use Healtheon services to shop the provider market and to manage benefits.

Healtheon/WebMD was founded in 1996 by Netscape founder Jim Clark. The company's name comes from the 1999 merger of Health eon.com and WebMD.com—the two biggest health-related Web sites.

The Santa Clara, California operation went public with its initial stock offering in 1999. It has about 700 employees and a market capitalization of about $9 billion.

EARNINGS PER SHARE PROGRESSION
None

REVENUE GROWTH   ★ ★ ★ ★
Past 4 years: 4,541 percent (161 percent per year)

STOCK GROWTH   ★
Healtheon/WebMD went public in 1999 and experienced rocky price performance.

CONSISTENCY   ★ ★
Positive earnings progression: None
Increased revenues: 4 consecutive years

STABILITY/VULNERABILITY   ★ ★
Competitors such as ENVOY have deep pockets and strong ties to health care, but Healtheon's early start is considerable.

HEALTHEON/WEBMD AT A GLANCE

Fiscal year ended: Dec. 31
Revenue in $ millions

	1995	1996	1997	1998	1999	4-Year Growth Avg. Annual (%)	Total (%)
Revenue ($)	2.2	11	13.4	48.8	102.1	161	4,541
Earnings/share ($)	-0.85	-2.83	-3.88	-1.54	-3.58	NA	NA
PE ratio range	NA	NA	NA	NA	NA		

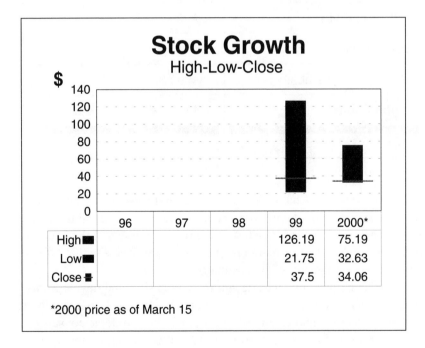

Stock Growth
High-Low-Close

$	96	97	98	99	2000*
High ■				126.19	75.19
Low ■				21.75	32.63
Close ■				37.5	34.06

*2000 price as of March 15

INTERNET BUSINESS
SERVICES

73
Razorfish, Inc.

107 Grand Street, 3rd Floor
New York, NY 10013
212-966-5960
Nasdaq: RAZF
www.razorfish.com

President and CEO: Jeffrey A. Dachis

Earnings Progression	
Revenue Growth	★ ★ ★
Stock Growth	★ ★
Consistency	★ ★
Stability/Vulnerability	★
Total Points	**8 points**

When discount broker Charles Schwab needed to redesign its trading floor Web site and online marketing presence, it turned to Razorfish to handle the job. When Intel wanted to demonstrate the capabilities of the Pentium III processor, it hired Razorfish to help set up a new Web site that offered an interactive relationship with consumers.

Razorfish helps companies design their Web sites and develops customized software to enable client companies to effectively operate their sites. The firm offers end-to-end solutions, including strategic consulting, design of information architectures and user interfaces, and technology services across platforms, devices, and networks.

The New York–based operation is international in scope, with offices in Amsterdam, Hamburg, Helsinki, London, Stockholm, and Oslo. Among its international customers are Siemens, Nokia, Nissan, Ericsson, and Finnair. In the United States, Razorfish has done projects for a variety of notable companies, including 3M, NBC, PBS, Fox Kids, Sallie Mae, Showtime Networks, Dell, and Compaq.

Currently, most of the company's projects are geared to traditional Web site development. But it has been incorporating advanced communications technologies, such as wireless, satellite, and broadband, for use with a variety of digital devices and information appliances, such as mobile phones and pagers.

The company has grown through internal expansion and an aggressive acquisition policy. It acquired five companies in 1998 and several more in 1999, including Electrokinetics, I-Cube, Lee Hunt, TSDesign, Fuel, Inc., and Tonga.

Although it competes in an increasingly crowded market, Razorfish should have little trouble adding new business. The Internet professional services market is expected to grow from $2.4 billion in 1997 to more than $33 billion by 2002, according to Forrester Research, Inc.

Founded in 1995, Razorfish went public with its initial stock offering in 1999. It has about 1,100 employees and a market capitalization of about $4 billion.

EARNINGS PER SHARE PROGRESSION
None

REVENUE GROWTH ★ ★ ★
Past 2 years: 2,640 percent (423 percent per year)

STOCK GROWTH ★ ★
Razorfish went public in 1999 and had strong growth after the IPO.

CONSISTENCY ★ ★
Positive earnings progression: None
Increased sales: 2 consecutive years

STABILITY/VULNERABILITY ★
Razorfish is a strong, young company, but it's in a highly competitive field.

RAZORFISH AT A GLANCE

Fiscal year ended: Dec. 31
Revenue in $ millions

	1995	1996	1997	1998	1999	2-Year Growth	
						Avg. Annual (%)	Total (%)
Revenue ($)	—	—	3.62	13.8	99.2	423	2,640
Earnings/share ($)	—	—	0.03	−0.01	−0.21	NA	NA
PE ratio range	—	—	NA	NA	NA		

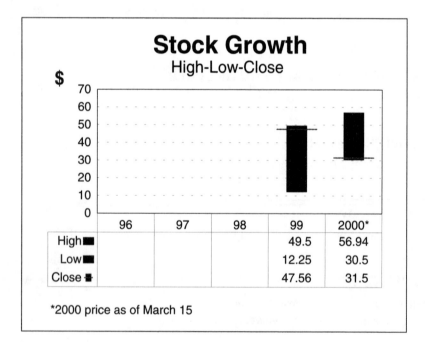

Stock Growth
High-Low-Close

$	96	97	98	99	2000*
High ■				49.5	56.94
Low ■				12.25	30.5
Close ■				47.56	31.5

*2000 price as of March 15

INTERNET HOLDING
COMPANIES

Internet Capital Group

435 Devon Park Drive, Building 800
Wayne, PA 19087
610-989-0111
Nasdaq: ICGE
www.icge.com

Chairman: Robert E. Keith, Jr.
President and CEO: Walter W. Buckley, III

Earnings Progression	
Revenue Growth	★ ★
Stock Growth	★ ★
Consistency	★
Stability/ Vulnerability	★ ★ ★
Total Points	**8 points**

Internet Capital Group is all business—all business-to-business e-commerce, that is.

The Wayne, Pennsylvania operation makes no products itself. Rather, it is a holding company that invests in other companies. It focuses strictly on Internet upstarts involved in e-commerce between businesses, with the goal of nurturing each property through to its initial public stock offering (IPO). Internet Capital often sells out its stake in companies after they go public.

Although business-to-business trade doesn't have the glamour of Web portals or e-tailing, the money-making potential is certainly attractive. Internet Capital was the top performing IPO of 1999.

When mulling an investment, Internet Capital analyzes the vertical market a company serves as much as the operation itself. It looks for markets with inherent inefficiencies that lend themselves to improvement via the Internet. If the market isn't overcrowded with start-ups, Internet Capital takes a position.

Ideally, the firm tries to buy about a 40 percent stake in each company, although it often ends up holding between 25 and 35 percent.

The top player in the Internet Capital stable is online market operator VerticalNet, which has emerged as the leader of its sector. Internet Capital owns stakes in other market operators, including Deja.com, BidCom, CommerX, and e-Chemicals.

Internet Capital also has ownership stakes in several e-commerce software companies, including ClearCommerce and Entegrity Solutions. It owns pieces of many consulting and services firms, including United Messaging, Benchmarking Partners, and U.S. Interactive.

Internet Capital has already cashed in positions held in portal giants Lycos and Excite and recently sold its stake in e-commerce software heavy Tradex to Ariba.

Founded in 1996, Internet Capital Group made its initial public stock offering in 1999. The company has about 100 employees and has a market capitalization of about $35 billion.

EARNINGS PER SHARE PROGRESSION
None

REVENUE GROWTH   ★ ★
Past year: 427 percent

STOCK GROWTH   ★ ★
Internet Capital went public in 1999 and experienced strong gains after its IPO.

CONSISTENCY   ★
Positive earnings progression: None
Increased revenue: 1 year

STABILITY/VULNERABILITY   ★ ★ ★
With risk spread across so many companies and market niches, Internet Capital Group should be in good shape when the booming e-commerce industry begins the inevitable process of winnowing down its players.

INTERNET CAPITAL GROUP AT A GLANCE

Fiscal year ended: Dec. 31
Revenue in $ millions

	1995	1996	1997	1998	1999	Avg. Annual (%)	Total (%)
						1-Year Growth	
Revenue ($)	—	—	—	3.13	16.5	427	427
Earnings/share ($)	—	—	—	0.14	−0.08	NA	NA
PE ratio range	—	—	—	NA	NA		

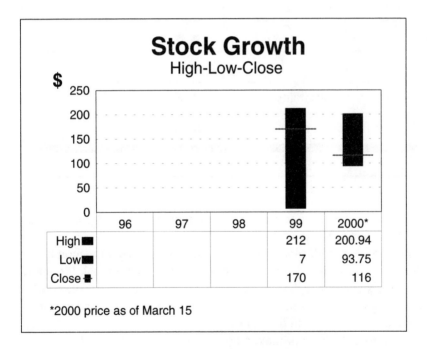

Stock Growth
High-Low-Close

$

	96	97	98	99	2000*
High				212	200.94
Low				7	93.75
Close				170	116

*2000 price as of March 15

75

Sycamore Networks

10 Elizabeth Drive
Chelmsford, MA 01824
978-250-2900
Nasdaq: SCMR
www.sycamorenet.com

Chairman: Gururaj Deshpande
President and CEO: Daniel E. Smith

Earnings Progression	★
Revenue Growth	★
Stock Growth	★ ★
Consistency	★
Stability/Vulnerability	★ ★ ★
Total Points	**8 points**

It used to be good enough for fiber-optic networks to be lightning fast. Now they have to be smart, too.

The problem with most fiber networks is that it can take months for technicians to configure new links for customers. But a breakthrough in fiber-optic switching technology now makes it possible to handle configuration tasks in hours from a computer screen that until now had to be performed by a technician in the field.

Sycamore Networks makes advanced data switches that can be inserted into existing fiber networks to facilitate the new switching technology. Simply put, Sycamore's technology makes it possible to design, maintain, and change fiber networks *in software,* instead of working directly with the actual hardware.

"Software-intensive" fiber configurations promise huge payoffs. For example, it has been standard procedure to set aside half a network's bandwidth for emergency bypass routing in case another network fails. That's not necessary with Sycamore's equipment, effectively doubling capacity without pulling a single new cable.

Sycamore's product line is anchored by the SN16000, a heavy-duty optical switch capable of routing individual fiber light-paths based on software settings. It also makes sophisticated devices used by network operators to set up "bandwidth-on-demand" customer circuits and to pack more revenue-generating data streams into a single optical pipe.

Sycamore's product line not only saves Internet backbone providers big money, it enables them to offer their customers more flexible services.

Sycamore Networks was founded in 1998 by the same team that started Cascade Communications, which is now owned by Lucent Technologies. The firm went public with its initial stock offering in 1999. It has about 150 employees and a market capitalization of about $25 billion.

EARNINGS PER SHARE PROGRESSION ★

Not applicable

REVENUE GROWTH ★

Not applicable

STOCK GROWTH ★ ★

The company had impressive performance after its 1999 IPO.

CONSISTENCY ★

Positive earnings progression: Not applicable
Increased sales: Not applicable

STABILITY/VULNERABILITY ★ ★ ★

Sycamore has a proven management team, great technology, and a boom market. Yet it must contend with such giants as Cisco Systems and Nortel Networks.

SYCAMORE NETWORKS AT A GLANCE

Fiscal year ended: July 31
Revenue in $ millions

	1995	1996	1997	1998	1999	0-Year Growth Avg. Annual (%)	Total (%)
Revenue ($)	—	—	—	—	11.3	NA	NA
Earnings/share ($)	—	—	—	—	−0.17	NA	NA
PE ratio range	—	—	—	—	NA		

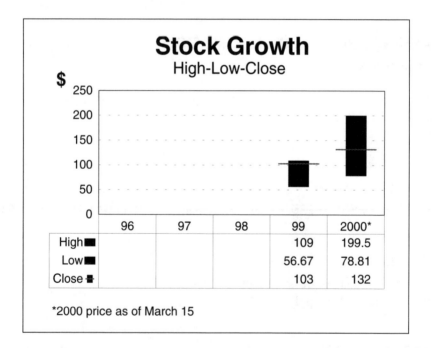

	96	97	98	99	2000*
High ■				109	199.5
Low ■				56.67	78.81
Close ■				103	132

*2000 price as of March 15

INTERNET BUSINESS
SERVICES

Cysive, Inc.

11480 Sunset Hills Road, Suite 200E
Reston, VA 20190
703-742-0865
Nasdaq: CYSV
www.cysive.com

Chairman, President, and CEO: Nelson A. Carbonell, Jr.

Earnings Progression	
Revenue Growth	★ ★ ★
Stock Growth	★ ★
Consistency	★
Stability/Vulnerability	★ ★
Total Points	**8 points**

Cysive helps e-commerce companies get more bang for their buck. The company is a software engineering firm that specializes in building highly customized Web sites that support large-scale e-businesses.

Cysive engineers helped Cisco Systems build its Internetworking Products Center, which is one of the world's largest e-commerce sites. Cysive has also built systems for DaimlerChrysler, Equifax Secure, First Union, and UUNET Technologies, among others.

The company redesigned the online auto sales site for Cars.com to handle extremely high user volumes and to incorporate real-time classified ad data from more than 130 affiliate newspapers.

The Reston, Virginia operation focuses on designing software systems that can handle high volumes of customer transactions, operate reliably 24 hours a day, and expand to meet the growth requirements of large-scale e-businesses. As a consulting house, Cysive focuses on several key operational issues, including:

- **Experienced engineers.** On average, Cysive engineers have ten years' experience in software development.
- **SWAT team approach.** Cysive tries to shorten the delivery time of a project by assigning a team of engineers to build each new site.

Cysive uses an advanced technology approach in building Web sites that incorporate all of the client company's procedures and rules into a core software application, and presents business functions to customers in a simple yet comprehensive format.

Cysive began operations in 1994 and went public with its initial stock offering in 1999. It has about 150 employees and a market capitalization of about $1 billion.

EARNINGS PER SHARE PROGRESSION

Earnings have become losses the past 2 years.

REVENUE GROWTH   ★ ★ ★

Past 2 years: 228 percent (81 percent per year)

STOCK GROWTH   ★ ★

Cysive went public in 1999 and experienced strong growth after the IPO.

CONSISTENCY   ★

Positive earnings progression: None
Increased revenue: 2 consecutive years

STABILITY/VULNERABILITY

Cysive is still a small, unproven player in a rapidly growing but highly competitive sector.

CYSIVE AT A GLANCE

Fiscal year ended: Dec. 31
Revenue in $ millions

	1995	1996	1997	1998	1999	2-Year Growth Avg. Annual (%)	Total (%)
Revenue ($)	—	—	7.71	9.14	25.3	81	228
Earnings/share ($)	—	—	0.19	0.10	−1.11	NA	NA
PE ratio range	—	—	NA	NA	NA		

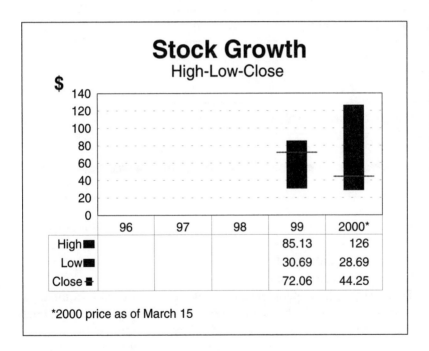

Stock Growth
High-Low-Close

$	96	97	98	99	2000*
High■				85.13	126
Low■				30.69	28.69
Close■				72.06	44.25

*2000 price as of March 15

Net2Phone

171 Main Street
Hackensack, NJ 07601
201-530-4000
Nasdaq: NTOP
www.net2phone.com

Chairman: Clifford M. Sobel
Vice Chairman and CEO: Howard S. Balter
President: Jonathan Fram

Earnings Progression	★
Revenue Growth	★ ★
Stock Growth	★ ★
Consistency	★
Stability/Vulnerability	★ ★
Total Points	**8 points**

Still dialing 10-10-22Whatever to save some coin on your long-distance calls?

Maybe you should talk to your computer and save even more.

How does a penny a minute sound?

That's right, those people you see muttering into their computers aren't necessarily on the brink of a breakdown. They're simply making "PC phone calls" over the Internet. And at a penny a minute for long distance calls, the crazy ones may be those of us who aren't yet talking to our computers.

With nearly half a million customers, Net2Phone is the biggest telephony carrier on the Internet. The Hackensack, New Jersey operation offers a range of services, including:

- **PC phone calls.** A personal computer equipped with microphone and speaker can call normal phones anywhere in the United States for a penny a minute. Customers outside the U.S. pay about a dime. The quality is not yet as good as a normal phone call, but improvements are coming.
- **Net2Phone Direct.** Customers can place Internet calls from normal phones by dialing a special access number anywhere in the U.S., Canada, and the United Kingdom. Pricing is rock bottom, at under a nickel a minute in most locations.
- **Click2Talk.** This service allows e-commerce companies to put an icon on their Web site customers can click to initiate a phone conversation with the site's customer support department.

Net2Phone has taken a leadership position in the PC phone market, and has forged marketing alliances with AOL Time Warner, and AT&T. AOL holds a large stake in the company and has negotiated to buy more.

Net2Phone, which was spun off from IDT Corp. in 1997, went public with its initial stock offering in 1999. The company has about 300 employees and a market capitalization of about $2 billion.

EARNINGS PER SHARE PROGRESSION ★
None

REVENUE GROWTH ★ ★
Past year: 177 percent

STOCK GROWTH ★ ★
Net2Phone went public in 1999 and had solid but rocky growth after its IPO.

CONSISTENCY ★
Positive earnings progression: None
Increased revenue: 1 year

STABILITY/VULNERABILITY ★ ★
Net2Phone is the leading player in this exciting sector, but will PC phoning catch on if traditional long distance rates keep falling?

NET2PHONE AT A GLANCE

Fiscal year ended: July 31
Revenue in $ millions

	1995	1996	1997	1998	1999	1-Year Growth Avg. Annual (%)	Total (%)
Revenue ($)	—	—	—	12.01	33.2	177	177
Earnings/share ($)	—	—	—	−0.11	−1.69	NA	NA
PE ratio range	—	—	—	NA	NA		

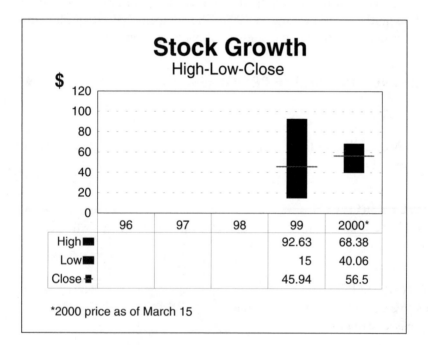

Stock Growth
High-Low-Close

$	96	97	98	99	2000*
High				92.63	68.38
Low				15	40.06
Close				45.94	56.5

*2000 price as of March 15

78
NextCard, Inc.

595 Market Street, Suite 1800
San Francisco, CA 94105
415-836-9792
Nasdaq: NXCD
www.nextcard.com

Chairman, President, and CEO: Jeremy R. Lent

Earnings Progression	
Revenue Growth	★ ★ ★
Stock Growth	★
Consistency	★ ★
Stability/Vulnerability	★ ★
Total Points	**8 points**

As if you don't already get enough offers for credit cards through the mail and from telemarketers calling your home, NextCard offers you the opportunity to apply for a credit card on the Internet.

The San Francisco operation is one of the leading issuers of consumer credit on the Net. Since its online marketing launch in late 1997, Next-Card has received applications for Visa credit cards from well over two million consumers.

You might see NextCard's banner ads as you surf the Web; the company runs about 12 million Internet ads a day. The ads typically offer a Visa card with a competitive interest rate and an introductory rate as low as 0 percent. Click on the banner ads, and you're led through an online application process that can be completed and approved within minutes.

NextCard customers can view their account balance online and transfer balances from other credit cards at the NextCard site.

The company also offers a couple of other features for its customers, including NextCard Rewards, an Internet-based incentives program that allows customers to earn points that can be redeemed for goods or services. It also has launched an online shopping service called GoShopping!

One of the keys to NextCard's success is the type of consumers who apply for its cards. They are all Internet users, which means that they tend to be more affluent professionals. They can afford to spend money while still paying their bills and maintaining a strong credit rating. As a result, the average balance of NextCard customers is nearly $3,000—twice the industry average. Yet, the company's net credit charge-offs are well below the industry average.

Founded in 1996, NextCard went public in 1999. It has about 250 employees and a market capitalization of about $2 billion.

EARNINGS PER SHARE PROGRESSION

Losses declined slightly the past year.

REVENUE GROWTH   ★ ★ ★

Past 2 years: 23,663 percent (1,445 percent per year)

STOCK GROWTH   ★

NextCard went public in 1999 and experienced rocky gains after its IPO.

CONSISTENCY   ★ ★

Positive earnings progression: 1 year
Increased revenue: 2 consecutive years

STABILITY/VULNERABILITY   ★ ★

NextCard has a good start, with a solid base of affluent customers and a good concept for continuing its growth. But, the consumer credit card market is highly competitive.

NEXTCARD AT A GLANCE

Fiscal year ended: Dec. 31
Revenue in $ millions

	1995	1996	1997	1998	1999	2-Year Growth Avg. Annual (%)	Total (%)
Revenue ($)	—	—	.093	.502	22.1	1,445	23,663
Earnings/share ($)	—	—	−1.08	−5.07	−4.61	NA	NA
PE ratio range	—	—	NA	NA	NA		

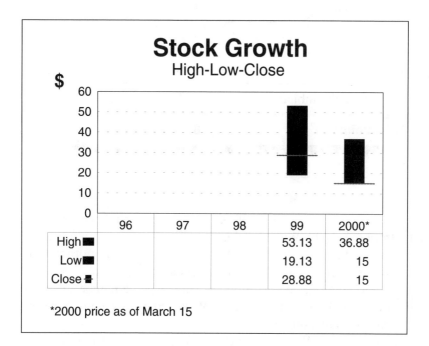

Stock Growth
High-Low-Close

	96	97	98	99	2000*
High				53.13	36.88
Low				19.13	15
Close				28.88	15

*2000 price as of March 15

INTERNET HOLDING
COMPANIES

79

Wit Capital Group, Inc.

826 Broadway, Sixth Floor
New York, NY 10003
212-253-4400
Nasdaq: WITC
www.witcapital.com

Chairman and Co-CEO: Robert H. Lessin
President and Co-CEO: Ronald Readmond

Earnings Progression	★
Revenue Growth	★ ★
Stock Growth	★
Consistency	★ ★
Stability/Vulnerability	★ ★
Total Points	**8 points**

When the World Wrestling Federation (WWF) went public with its initial stock offering in 1999, Wit Capital Group muscled its way into the deal to help move Stone Cold Steve Austin and the WWF's other foul-mouthed fighters from your TV set into your stock portfolio.

The New York–based operation has comanaged a number of initial public offerings (IPOs), including the WWF, ShopNow.com, NetZero, and Earthweb, among others.

Founded in 1996, Wit was the nation's first online investment banking firm. For its online brokerage customers, Wit offers access to securities such as IPOs and secondary offerings the company claims would previously have been available only to institutions and wealthy investors.

For companies interested in issuing stock, Wit offers a broad range of investment banking and advisory services, including access to capital sources through distribution of deals and related materials via the Internet. Wit also offers stock issuers the opportunity to keep their companies in front of investors through online research and other after-market materials published by its team of analysts.

In addition to serving its two key markets—investors and stock issuers—the company has attempted to build its business through acquisitions. In 1999, it acquired SoundView Technology Group, an investment banking firm that focuses on technology stocks. The $320 million SoundView acquisition put Wit in a new league, because the firm can now provide coverage of more than 200 companies in the technology and Internet sectors.

The company, which is 20 percent owned by Goldman Sachs, went public with its IPO in 1999. It has about 150 employees and a market capitalization of about $1 billion.

EARNINGS PER SHARE PROGRESSION   ★
Losses decreased the past year.

REVENUE GROWTH   ★ ★
Past year: 2,282 percent

STOCK GROWTH   ★
Wit experienced rocky growth after its 1999 IPO.

CONSISTENCY   ★ ★
Positive earnings progression: 1 year
Increased revenue: 1 year

STABILITY/VULNERABILITY   ★ ★
Still a small player in the investment banking business, Wit seems to be doing a good job of carving out a unique niche.

WIT CAPITAL GROUP AT A GLANCE

Fiscal year ended: Dec. 31
Revenue in $ millions

	1995	1996	1997	1998	1999	1-Year Growth Avg. Annual (%)	Total (%)
Revenue ($)	—	—	—	2.04	48.6	2,282	2,282
Earnings/share ($)	—	—	—	–1.22	–0.99	NA	NA
PE ratio range	—	—	—	NA	NA		

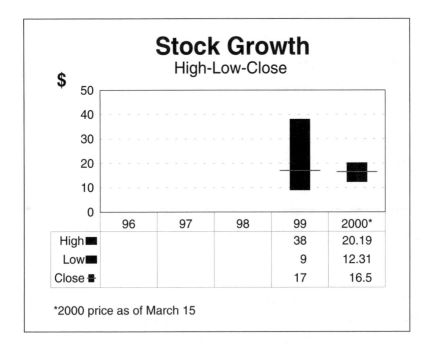

Stock Growth
High-Low-Close

$	96	97	98	99	2000*
High ■				38	20.19
Low ■				9	12.31
Close ■				17	16.5

*2000 price as of March 15

80
Worldgate
Communications, Inc.

3190 Tremont Avenue
Trevose, PA 19053
215-354-5100
Nasdaq: WGAT
www.wgate.com

Chairman, President, and CEO: Hal Krisbergh

Earnings Progression	★
Revenue Growth	★ ★ ★
Stock Growth	
Consistency	★ ★
Stability/Vulnerability	★ ★
Total Points	**8 points**

WorldGate Communications can transform your TV into a high-speed Web browser. The company's Internet access technology, which it makes available exclusively through cable TV services, helps turn channel surfers into Web surfers.

Using WorldGate's system, TV viewers can browse the Web and write and receive e-mail through the use of a remote control pad or wireless keyboard. The WorldGate technology, which is integrated into special cable set-up boxes, generally operates at two to four times the speed of a standard 56K PC modem. And, because the WorldGate system remains wired to the Internet 100 percent of the time, there's no wasted time reconnecting.

WorldGate has also developed a picture-in-picture capability that allows viewers to surf the Web, while still watching their television program. WorldGate's Internet service is available only to cable TV subscribers, and not to PC users or TV satellite dish customers.

The Philadelphia-based operation recently introduced its new Channel HyperLinking technology, which is designed to allow TV viewers to link instantly to related interactive Web sites where they can find additional information on or place an order for a product or service. The technology is attractive to broadcasters and advertisers because it helps merge TV advertising, electronic commerce, and information delivery into a single medium.

WorldGate has already signed up more than 70 Channel HyperLinking partners, including CNN, E!, Showtime, A&E, and Lifetime.

WorldGate has quickly expanded its cable Internet service worldwide, with customers in more than 15 countries in Asia, Europe, and South America. The company's service is ideal in certain international markets where PCs and phone lines are scarce.

Founded in 1995, the company has more than 12,000 customers. It has a market capitalization of about $1 billion. WorldGate went public with its initial stock offering in 1999.

EARNINGS PER SHARE PROGRESSION ★
Losses decreased the past year.

REVENUE GROWTH ★ ★ ★
Past 2 years: 3,864 percent (530 percent per year).

STOCK GROWTH
WorldGate experienced rocky performance after its 1999 IPO.

CONSISTENCY ★ ★
Positive earnings progression: 1 year
Increased revenue: 2 consecutive years

STABILITY/VULNERABILITY ★ ★
WorldGate is a young, unproven company, but it is pioneering a technology that seems to have a lot of growth potential.

WORLDGATE COMMUNICATIONS AT A GLANCE

Fiscal year ended: Dec. 31
Revenue in $ millions

	1995	1996	1997	1998	1999	2-Year Growth Avg. Annual (%)	Total (%)
Revenue ($)	—	—	.141	1.02	5.59	530	3,864
Earnings/share ($)	—	−0.33	−1.81	−2.33	−1.91	NA	NA
PE ratio range	—	NA	NA	NA	NA		

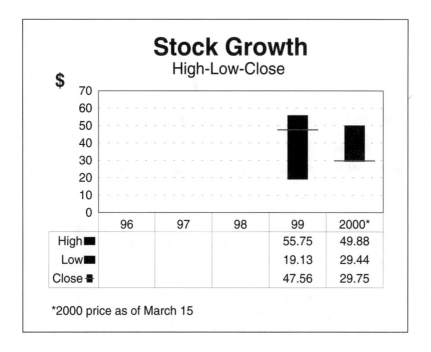

Stock Growth
High-Low-Close

	96	97	98	99	2000*
High				55.75	49.88
Low				19.13	29.44
Close				47.56	29.75

*2000 price as of March 15

INTERNET BUSINESS
SERVICES

81

Interliant, Inc.

Two Manhattanville Road
Purchase, NY 10577
914-640-9000
Nasdaq: INIT
www.interliant.com

Co-Chairman: Leonard Fassler
Co-Chairman: Bradley Feld
CEO: Stephen Maggs
President: James Lidestri

Earnings Progression	
Revenue Growth	★ ★
Stock Growth	★ ★
Consistency	★
Stability/Vulnerability	★ ★
Total Points	**7 points**

Need a Web presence? Interliant can get you started—and keep you running. The Purchase, New York operation is a Web site host for more than 40,000 customers. Interliant makes it easy and inexpensive for companies to establish and operate a Web site without going to the trouble of building and maintaining an internal network infrastructure.

The company has three state-of-the-art Web hosting data centers in Atlanta, Houston, and Washington, D.C., with high-speed network connectivity and uninterruptible power supplies to keep its clients' sites up and running 24 hours a day.

Interliant offers several hosting options, including:

- **Virtual hosting.** The firm provides site hosting for multiple customers on a server Interliant owns and operates. The virtual hosting option is for customers with simple or moderately used sites.

- **Dedicated hosting.** Interliant can assign a server specifically to a single customer who needs to host high-traffic or complex Web sites and applications, but wants to avoid incurring significant infrastructure and overhead costs.
- **Colocated hosting.** Interliant can house and manage servers owned by its customers.
- **Application hosting.** The firm can manage online software applications for customers through the Lotus Notes/Domino platform. It also hosts such applications such as legal automation, sales automation, and online training that run on remote servers its customers access and use through the Internet.
- **Groupware hosting.** The company's groupware software applications enable people from remote locations to work together on the same applications. Options include e-mail and other messaging methods, project team collaboration and document sharing, business process automation and workflow, and document libraries.

Interliant has formed strategic alliances with leading technology companies, including Dell, IBM, Lotus, Microsoft, BMC, and Network Solutions.

Interliant went public with its initial stock offering in 1999. It has about 500 employees and a market capitalization of about $2 billion.

EARNINGS PER SHARE PROGRESSION
None

REVENUE GROWTH ★★
Past year: 859 percent

STOCK GROWTH ★★
Interliant went public in 1999 and had very strong growth after the IPO.

CONSISTENCY ★
Positive earnings progression: None
Increased revenue: 1 year

STABILITY/VULNERABILITY ★★
With its infrastructure already in place, Interliant appears to be on stable footing, but it's a long way from profitability.

INTERLIANT AT A GLANCE

Fiscal year ended: Dec. 31
Revenue in $ millions

	1995	1996	1997	1998	1999	1-Year Growth Avg. Annual (%)	Total (%)
Revenue ($)	—	—	—	4.91	47.1	859	859
Earnings/share ($)	—	—	—	–1.06	–1.49	NA	NA
PE ratio range	—	—	—	NA	NA		

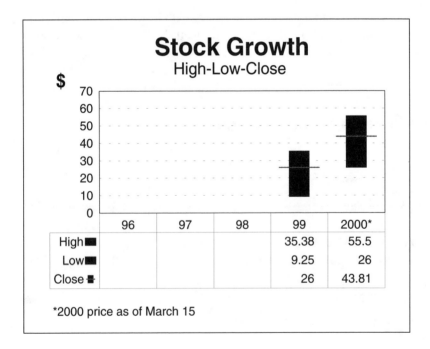

Stock Growth
High-Low-Close

$	96	97	98	99	2000*
High				35.38	55.5
Low				9.25	26
Close				26	43.81

*2000 price as of March 15

E-TAILING

82
Priceline.com, Inc.

Five High Ridge Park
Stamford, CT 06905
203-705-3000
Nasdaq: PCLN
www.priceline.com

Chairman and CEO: Richard Braddock
Vice Chairman and Founder: Jay S. Walker
President: Daniel Schulman

Earnings Progression	
Revenue Growth	★ ★ ★
Stock Growth	★
Consistency	★
Stability/Vulnerability	★ ★
Total Points	**7 points**

"Name your price and save!" That's the promise of Priceline.com, an e-tailing operation that invites consumers to bid on plane tickets and other products and services in the hopes of getting discount prices well below the standard fares.

In addition to airlines tickets, Priceline.com also offers a growing list of other products and services, including hotel rooms, new cars, home mortgages, and home equity loans.

The Stamford, Connecticut operation has been a pioneer in what it terms a "demand collection system" in which consumers guarantee their bids with a credit card while Priceline.com looks for a seller. The company either communicates the bid directly to a seller or accesses the seller's private database to determine whether the customer's offer can be fulfilled on the basis of pricing information and rules established by the seller.

The concept has attracted a strong response by consumers, although the company was still very much in the red through its first two years of operation in 1998 and 1999. Priceline.com's revenue comes through marketing fees from the sale of the products or services it facilitates. For instance, when a customer buys a new car through Priceline.com, the company receives a fixed fee from both the customer and the car dealer after the transaction is consummated.

Priceline.com started out with a bang. Within 14 months after the company launched its service in April 1998, it had received offers for more than five million plane tickets. Of those bids, about 762,000 resulted in actual sales of airline tickets.

The company is aggressively moving into other areas, such as retail merchandise and consumer-to-consumer sales.

Priceline.com was founded in July 1997 and went public with its initial stock offering in 1999. The company has about 300 employees and a market capitalization of about $9 billion.

EARNINGS PER SHARE PROGRESSION
The company experienced increasing losses the past 2 years.

REVENUE GROWTH ★ ★ ★
Past year: 1,270 percent

STOCK GROWTH ★
Priceline.com went public in 1999 and had rocky performance after the IPO.

CONSISTENCY ★
Positive earnings progression: None
Increased sales: 1 year

STABILITY/VULNERABILITY ★ ★
Priceline.com is the leader and original pioneer of this unique business concept, but its losses mounted quickly through its first two years of operations.

PRICELINE.COM AT A GLANCE

Fiscal year ended: Dec. 31
Revenue in $ millions

	1995	1996	1997	1998	1999	1-Year Growth Avg. Annual (%)	Total (%)
Revenue ($)	—	—	—	35.2	482.4	1,270	1,270
Earnings/share ($)	—	—	−0.05	−1.16	−6.99	NA	NA
PE ratio range	—	—	NA	NA	NA		

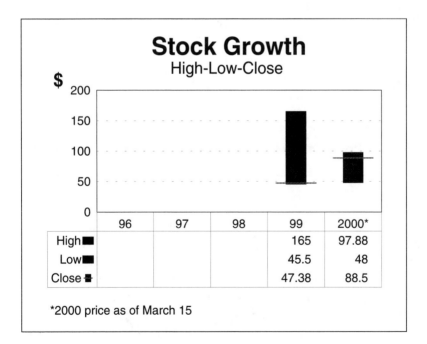

Stock Growth
High-Low-Close

	96	97	98	99	2000*
High■				165	97.88
Low■				45.5	48
Close■				47.38	88.5

*2000 price as of March 15

Scient Corp. Inc.

INTERNET BUSINESS
SERVICES

One Front Street, 28th Floor
San Francisco, CA 94111
415-733-8200
Nasdaq: SCNT
www.scient.com

Chairman: Eric Greenberg
President and CEO: Bob Howe

Earnings Progression	
Revenue Growth	★ ★
Stock Growth	★ ★
Consistency	★
Stability/Vulnerability	★ ★
Total Points	**7 points**

Go big or go home. That's the advice Scient gives clients mulling their e-commerce strategies. The San Francisco–based Web consulting firm tells its customers that they must adapt their businesses to the Web, not the other way around.

Scient designs and develops e-commerce Web sites for both pure Internet companies and traditional Fortune 500 corporations. Its client list includes the likes of Chase Manhattan and Gateway Computer.

The blue-suit consulting firms have made billions implementing internal corporate computer systems that are now having trouble working with the Internet. This is a big problem, because corporations are being driven to interact with their customers and suppliers over the Web.

With that in mind, Scient's consultants encourage clients to boldly rethink business strategy from scratch before making the first move on a corporate e-commerce Web site. E-commerce presents substantial risks to all companies, and the Scient Approach methodology is to manage it by embracing radical changes instead of taking an incremental approach.

Customers have responded. In just two years, Scient has become a major factor in e-commerce consulting. In a business where head count is almost as important as revenues, the company has been able to increase its consultant roster at a rapid pace.

Before founding Scient in 1997, Chairman Eric Greenberg had been a vice president at the technology research firm Gartner Group and later helped start rival Web consulting firm Viant.

Greenberg surprised everybody by bringing in President and CEO Robert Howe to run Scient. Howe served as a senior executive with IBM, where he ran Big Blue's global consulting business.

The company went public with its initial stock offering in 1999. It has 600 employees and has a market capitalization of about $6 billion.

EARNINGS PER SHARE PROGRESSION
None

REVENUE GROWTH ★★
Past year: 11,464 percent

STOCK GROWTH ★★
Scient had outstanding growth after its 1999 IPO.

CONSISTENCY ★
Positive earnings progression: None
Increased revenue: 1 year

STABILITY/VULNERABILITY ★★
The company is off to a great start in a market that most feel will get several times bigger over the next few years.

SCIENT CORP. AT A GLANCE

Fiscal year ended: March 31
Revenue in $ millions

	1995	1996	1997	1998	1999	1-Year Growth Avg. Annual (%)	Total (%)
Revenue ($)	—	—	—	.179	20.7	11,464	11,464
Earnings/share ($)	—	—	—	−0.10	−.084	NA	NA
PE ratio range	—	—	—	NA	NA		

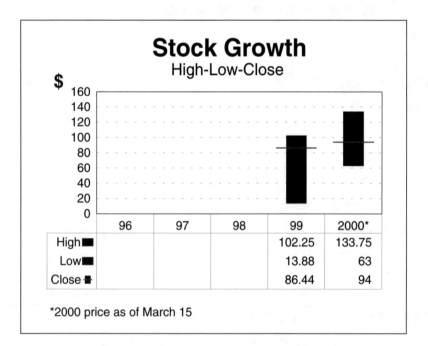

Stock Growth
High-Low-Close

$	96	97	98	99	2000*
High ■				102.25	133.75
Low ■				13.88	63
Close ■				86.44	94

*2000 price as of March 15

E-COMMERCE

PurchasePro.com, Inc.

3291 North Buffalo Drive, Suite 2
Las Vegas, NV 89129
702-316-7000
Nasdaq: PPRO
www.purchasepro.com

Chairman and CEO: Charles E. Johnson
President: Christopher P. Carton

Earnings Progression	
Revenue Growth	★ ★
Stock Growth	★ ★
Consistency	★
Stability/Vulnerability	★ ★
Total Points	**7 points**

PurchasePro.com has created a network of online marketplaces for commercial buyers and sellers from a broad range of industries.

The Las Vegas operation has set up a number of public and private online "digital marketplaces" that enable its member companies to participate as either buyers or sellers or both.

PurchasePro.com member companies enjoy several benefits when using its online network to buy supplies and other products. They can save money through reduced processing costs and competitive online comparison shopping, and they can manage the corporate purchasing process by setting up online purchasing policies and auditing and evaluating purchases made by their employees.

Suppliers can cut costs on sales, marketing, and administration, and can reach a wider universe of potential customers. The system also gives member companies a constant presence on the Web. Pricing, product information, and service policies are all readily available to potential customers 24 hours a day, seven days a week. Product ordering and payment also can be done online.

PurchasePro.com targets small and medium-sized businesses, which constitute about 99 percent of all U.S. businesses.

The firm has already helped set up online business-to-business commerce marketplaces for a number of corporations and organizations and is currently involved in sales and marketing relationships with Sprint, Office Depot, Advanstar Communications, Primavera Systems, DigitalWork, Workflow Management, Zoomtown.com, the Greater Phoenix Chamber of Commerce, and the American Association of Franchisees and Dealers.

Incorporated in 1996, PurchasePro.com went public with its initial stock offering in 1999. The company has about 200 employees and a market capitalization of about $3 billion.

EARNINGS PER SHARE PROGRESSION
None

REVENUE GROWTH ★★
Past year: 260 percent

STOCK GROWTH ★★
PurchasePro.com went public in 1999 and had outstanding gains after the IPO.

CONSISTENCY ★
Positive earnings progression: None
Increased sales: 1 year

STABILITY/VULNERABILITY ★★
Can PurchasePro.com grow into a dominant player in the competitive business-to-business e-commerce field?

PURCHASEPRO.COM AT A GLANCE

Fiscal year ended: Dec. 31
Revenue in $ millions

	1995	1996	1997	1998	1999	Avg. Annual (%)	Total (%)
						1-Year Growth	
Revenue ($)	—	—	—	1.67	6.02	260	260
Earnings/share ($)	—	—	—	−0.57	−3.95	NA	NA
PE ratio range	—	—	—	NA	NA		

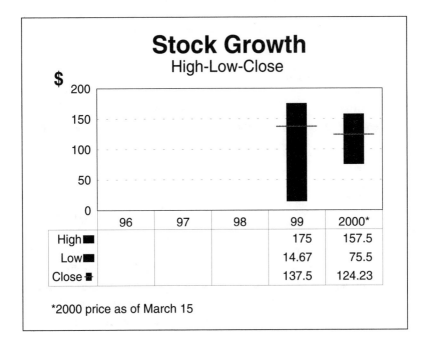

Stock Growth
High-Low-Close

	96	97	98	99	2000*
High ■				175	157.5
Low ■				14.67	75.5
Close ■				137.5	124.23

*2000 price as of March 15

SOFTWARE

85

webMethods, Inc.

3877 Fairfax Ridge Road, 4th Floor
Fairfax, VA 22030
703-460-2500
Nasdaq: WEBM
www.webmethods.com

Chairman, President, and CEO: Phillip Merrick

Earnings Progression	
Revenue Growth	★
Stock Growth	★ ★
Consistency	★
Stability/Vulnerability	★ ★ ★
Total Points	**7 points**

E-commerce can do more than just help companies cut better deals. Using webMethods software, companies also can map together incompatible internal systems so that inventory, accounting, and other business data can be freely exchanged between trading partners. Inter-company integration smooths operations, saves time and money, and boosts quality.

webMethods has emerged as a leading vendor of business-to-business (B2B) integration software. The Fairfax, Virginia operation's software is based on a breakthrough technology called XML (eXtensible Markup Language).

In much the same way that HTML code made all computer models Web compatible in the mid-1990s, XML is making everybody's databases compatible. The compatibility allows corporations to do business on a more intimate basis with little of the costs and bureaucratic delays most purchasing departments face.

Integrating otherwise incompatible systems isn't easy. Large corporations have had to operate within a veritable Tower of Babel for years. There are several competing data exchange standards, as well as dozens of proprietary formats for database products and Enterprise Requirements Planning (ERP) applications software systems.

The engineers at webMethods managed to make all those divergent formats compatible through its XML breakthrough. Now webMethods is racing to land as many major accounts as possible. Its fast-growing list of customers includes Dell, Barnesandnoble.com, and DHL WorldWide.

webMethods has also been busy forging technology alliances with such elite software players as SAP, S1, and Ariba and has aligned with big consulting firms in KPMG, Deloitte, Computer Sciences, and EDS. This puts webMethods in the middle of the B2B e-commerce revolution.

The company went public with its initial stock offering in 2000. It has about 200 employees and a market capitalization of about $10 billion.

EARNINGS PER SHARE PROGRESSION
Not applicable

REVENUE GROWTH ★
Not applicable

STOCK GROWTH ★ ★
WebMethods had a large run-up after its 2000 IPO.

CONSISTENCY ★
Increased earnings per share: Not applicable
Increased sales: Not applicable

STABILITY/VULNERABILITY ★ ★ ★
The company is treading on turf traditionally held by Microsoft and Oracle, but it has a solid lead in its niche.

WEBMETHODS AT A GLANCE

Fiscal year ended: March 31
Revenue in $ millions

	1995	1996	1997	1998	1999	0-Year Growth Avg. Annual (%)	Total (%)
Revenue ($)	—	—	—	—	4.46	NA	NA
Earnings/share ($)	—	—	—	—	−0.71	NA	NA
PE ratio range	—	—	—	—	NA		

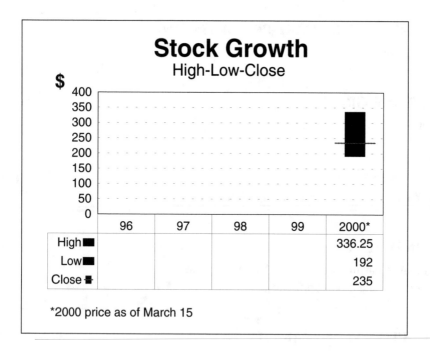

*2000 price as of March 15

86

Network Access Solutions Corp.

100 Carpenter Drive
Sterling, VA 20164
703-742-7700
Nasdaq: NASC
www.nas-corp.com

Chairman, President, and CEO: Jonathan P. Aust

Earnings Progression	
Revenue Growth	★ ★
Stock Growth	★ ★
Consistency	★
Stability/Vulnerability	★ ★
Total Points	**7 points**

Speed pays. That's why Network Access Solutions (NAS) is stringing high-speed data lines throughout the Northeast and Mid-Atlantic regions.

The Internet backbone provider solves both ends of the bandwidth problem with backbone links running from Boston to Norfolk, and metropolitan access networks that make slow-poke normal copper phone lines run like lightning.

The Virginia-based operation's hallmark CopperNet service can hook a business up to the Internet—and also connect any remote locations throughout the Northeast. NAS handles the "last mile" between its backbone and customers with Digital Subscriber Line (DSL) circuits that run up to seven megabits per second—substantially faster than dial-up modems. In addition to greatly increasing speed and efficiency, CopperNet can save companies as much as 70 percent in voice/data communications expenses.

NAS offers its customers a full line of telecom products and services. It sells telecom equipment and design and set-up services and will manage and secure customer networks.

The Virginia-based operation's service region is home to about one-third of the world's data communications traffic and the densest collection of businesses in the United States.

NAS has been busy the past two years setting up a DSL high-speed network that should be accessible to nearly 100 percent of the businesses in the Bell Atlantic region. The company is focusing its efforts on the business sector of the broadband market and is leading the industry in revenue per line metrics for access-based services.

Founded in 1994, NAS went public with its initial stock offering in 1999. The company has about 150 employees and a market capitalization of about $1 billion.

EARNINGS PER SHARE PROGRESSION
None

REVENUE GROWTH   ★ ★
Past year: 50 percent

STOCK GROWTH   ★ ★
Network Access Solutions went public in 1999 and experienced strong gains after its IPO.

CONSISTENCY   ★
Positive earnings progression: None
Increased revenue: 1 year

STABILITY/VULNERABILITY   ★ ★
The need for more bandwidth is going to continue to grow, and NAS is well positioned to profit from that demand. However, it is still a new, small player in the crowded network services business.

NETWORK ACCESS SOLUTIONS AT A GLANCE

Fiscal year ended: Dec. 31
Revenue in $ millions

	1995	1996	1997	1998	1999	1-Year Growth Avg. Annual (%)	Total (%)
Revenue ($)	—	—	—	11.6	17.4	50	50
Earnings/share ($)	—	—	—	−0.09	−0.96	NA	NA
PE ratio range	—	—	—	NA	NA		

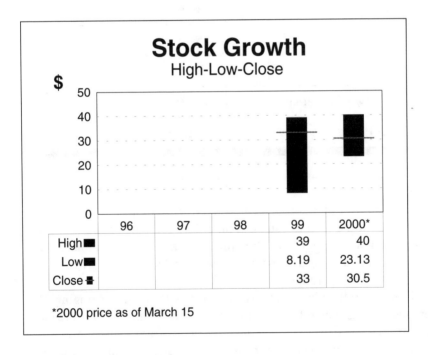

Stock Growth
High-Low-Close

$	96	97	98	99	2000*
High ■				39	40
Low ■				8.19	23.13
Close ■				33	30.5

*2000 price as of March 15

SOFTWARE

87
Art Technology Group

25 First Street
Cambridge, MA 02144
617-386-1000
Nasdaq: ARTG
www.atg.com

Chairman: Joseph T. Chung
President and CEO: Jeet Singh

Earnings Progression	
Revenue Growth	★ ★
Stock Growth	★ ★
Consistency	★
Stability/Vulnerability	★ ★
Total Points	**7 points**

You wouldn't build a corporate headquarters without a plan. Yet most companies, in the rush to establish an online presence, build their Web sites without a blueprint. Too often the result has been e-commerce sites that are hard to use, hard to maintain, and even harder to improve.

Time to call an architect.

That's why the phones at Art Technology Group keep ringing. The Cambridge, Massachusetts operation offers an e-commerce software package called Dynamo that is used to run some of the world's busiest Web sites.

Dynamo is earning praise for a tight architecture that makes it easy for customers to install and maintain. Used both for e-tailing and business-to-business e-commerce, the Dynamo product suite includes:

- **Dynamo Personalization Server.** This platform is used to build customer profiles and to target Web site content by profile. It lets nontechnical managers use business rules to target customers.

- **Dynamo Commerce Server.** This module is used to create e-storefronts and to personalize the content each visitor sees. It has built-in tools for product searching, registering customers, and handling online sales transactions.
- **Dynamo Application Server.** This is the software engine that serves up Web pages to site visitors. It compiles and stages the content that goes into Web pages and handles the high volume of download requests that big Web sites must withstand.

Like most high-end Web site packages, Dynamo is part software package and part programming tool kit. Customers use the product's programming tools to "build out" the various modules in such a way that they're customized to specific needs.

Dynamo customers include RealNetworks, Hilton Hotels, Bell South, Sun Microsystems, and other major companies.

Art Technology Group went public with its initial stock offering in 1999. The company has about 170 employees and a market capitalization of about $4 billion.

EARNINGS PER SHARE PROGRESSION
Art Technology's losses increased slightly from 1998 to 1999.

REVENUE GROWTH ★ ★
Past year: 166 percent

STOCK GROWTH ★ ★
Art Technology went public in 1999 and experienced strong gains after the IPO.

CONSISTENCY ★
Positive earnings progression: None
Increased revenue: 1 year

STABILITY/VULNERABILITY ★ ★
Art Technology Group must work hard to keep up with new technology and changing market conditions in the cutthroat software market, but its strong product line and big customer base will help.

ART TECHNOLOGY GROUP AT A GLANCE

Fiscal year ended: Dec. 31
Revenue in $ millions

	1995	1996	1997	1998	1999	1-Year Growth Avg. Annual (%)	Total (%)
Revenue ($)	—	—	—	12.1	32.1	166	166
Earnings/share ($)	—	—	—	−0.50	−0.54	NA	NA
PE ratio range	—	—	—	NA	NA		

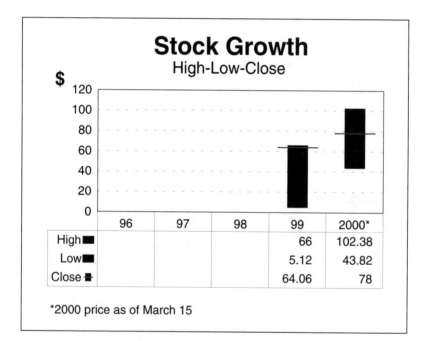

Stock Growth
High-Low-Close

	96	97	98	99	2000*
High				66	102.38
Low				5.12	43.82
Close				64.06	78

*2000 price as of March 15

INTERNET BUSINESS
SERVICES

AppNet, Inc.

6707 Democracy Boulevard
Bethesda, MD 20817
301-493-8900
Nasdaq: APNT
www.appnet.com

Chairman, President, and CEO: Ken S. Bajaj

Earnings Progression	
Revenue Growth	★ ★
Stock Growth	★ ★
Consistency	★
Stability/Vulnerability	★ ★
Total Points	**7 points**

Deciding to roll out an e-commerce strategy can invite big trouble. Even with the best of intentions, Web neophytes can end up with an e-commerce site that is confusing, crash prone, and poorly matched with internal corporate computer systems. The Web is littered with such sites.

AppNet is an Internet professional services firm that understands the ways of the Web. It takes on large corporate Web site development projects, handling every technical detail of the project from start to finish. The company's client roster includes Ford, America Online, Sprint, Baxter Healthcare, and other leading corporations.

The Bethesda, Maryland operation offers a comprehensive suite of products and services, including:

- **Strategic consulting.** Before starting development, a rigorous review of the client's market position and e-commerce requirements is necessary to plan the project.

- **Interactive media services.** The firm offers interactive marketing campaign development, including advertising strategy design, media buying, ad placement, and promotions.
- **Internet applications development.** AppNet's programmers design and write the client's Web site software and integrate it with internal computers.
- **dot-com Solutions.** This is a software product targeted for use by pure Internet companies such as start-up e-tailers to run their Web businesses.
- **Hosting and management services.** Clients can "outsource" their Web sites by contracting for AppNet to operate and manage them in its own data centers.

Dependence on the ability to recruit technical employees can stunt a consulting firm's growth. AppNet's diversification into software and outsourcing services hedges against this peril, and differentiates the company from most of its competitors.

Prior to founding AppNet, company President Ken Bajaj served as vice chairman of Wang Laboratories and vice president of Electronic Data Systems. AppNet completed its initial public stock offering in 1999. The firm has a market capitalization of about $2 billion.

EARNINGS PER SHARE PROGRESSION
AppNet's losses have increased in its 2 years of reported financials.

REVENUE GROWTH ★ ★
Past year: 520 percent (520 percent per year)

STOCK GROWTH ★ ★
The company went public in 1999 and enjoyed strong stock price gains.

CONSISTENCY ★
Increased earnings per share: None
Increased revenue: 1 year

STABILITY/VULNERABILITY ★ ★
A consulting firm is only as good as its last project, but AppNet's diversification blunts some of that risk.

APPNET AT A GLANCE

Fiscal year ended: Dec. 31
Revenue in $ millions

	1995	1996	1997	1998	1999	Avg. Annual (%)	Total (%)
						1-Year Growth	
Revenue ($)	—	—	—	17.7	109.7	520	520
Earnings/share ($)	—	—	—	–1.19	–3.19	NA	NA
PE ratio range	—	—	—	NA	NA		

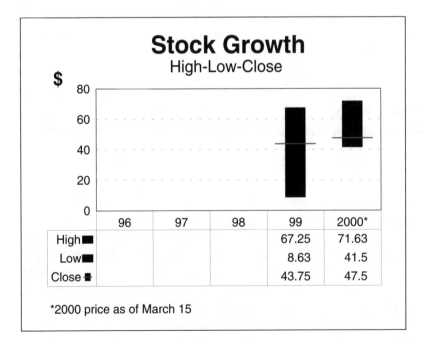

Stock Growth
High-Low-Close

	96	97	98	99	2000*
High				67.25	71.63
Low				8.63	41.5
Close				43.75	47.5

*2000 price as of March 15

SOFTWARE

89
Viador, Inc.

167 Second Avenue
San Mateo, CA 94401
650-685-3000
Nasdaq: VIAD
www.viador.com

Chairman, President, and CEO: Stan X. Wang

Earnings Progression	
Revenue Growth	★ ★
Stock Growth	★ ★
Consistency	★
Stability/Vulnerability	★ ★
Total Points	**7 points**

Most of us think of an Internet portal as a place where individuals enter the Web, browse through news and stock quotes, read their e-mail, and link to other sites. A portal is a person's home on the Internet, so to speak. But what's a business portal? It's an employee's home on the Internet, a single Web site where employees and select trading partners go to do electronic paperwork, generate reports, conduct meetings, and handle other functions. A business portal is a virtual corporate headquarters.

Viador's E-Portal software has given thousands of businesses the ability to develop high-quality, high-performance business portals at a relatively low cost. Viador's E-Portal Suite allows customers to choose from several modules to build a portal that fits their needs:

- **Viador Information Center.** This is the server software that organizes information and downloads it to users.

- **Viador Sage.** Users interact with the portal through Viador's own Web browser, which has special capabilities for using internal data that normal browsers can't handle.
- **Viador Gateway.** These are the software drivers that hook the portal up to corporate databases.
- **Viador Sentinel.** This software gives suppliers and preferred customers secured entry into the business portal.
- **Viador Administrator.** This management console is used to keep track of users, data, and other activity in the portal.
- **Viador SDK.** Computer programmers use this software development kit to customize the business portal.

The business portal market is growing quickly, because portals have become indispensable to the e-business strategies of most corporations. Among Viador's leading customers are IBM, Charles Schwab, Hewlett-Packard, Amazon.com, Xerox, and Sprint.

The San Mateo, California operation went public with its initial stock offering in 1999. Viador has about 110 employees and a market capitalization of about $600 million.

EARNINGS PER SHARE PROGRESSION
None

REVENUE GROWTH ★ ★
Past year: 164 percent

STOCK GROWTH ★ ★
Viador had strong growth after its 1999 IPO.

CONSISTENCY ★
Positive earnings progression: None
Increased revenue: 1 year

STABILITY/VULNERABILITY ★ ★
Corporate software giants such as SAP, PeopleSoft, and Baan are coming up with similar products, but Viador has the early lead.

VIADOR AT A GLANCE

Fiscal year ended: Dec. 31
Revenue in $ millions

	1995	1996	1997	1998	1999	1-Year Growth Avg. Annual (%)	Total (%)
Revenue ($)	—	—	—	3.82	10.1	164	164
Earnings/share ($)	—	—	—	−1.75	−2.31	NA	NA
PE ratio range	—	—	—	NA	NA		

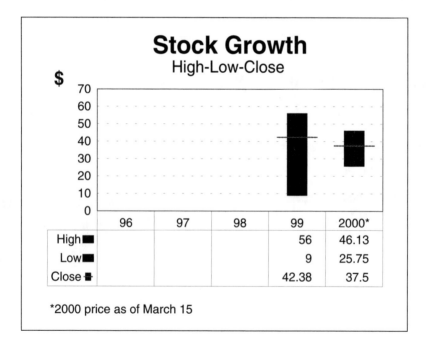

Stock Growth
High-Low-Close

$	96	97	98	99	2000*
High ■				56	46.13
Low ■				9	25.75
Close ■				42.38	37.5

*2000 price as of March 15

F5 Networks, Inc.

INFRASTRUCTURE

200 First Avenue West, Suite 500
Seattle, WA 98119
206-505-0800
Nasdaq: FFIV
www.f5.com

Chairman, President, and CEO: Jeffrey S. Hussey

Earnings Progression	
Revenue Growth	★ ★ ★
Stock Growth	★
Consistency	★ ★
Stability/Vulnerability	★
Total Points	**7 points**

Sometimes getting there has more to do with how fast you can get out of the garage than how fast your car is. Internet traffic has taxed traditional computer room management tools because they were designed to handle local traffic, rather than to download requests from users all over the planet.

F5 Networks helps Internet traffic move more smoothly by making traffic management systems that control activity within a data center based on fluctuating traffic patterns and system availability status. That helps users navigate the Internet faster.

The Seattle operation's products help Web site operators guarantee "quality control" by balancing traffic loads to a site's best available resource at any given moment. The company's product line includes:

- **BIG/ip.** A series of five products is used to balance the flow of Internet traffic within a computer room.

- **3DNS.** Balances traffic between computer rooms at different sites.
- **GlobalSite.** This hardware tool is designed to stage and download Web pages.
- **SeeIT.** Monitors Web site performance in real time, graphs performance trends, and triggers alarms when appropriate.

F5's systems help appease Web users who are becoming less tolerant of slow-performing sites—making traffic management systems a competitive weapon among Web sites. Leading customers include major Internet service providers such as PSINet and MCI WorldCom, and big Web site operators such as Hewlett-Packard and Microsoft.

Because Cisco's Traffic Director product has a 50 percent share of the Internet traffic management market, F5 is packaging its technology into the products of Cisco's competitors, such as 3Com.

F5 went public with its initial stock offering in 1999. It has about 200 employees and a market capitalization of about $3 billion.

EARNINGS PER SHARE PROGRESSION
Losses have increased the past 2 years.

REVENUE GROWTH ★ ★ ★
Past 2 years: 12,040 percent (1,000 percent per year)

STOCK GROWTH ★
F5 went public in 1999 and had solid gains after the IPO.

CONSISTENCY ★ ★
Positive earnings progression: None
Increased revenue: 2 consecutive years

STABILITY/VULNERABILITY ★
F5 must stay one step ahead on technology to avoid being crushed by Cisco and other competitors.

F5 NETWORKS AT A GLANCE

Fiscal year ended: Sept. 30
Revenue in $ millions

	1995	1996	1997	1998	1999	2-Year Growth Avg. Annual (%)	Total (%)
Revenue ($)	—	—	.229	4.89	27.8	1,000	12,040
Earnings/share ($)	—	—	−0.24	−0.61	−0.86	NA	NA
PE ratio range	—	—	NA	NA	NA		

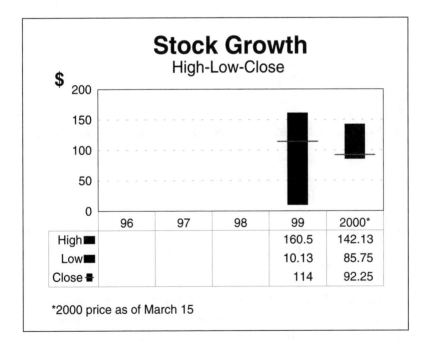

Stock Growth
High-Low-Close

$	96	97	98	99	2000*
High ■				160.5	142.13
Low ■				10.13	85.75
Close ■				114	92.25

*2000 price as of March 15

INTERNET BUSINESS
SERVICES

91

CyberSource Corp.

550 S. Winchester Road, Suite 301
San Jose, CA 95128
408-556-9100
Nasdaq: CYBS
www.cybersource.com

Chairman, President, and CEO: William S. McKiernan

Earnings Progression	
Revenue Growth	★ ★
Stock Growth	★ ★
Consistency	★
Stability/Vulnerability	★ ★
Total Points	**7 points**

CyberSource is in a prime position to profit handsomely from the explosion in online shopping. The company has been a pioneer in the development of e-commerce transaction services and Internet fraud detection. Cyber-Source should continue to grow as the volume of online purchases soars.

Based in San Jose, California, CyberSource provides online transaction services—accepting credit cards and processing orders—for nearly 1,000 Internet merchants in 26 countries. Among its leading customers are Amazon.com, Compaq Computer, Nike.com, 3M, Buy.com, Casio, and Egghead.com. Visa, the credit card giant, is among the leading investors in CyberSource.

In addition to e-tailing transaction processing, CyberSource also offers tax calculation services, risk management, distribution control services, delivery address verification, and fulfillment management services. The extra services account for about one-third of the firm's total revenue.

Fraud screening is one of CyberSource's most successful offerings. Not only does the company's transaction software accept credit card payments, it also automatically checks to make sure the credit card is valid.

The extra services offered by CyberSource have helped set it apart from the crowd of companies that simply handle the low-margin business of clearing credit card transactions. By bundling transaction processing with its array of other related services, CyberSource has been able to attract more customers, while realizing higher margins.

For merchants, using CyberSource allows them to focus on their core business, while avoiding the time and costs involved in developing and managing a complex e-commerce infrastructure.

CyberSource was founded in 1994 as Software.net, an online store that was later renamed Beyond.com and spun off as a separate stock in 1998. CyberSource opened its transaction processing business in 1997. The company went public with its initial stock offering in 1999. It has about 200 employees and a market capitalization of about $1 billion.

EARNINGS PER SHARE PROGRESSION
Losses increased the past year.

REVENUE GROWTH ★ ★
Past year: 282 percent

STOCK GROWTH ★ ★
CyberSource went public in 1999 and had strong but rocky growth after the IPO.

CONSISTENCY ★
Positive earnings progression: None
Increased revenue: 1 year

STABILITY/VULNERABILITY ★ ★
CyberSource serves a rapidly growing customer base, so the potential for growth is enormous. It does face a strong challenge from a growing field of competitors, but CyberSource is among the leaders of the niche.

CYBERSOURCE AT A GLANCE

Fiscal year ended: Dec. 31
Revenue in $ millions

	1995	1996	1997	1998	1999	1-Year Growth Avg. Annual (%)	Total (%)
Revenue ($)	—	—	—	3.38	12.9	282	282
Earnings/share ($)	—	—	—	−2.08	−2.50	NA	NA
PE ratio range	—	—	—	NA	NA		

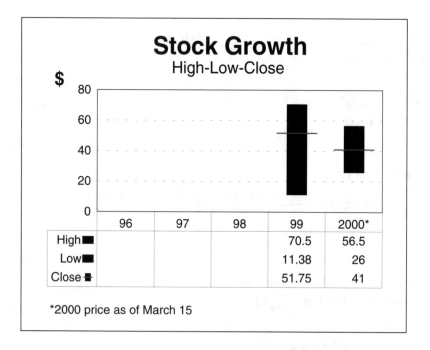

	96	97	98	99	2000*
High				70.5	56.5
Low				11.38	26
Close				51.75	41

*2000 price as of March 15

Digital River, Inc.

INTERNET BUSINESS
SERVICES

9625 West 76th Street, Suite 150
Eden Prairie, MN 55444
612-253-1234
Nasdaq: DRIV
www.digitalriver.com

CEO: Joel A. Ronning
President: Perry W. Steiner

Earnings Progression	
Revenue Growth	★ ★ ★ ★
Stock Growth	
Consistency	★ ★
Stability/Vulnerability	★
Total Points	**7 points**

It might seem only natural that software companies would run their own e-commerce sites. But in the highly competitive software industry, most companies have neither the time nor the resources to make a go of running an e-store. That's why a growing number of software makers are turning to Digital River to build them an online outlet.

Digital River is the world leader in digital product delivery. It operates e-stores for corporate clients under their own corporate brands and delivers products via download over the Internet.

The company's Web site holds the world's largest online software library, with more than 100,000 digital products. The Minneapolis operation has built a technical infrastructure specially designed for e-tailing digital products. Its services include:

- **E-store operation.** Digital River operates client e-stores on an "outsource" basis.

- **Digital delivery.** The company has developed special systems to let customers purchase and download software products and to automatically update them with new versions and bug-fix patches.
- **Physical fulfillment.** Digital River also operates a warehouse to fill orders in such physical media as CD-ROM, floppy disk, and digital computer tape cassette.
- **Marketing services**. A team of online merchants assists clients with product launches, customer analysis, and leveraging the company's network of affiliated e-tailers.

Founded in 1994, the company's roster of software publisher clients has grown to more than 6,000, including Sega, Xerox, IBM/Lotus, Qualcomm, and Corel. Digital River also has branched off into outsourcing deals with brick-and-mortar powerhouses Wal-Mart and Kmart.

The company went public with its initial stock offering in 1998. It has about 150 employees and a market capitalization of about $1 billion.

EARNINGS PER SHARE PROGRESSION

The company has had a string of increasing losses.

REVENUE GROWTH ★ ★ ★ ★

Past 3 years: 67,557 percent (778 percent per year)

STOCK GROWTH

Past year: Down 3.5 percent
Dollar loss: $10,000 over 1 year would have declined to $9,650.

CONSISTENCY ★ ★

Positive earnings progression: None
Increased revenue: 3 consecutive years

STABILITY/VULNERABILITY ★

The company's unique technical infrastructure is a valuable asset, but the online software business will be highly competitive.

DIGITAL RIVER AT A GLANCE

Fiscal year ended: Dec. 31
Revenue in $ millions

	1995	1996	1997	1998	1999	3-Year Growth Avg. Annual (%)	Total (%)
Revenue ($)	—	.111	2.47	20.9	75.1	778	67,557
Earnings/share ($)	−0.03	−0.13	−0.46	−1.01	−1.35	NA	NA
PE ratio range	NA	NA	NA	NA	NA		

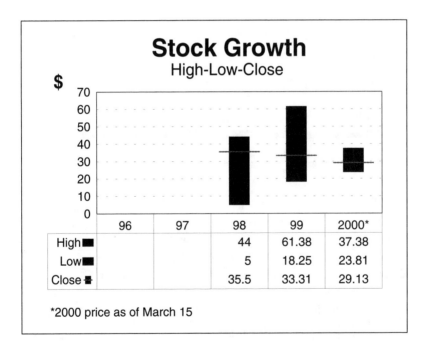

Stock Growth
High-Low-Close

	96	97	98	99	2000*
High ■			44	61.38	37.38
Low ■			5	18.25	23.81
Close ■			35.5	33.31	29.13

*2000 price as of March 15

SOFTWARE

93

Macromedia, Inc.

600 Townsend Street
San Francisco, CA 94103
415-252-2000
Nasdaq: MACR
www.macromedia.com

Chairman, President, and CEO: Robert K. Burgess

Earnings Progression	★ ★
Revenue Growth	★ ★
Stock Growth	
Consistency	★
Stability/Vulnerability	★
Total Points	**6 points**

Macromedia's mission is to add life to the Web. The San Francisco–based company makes tools that help designers put motion, sound, and interactivity into their Web pages.

Founded in 1992, Macromedia originally made tools to develop multimedia software for local networks. It translated that early technology into a quick start in Internet software. Its suite of development tools covers the gamut of Web programming needs:

- **Dreamweaver.** The company's flagship product, Dreamweaver is a workbench for Web site design and production. It's the world's top-selling product for visual Web site design by a wide margin.
- **Fireworks.** This product is used to produce such Web graphics as animations, buttons, and page layouts.
- **Flash.** This is a tool for integrating graphics, animation, MP3 audio, and interactivity into Web sites.

- **Authorware.** This is used for producing training applications for delivery over the Web, local networks, or CD-ROMs.

Some Macromedia products have almost gained the status of industry standards. For example, Flash ships with Microsoft Windows operating system and with both Microsoft Internet Explorer and AOL Netscape browsers. In addition, IBM, BroadVision, and others design their Web server platforms so customers can use Dreamweaver to customize their sites.

The company has expanded beyond front-end development tools with its Macromedia eBusiness Infrastructure framework. The framework adds such back-end features as the ability to manage site content, personalize interaction with repeat visitors, and analyze Web site traffic.

Macromedia's customer list includes such diverse names as E*Trade, Pruduential, Volkswagen, and hundreds more. Its future is bright, because pressure for Internet multimedia is likely to build as fatter bandwidth is installed to homes and businesses.

Macromedia went public with its initial stock offering in 1994. It has about 600 employees and a market capitalization of about $4 billion.

EARNINGS PER SHARE PROGRESSION ★ ★
Earnings growth past 4 years: 132 percent (24 percent per year)

REVENUE GROWTH ★ ★
Past 4 years: 179 percent (29 percent per year)

STOCK GROWTH
Past 4 years: 40 percent (9 percent per year)
Dollar growth: $10,000 over 4 years would have grown to $14,000.

CONSISTENCY ★
Increased earnings per share: 2 of the past 4 years
Increased revenue: 3 of the past 4 years

STABILITY/VULNERABILITY ★
Macromedia faces formidable competitors in Adobe, Microsoft, and others, but it has carved out a strong position in its niche.

MACROMEDIA AT A GLANCE

Fiscal year ended: March 31
Revenue in $ millions

	1995	1996	1997	1998	1999	4-Year Growth Avg. Annual (%)	4-Year Growth Total (%)
Revenue ($)	53.7	116.7	107.4	113.1	149.9	29	179
Earnings/share ($)	0.19	0.59	−0.16	−0.16	0.44	24	132
PE ratio range	55-335	24-91	NA	NA	60-203		

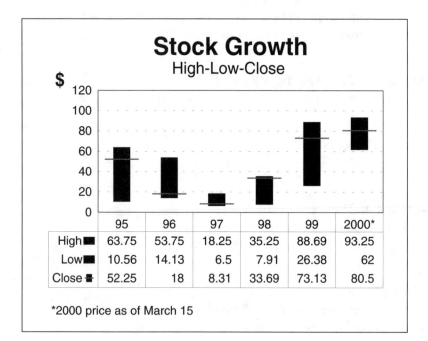

Stock Growth
High-Low-Close

$	95	96	97	98	99	2000*
High	63.75	53.75	18.25	35.25	88.69	93.25
Low	10.56	14.13	6.5	7.91	26.38	62
Close	52.25	18	8.31	33.69	73.13	80.5

*2000 price as of March 15

94

FirePond, Inc.

890 Winter Street
Waltham, MA 02451
781-487-8400
Nasdaq: FIRE
www.firepond.com

Chairman, President, and CEO: Klaus P. Besier

Earnings Progression	
Revenue Growth	★
Stock Growth	★
Consistency	★
Stability/Vulnerability	★ ★
Total Points	**5 points**

Business on the Web is starting to get personal. E-commerce companies that can tailor their offerings to individual customers will have a leg up in the increasingly competitive online market.

FirePond makes e-commerce software that allows companies to get more personal with their customers. Its software enables companies to offer targeted products, services, and content when a customer is preparing to buy—either on an e-commerce Web site or from a direct salesperson, distributor, or dealer.

The Waltham, Massachusetts operation's signature FirePond Application Suite software gives companies the ability to share customer information obtained from e-commerce sales transactions with traditional sales channels. The software can collect information about individual customer behavior, preferences, and transaction activity. That information can be used to improve individual customer relationships and tailor product offerings, services, and sales strategies to increase customer retention.

Some of the world's largest companies use FirePond e-commerce software, including General Motors, IBM, ADP, and Hitachi.

The FirePond Application Suite was recently honored by the Denali Group as the "Best use of the Internet to improve sales and marketing," based on the fact that the software suite is among the first to combine technology-enabled selling with partner relationship management technologies and sales force automation.

Founded in 1983, FirePond went public with its initial stock offering in 2000. The company has about 350 employees and a market capitalization of about $3 billion.

EARNINGS PER SHARE PROGRESSION

The company experienced increased losses the past year.

REVENUE GROWTH ★

Past year: 18 percent

STOCK GROWTH ★

FirePond went public in 2000.

CONSISTENCY ★

Positive earnings progression: None
Increased revenue: 1 year

STABILITY/VULNERABILITY ★ ★

FirePond has been in business for more than 15 years, so it is a well-established operation. Since shifting its emphasis to the Internet, however, it is a long way from profitability.

FIREPOND AT A GLANCE

Fiscal year ended: Oct. 31
Revenue in $ millions

	1995	1996	1997	1998	1999	1-Year Growth Avg. Annual (%)	Total (%)
Revenue ($)	—	—	—	29	34.3	18	18
Earnings/share ($)	—	—	—	−0.90	−2.88	NA	NA
PE ratio range	—	—	—	NA	NA		

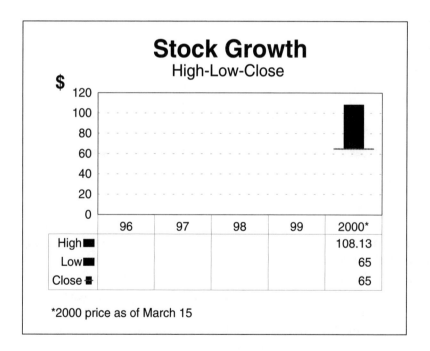

Stock Growth
High-Low-Close

$	96	97	98	99	2000*
High ■					108.13
Low ■					65
Close ■					65

*2000 price as of March 15

INTERNET BUSINESS
SERVICES

95

Mail.com, Inc.

11 Broadway, 6th Floor
New York, NY 10004
212-425-4200
Nasdaq: MAIL
www.mail.com

Chairman and CEO: Gerald Gorman
President: Gary Millin

Earnings Progression	
Revenue Growth	★
Stock Growth	★
Consistency	★
Stability/Vulnerability	★ ★
Total Points	**5 points**

It's a long way from the Pony Express. Mail.com has helped build the new global postal system, assigning about 10 million e-mail boxes for companies and consumers around the world and processing more than 150 million e-mail messages a month.

The New York operation sets up e-mail boxes for Internet users through its own Web site; through Internet service providers, such as Prodigy and EarthLink; through corporations, such as Continental Airlines and GTE; and through more than 40 high-traffic Web site partners, such as CNET, DellNet, NBC, and Snap.com.

Mail.com generates revenue primarily from advertising sales, the sale of domain names, and e-mail service outsourcing fees. The company delivers more than 200 million advertisements per month.

Mail.com also offers several related services, including:

- **MailZone.** This service blocks incoming and outgoing e-mail that contains viruses, large attachments that clog systems, and objectionable messages of a sexual, racial, or profane nature. The company has about 200,000 MailZone customers.
- **Anti-spam protection.** Mail.com has teamed with Brightmail to offer companies protection from unsolicited bulk e-mail known as "spam" that tends to bog down e-mail systems and bury employees in e-mail solicitations.
- **Premium e-mail boxes.** For an extra fee of about $3 a month, consumers can sign up for e-mail boxes with special names.
- **Special Delivery.** The company offers advertisers a permission-based e-mail marketing service that reaches an audience of customers who have asked to receive information on products and services via e-mail.

Incorporated in 1994, Mail.com launched its e-mail service in 1996 under the name iName. It changed to its current name in 1999, the same year it went public with its initial stock offering. The company has about 125 employees and a market capitalization of about $700 million.

EARNINGS PER SHARE PROGRESSION
None

REVENUE GROWTH ★
Past year: 342 percent

STOCK GROWTH ★
Mail.com went public in 1999 and had solid but rocky gains after its IPO.

CONSISTENCY ★
Positive earnings progression: None
Increased revenue: 1 year

STABILITY/VULNERABILITY ★ ★
Mail.com is a strong player in the e-mail market, which is growing by 100 million new e-mail boxes per year. It has added some new services to bump up revenue but still appears to be a long way from profitability.

MAIL.COM AT A GLANCE

Fiscal year ended: Dec. 31
Revenue in $ millions

	1995	1996	1997	1998	1999	1-Year Growth Avg. Annual (%)	Total (%)
Revenue ($)	—	—	—	1.49	6.59	342	342
Earnings/share ($)	—	—	—	−0.83	−1.86	NA	NA
PE ratio range	—	—	—	NA	NA		

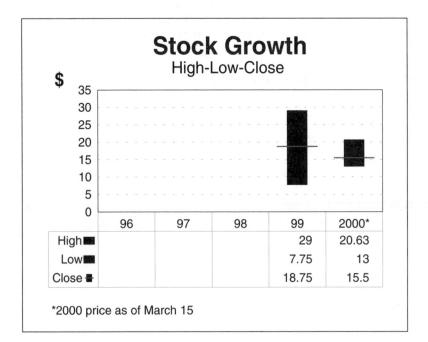

Stock Growth
High-Low-Close

$	96	97	98	99	2000*
High				29	20.63
Low				7.75	13
Close				18.75	15.5

*2000 price as of March 15

MEDIA AND
ENTERTAINMENT

96

MP3.com, Inc.

4790 Eastgate Mall
San Diego, CA 92121
858-623-7000
Nasdaq: MPPP
www.mp3.com

Chairman and CEO: Michael L. Robinson
President: Robin Richards

Earnings Progression	
Revenue Growth	★ ★ ★
Stock Growth	
Consistency	★
Stability/Vulnerability	★
Total Points	**5 points**

Is there a difference between MP3 and MP3.com? Yes, and a big one: MP3 is a data compression format that makes it possible to download music files over the Internet. MP3.com is a company that operates a Web site based on the format, a technology it didn't develop and does not own.

The MP3 format has exploded in popularity because it bypasses traditional music industry distribution, giving independent artists open access to markets and providing listeners with virtually unlimited choice. The idea behind MP3.com is that digital music will transform the music industry, and the company at the forefront of the revolution will reap big profits.

Although thousands of sites offer MP3 content, MP3.com is fast positioning itself as the place where artists and listeners can find one another. Its services include:

- **Music downloads.** Listeners can download songs or even whole albums for free.

- **Webcasts.** The company broadcasts live concerts over the Internet.
- **E-store.** About 15 percent of revenues are generated from sales of music CDs and related merchandise.
- **Music publishing.** MP3.com is signing thousands of artists to a standard deal that lets the company manufacture and distribute their albums for half the profits.

Most of its revenues still come from ad sales. The San Diego operation plans to boost the e-tailing revenue mix and hopes to eventually emerge as a music publishing powerhouse alongside the likes of Sony.

The company has entered into a joint marketing agreement with media giant Cox Enterprises and signed a $150 million marketing deal with Groupe Arnault, the French consumer products holding company.

MP3.com was founded in 1997 by Michael Robinson and Robin Richards, both with backgrounds as Internet media entrepreneurs. It went public with an initial stock offering in 1999. MP3.com has about 250 employees and a market capitalization of about $2 billion.

EARNINGS PER SHARE PROGRESSION
None

REVENUE GROWTH   ★ ★ ★
Past year: 1,788 percent

STOCK GROWTH
MP3 went public in 1999 and had an up-and-down performance.

CONSISTENCY   ★
Positive earnings progression: None
Increased revenue: 1 year

STABILITY/VULNERABILITY   ★
MP3.com's early market presence and growing brand recognition are valuable, but building a new business in the entertainment industry is always a tough proposition.

MP3.COM AT A GLANCE

Fiscal year ended: Dec. 31
Revenue in $ millions

	1995	1996	1997	1998	1999	1-Year Growth Avg. Annual (%)	1-Year Growth Total (%)
Revenue ($)	—	—	—	1.16	21.9	1,788	1,788
Earnings/share ($)	—	—	—	−0.01	−0.77	NA	NA
PE ratio range	—	—	—	NA	NA		

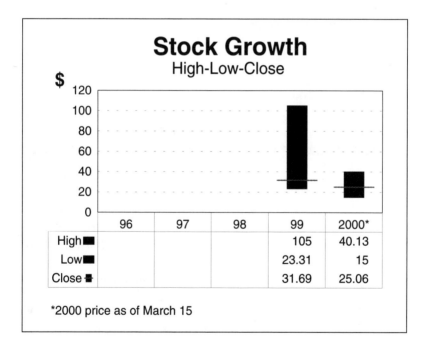

Stock Growth
High-Low-Close

	96	97	98	99	2000*
High ■				105	40.13
Low ■				23.31	15
Close ■				31.69	25.06

*2000 price as of March 15

INTERNET BUSINESS
SERVICES

97

ShopNow.com, Inc.

411 First Avenue S., Suite 200 N.
Seattle, WA 98104
206-223-1996
Nasdaq: SPNW
www.shopnow.com

Chairman and CEO: Dwayne M. Walker
President: Joe E. Arciniega, Jr.

Earnings Progression	
Revenue Growth	★ ★
Stock Growth	★
Consistency	★
Stability/Vulnerability	★
Total Points	**5 points**

ShopNow.com offers an online marketplace for both consumers and merchants. The company sells merchandise from 50,000 businesses and offers a wide range of e-commerce services from Web site construction to advertising and merchandising.

The company's portal, ShopNow.com, is an online marketplace that connects millions of buyers and sellers worldwide.

The Seattle operation also operates a business-to-business portal, b2b Now.com, that offers a range of e-commerce products and services, including:

- **Business directory.** The site has a directory of more than 500,000 businesses.
- **Transaction services.** ShopNow.com offers secure payment and order processing services for its merchant clients, as well as online check acceptance, online escrow services, and fraud detection.

340

- **Business solutions.** The site offers online marketing services, e-commerce enabling services, and hosting and maintenance services to help its clients build and operate online stores.
- **Specials and offers.** Through b2bNow.com companies can find business products or barter for services or products.
- **Internet tools.** The company can customize your site, monitor your site, or register a domain name.

The company generates income through online advertising, referral fees, and business service fees.

The ShopNow.com portal has been growing rapidly, with 21 million visits in the fourth quarter of 1999, compared with just 7 million the previous quarter.

Founded in 1994, ShopNow.com went public with its initial stock offering in 1999. The company has about 300 employees and a market capitalization of about $600 million.

EARNINGS PER SHARE PROGRESSION

None

REVENUE GROWTH ★★

Past year: 417 percent

STOCK GROWTH ★

ShopNow.com had modest growth after its 1999 IPO.

CONSISTENCY ★

Positive earnings progression: None
Increased sales: 1 year

STABILITY/VULNERABILITY ★

ShopNow.com has an interesting concept, but it is still young, small, and far from profitable.

SHOPNOW.COM AT A GLANCE

Fiscal year ended: Dec. 31
Revenue in $ millions

	1995	1996	1997	1998	1999	Avg. Annual (%)	Total (%)
						1-Year Growth	
Revenue ($)	—	—	—	7.15	37	417	417
Earnings/share ($)	—	—	—	−6.60	−9.71	NA	NA
PE ratio range	—	—	—	NA	NA		

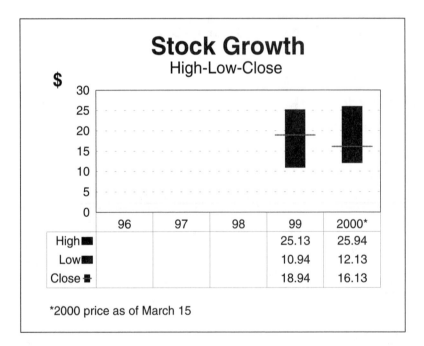

Stock Growth
High-Low-Close

	96	97	98	99	2000*
High ■				25.13	25.94
Low ■				10.94	12.13
Close ■				18.94	16.13

*2000 price as of March 15

98

Ask Jeeves, Inc.

5858 Horton Street, Suite 350
Emeryville, CA 94608
510-985-7400
Nasdaq: ASKJ
www.ask.com

President and CEO: Robert W. Wrubel

Earnings Progression	
Revenue Growth	★ ★
Stock Growth	★
Consistency	★
Stability/Vulnerability	★
Total Points	**5 points**

Got a question? Ask Jeeves. You won't get a direct answer, but you will be directed to a Web site that will very likely give you the answer.

In simple terms, Ask Jeeves is a Web search engine that speaks English. Instead of typing a word or a string of related words into a normal search engine, the user asks a complete question. Ask Jeeves responds with one or more related questions. The user clicks on the question that is most appropriate and is taken to a Web site that provides the answer.

For instance, ask "Where is Brussels?" and Jeeves responds with three options: "Where can I find a city guide to Brussels, Belgium?" "Where can I find an encyclopedia article on Brussels, Belgium?" and "Where is Brussels, Belgium?" Click on the latter and the search engine takes you to the MSN Expedia Maps site, where it displays a map of Belgium highlighting Brussels.

How does Ask Jeeves work? When you type in a question, Ask Jeeves automatically scans the words in the question, searches through its database for similar questions for which it already has an answer, then lists those questions for the user. The company also keeps about 40 people on hand who watch for questions that have no answers in the database and who manually find the answers on the Web.

Ask Jeeves ranks in the top 12 among all Web search engines with about 2 million unique visitors per month. Yahoo! is number one with more than 30 million unique monthly visitors.

Ask Jeeves also sets up corporate answering services to direct customers to the correct answers for their online questions. For instance, Ask Jeeves designed a question-and-answer service for Marthastewart.com that fields questions on weddings and wedding preparations. The firm also set up a Q&A site for Dell Computer, called "Ask Dudley," that helps Dell customers find answers to technical questions about their PCs.

Founded in 1996, the Emeryville, California operation went public with its initial stock offering in 1999. It has about 320 employees and a market capitalization of about $3 billion.

EARNINGS PER SHARE PROGRESSION
Ask Jeeves has seen its losses rise the past 3 years.

REVENUE GROWTH   ★ ★
Past year: 3,475 percent

STOCK GROWTH   ★
Ask Jeeves went public in 1999 and had up-and-down performance after its IPO.

CONSISTENCY   ★
Increased earnings per share: None
Increased revenue: 1 year

STABILITY/VULNERABILITY   ★
Neat concept, but Ask Jeeves is a long way from profitability, and it is competing in a very crowded market.

ASK JEEVES AT A GLANCE

Fiscal year ended: Dec. 31
Revenue in $ millions

	1995	1996	1997	1998	1999	1-Year Growth Avg. Annual (%)	Total (%)
Revenue ($)	—	0	0	0.593	21.2	3,475	3,475
Earnings/share ($)	—	−0.08	−0.135	−0.51	−2.14	NA	NA
PE ratio range	—	NA	NA	NA	NA		

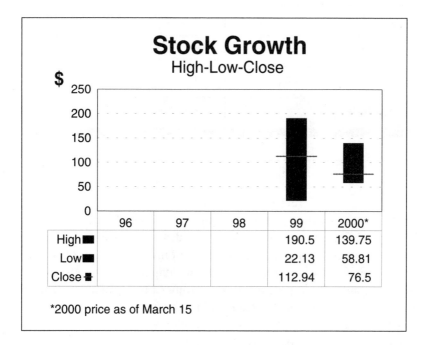

Stock Growth
High-Low-Close

	96	97	98	99	2000*
High ■				190.5	139.75
Low ■				22.13	58.81
Close ■				112.94	76.5

*2000 price as of March 15

E-COMMERCE

Entrade, Inc.

500 Central Avenue
Northfield, IL 60093
847-441-6650
NYSE: ETA
www.entrade.com

President and CEO: Mark F. Santacrose

Earnings Progression	
Revenue Growth	
Stock Growth	★ ★ ★
Consistency	
Stability/Vulnerability	★
Total Points	**4 points**

In Internet jargon, B2B refers to business-to-business commerce. Entrade specializes in the creation of B2B e-commerce marketplaces.

The Northfield, Illinois operation provides services to e-commerce companies to facilitate the purchase and sale of inventory, equipment, and other assets. Its technology enables its client companies to conduct online transactions, auctions, e-procurement, customer management, inventory management, and asset management and recovery.

Entrade's primary emphasis is on heavy industrial product sales. Its e-commerce tools are customized around sales, distribution, asset and inventory management, and procurement needs.

Entrade offers a variety of online services to help B2B operations, including:

- **Sales and marketing.** Through Entrade's systems, companies can set up a secure, functional online catalog sales and distribution system.
- **Procurement.** Entrade's technologies and commercial applications enable client companies to set up a real-time procurement presence within a customized community of vendor participants. Features include cataloging, open bid, ordering, payment, accounting, shipment, and transaction processing on an electronic platform customized for each client.
- **Account management.** Organizations can maintain and share data globally to provide sales support systems or improve customer service.
- **Inventory and asset management.** Through the Entrade system, organizations can instantly access, query, transact, ship, and document inventory transfers.

The company also helps build B2B online communities, focusing on specific business sectors by setting up alliances with industry leaders in those sectors.

Entrade went public with its initial stock offering in 1999. It has only ten employees and a market capitalization of about $500 million.

EARNINGS PER SHARE PROGRESSION
None

REVENUE GROWTH
No revenue reported

STOCK GROWTH ★ ★ ★
Past 4 years: 567 percent (60 percent per year)
Dollar growth: $10,000 over 4 years would have grown to $66,700

CONSISTENCY
Positive earnings progression: None
Increased revenue: None

STABILITY/VULNERABILITY ★
Good concept, but how seriously can you take a company with only ten employees? At least personnel overhead is at a minimum.

ENTRADE AT A GLANCE

Fiscal year ended: Dec. 31
Revenue in $ millions

	1995	1996	1997	1998	1999	1-Year Growth Avg. Annual (%)	Total (%)
Revenue ($)	—	120.7	125	0	0	3.5	NA
Earnings/share ($)	—	0.32	−0.07	−0.78	−0.74	NA	NA
PE ratio range	—	NA	NA	NA	NA		

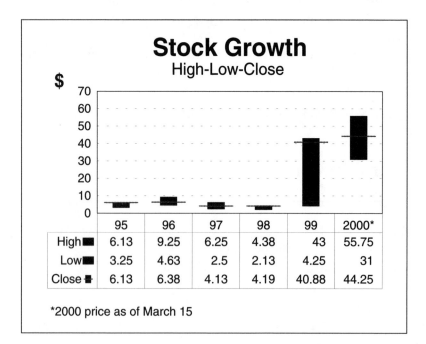

Stock Growth
High-Low-Close

$	95	96	97	98	99	2000*
High ■	6.13	9.25	6.25	4.38	43	55.75
Low ■	3.25	4.63	2.5	2.13	4.25	31
Close ■	6.13	6.38	4.13	4.19	40.88	44.25

*2000 price as of March 15

E-TAILING

100

Drugstore.com, Inc.

13920 Southeast Eastgate Way, #300
Bellevue, WA 98005
425-372-3200
Nasdaq: DSCM
www.drugstore.com

Chairman, President, and CEO: Peter M. Neupert

Earnings Progression	
Revenue Growth	★ ★
Stock Growth	
Consistency	
Stability/Vulnerability	★
Total Points	**3 points**

Going to the drugstore is seldom fun but usually necessary. Drugstore.com may not be able to make the chore entertaining, but it is making it more efficient.

With former Microsoft Vice President Peter Neupert at the helm, the company has set out to do more than just fill prescriptions at cut-rate prices. It uses technology to enhance the pharmacy shopping experience.

The Bellevue, Washington operation handles an inventory of thousands of the same health, beauty, wellness, and personal care products found in the typical brick-and-mortar drugstore. It also offers users a variety of online tools such as online experts, wellness guides, free newsletters, and e-mail reminders to refill a prescription.

Drugstore.com has received high marks for its Web site. It was recently ranked as the best online pharmacy by Gomez Advisors, an e-commerce consumer research firm. Drugstore.com has become a favorite investment of Amazon.com, which acquired a 27 percent stake in the business.

The company's business model is built on partnerships with brick-and-mortar retailers. It has an agreement with Rite Aid, the third-largest pharmacy chain in the United States, to sell from its inventory and has teamed with GNC to sell its vitamins and nutritional supplements.

The deal with Rite Aid gives the company enormous buying clout and offers customers the convenience of being able to pick up prescriptions at Rite Aid stores. Some analysts see the Rite Aid connection as a weakness because of the giant drugstore chain's recent financial problems. But Drugstore.com has contracted directly with the insurance clearinghouses for prescription reimbursement, making it safe on that front.

The company made its initial public stock offering in 1999. It has a market capitalization of about $1 billion.

EARNINGS PER SHARE PROGRESSION

Earnings increased from 1998 to 1999.

REVENUE GROWTH   ★ ★

Strong sales in its first year

STOCK GROWTH

The stock went public in 1999, and slid to new lows in 2000.

CONSISTENCY

Positive earnings progression: None
Increased revenue: Not applicable

STABILITY/VULNERABILITY   ★

The company faces big competition from CVS.com, PlanetRX.com, and Walgreens, but its sharp e-store interface and great services should serve it well.

DRUGSTORE.COM AT A GLANCE

Fiscal year ended: Dec. 31
Revenue in $ millions

	1995	1996	1997	1998	1999	0-Year Growth Avg. Annual (%)	Total (%)
Revenue ($)	—	—	—	—	34.8	NA	NA
Earnings/share ($)	—	—	—	−0.98	−3.52	NA	NA
PE ratio range	—	—	—	NA	NA		

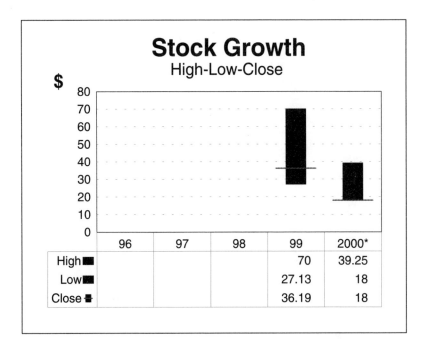

	96	97	98	99	2000*
High ■				70	39.25
Low ■				27.13	18
Close ■				36.19	18

Honorable Mention Internet Stocks

About.com	BOUT	Genesisintermedia.com	GENI
Accrue Software	ACRU	Go2Net Inc.	GNET
Agile Software	AGIL	GoTo.com Inc.	GOTO
Akamai Technologies	AKAM	HeadHunter.net	HHNT
Alloy Online	ALOY	HomeCom Communications	HCOM
Applied Micro	AMCC	Homestore.com	HOMS
AppliedTheory	ATHY	Hoover's Inc.	HOOV
Audible	ADBL	HotJobs.com	HOTJ
Autobytel	ABTL	ImageX.com	IMGX
Autoweb.com	AWEB	Infonautics	INFO
Axent Technologies	AXNT	InsWeb Corp.	INSW
Beyond.com	BYND	Interactive Intelligence	ININ
Braun Consulting	BRNC	Interactive Pictures	IPIX
Breakaway	BWAY	Intermedia Communications	ICIX
CareerBuilder	CBDR	Internet America	GEEK
Cendant Corp.	CD	Internet.com	INTM
Cheap Tickets	CTIX	Inter-Tel	INTL
Clarent Corp.	CLRN	InterVU	ITVU
Cobalt Group, The	CBLT	InterWorld	INTW
Com21	CMTO	Intraware	ITRA
CommScope	CTV	Intuit	INTU
Concur Technologies	CNQR	iTurf Inc.	TURF
Crossroads Systems, Inc.	CRDS	iVillage Inc.	IVIL
Cyberian Outpost	COOL	iXL	IIXL
CyberShop.com	CYSP	JFAX.com	JFAX
Diamond Tech.	DTPI	Juno Online Services	JWEB
Digex	DIGX	Kana Communications	KANA
Digital Island	ISLD	Keynote Systems, Inc.	KEYN
DLJ Direct	DIR	Launch Media	LAUN
EarthWeb	EWBX	Litronic	LTNX
Egghead.com Inc.	EGGS	LookSmart	LOOK
E-Loan.com	EELN	MapQuest.com	MQST
Engage Technologies	ENGA	Marimba	MRBA
eToys	ETYS	MarketWatch.com	MKTW
FlashNet Communications	FLAS	Micromuse	MUSE
Free Markets	FMKT	MMC Networks	MMCN
Freeshop.com, Inc.	FSHP	Modem Media.P/T	MMPT
FVC.COM	FVCX	Mortgage.com	MDCM

MyPoints.com	MYPT	RMI.NET	RMII
N2H2	NTWO	Rogue Wave Software	RWAV
NAVIDEC	NVDC	SalesLogix Corp.	SLGX
NEON Systems	NESY	Sapient	SAPE
Net.B@nk	NTBK	Silknet Software	SILK
NetGravity Inc.	NETG	Software.com	SWCM
NetObjects	NETO	Splitrock Services	SPLT
Netopia	NTPA	SportsLine USA Inc.	SPLN
Netro Corp.	NTRO	StarMedia Network	STRM
Netsilicon, Inc.	NSIL	Talk City	TCTY
Network Associates	NETA	Tanning Technology	TANN
NFront.com	NFNT	TD Waterhouse Group	TWE
NorthPoint Communications	NPNT	TheStreet.com	TSCM
Onlinetradinginc.com	LINE	theglobe.com	TGLO
ONSALE	ONSL	Tumbleweed	
Packeteer	PKTR	Communications	TMWD
Paradyne Networks, Inc.	PDYN	Tut Systems	TUTS
PcOrder.com	PCOR	US Internetworking	USIX
Peapod	PPOD	Viant Corp.	VIAN
Persistence Software	PRSW	Viatel Inc.	VYTL
Pilot Network Services	PILT	Vitria Tech.	VITR
PlanetRX.com	PLRX	VocalTec Communications	VOCL
Portal Software	PRSF	V-ONE	VONE
Preview Travel Inc.	PTVL	Voyager.net	VOYN
Primus Knowledge Solutions	PKSI	Wall Data Inc.	WALL
Prodigy Communications	PRGY	WinStar Communications	WCII
Quest Software	QSFT	Xoom.com	XMCM
Qwest Communications	QWST	ZDnet	ZDZ
Ramp Networks	RAMP	ZipLink	ZIPL
Red Hat Software Inc.	RHAT		

The 100 Best Internet Stocks by Sector

Infrastructure (18)
Ariba, Inc.
Broadcom Corp.
Brocade Communications
Carrier Access Corp.
Cisco Systems, Inc.
Copper Mountain Networks, Inc.
Extreme Networks, Inc.
F5 Networks, Inc.
Foundry Network, Inc.
Harmonic, Inc.
JDS Uniphase
Juniper Networks, Inc.
NetScout Systems, Inc.
Network Appliance, Inc.
Optibase Ltd.
Redback Networks, Inc.
Sycamore Networks
Terayon Communications Systems

ISPs and Portals (15)
America Online Time Warner, Inc.
Ask Jeeves, Inc.
China.com Corp.
Concentric Networks Corp.
Covad Communications Group
EarthLink Network, Inc.
Excite@Home Corp.
Global Crossing Ltd.
Lycos, Inc.
Network Access Solutions Corp.
PSINet, Inc.
ShopNow.com, Inc.
Verio, Inc.
WorldGate Communications, Inc.
Yahoo! Inc.

Internet Business Services (18)
AppNet, Inc.
Critical Path, Inc.
CyberSource Corp.
Cysive, Inc.
Digital River, Inc.
DoubleClick, Inc.
Exodus Communications
InterCept Group, Inc., The
Interliant, Inc.
ISS Group, Inc.
Mail.com, Inc.
Media Metrix, Inc.
National Information Consortium, Inc.
Razorfish, Inc.
Scient Corp., Inc.
24/7 Media, Inc.
TeleTech Holdings, Inc.
VeriSign, Inc.

Software (22)
Allaire, Inc.
Art Technology Group
BackWeb Technologies Ltd.
BroadVision, Inc.
Check Point Software Technologies
Entrust Technologies, Inc.
FirePond, Inc.
Inktomi Corp.
Liberate Technologies
Macromedia, Inc.
Mecury Interactive Corp.
Net Perceptions
Open Market, Inc.
Phone.com, Inc.
RealNetworks, Inc.
Sagent Technology, Inc.
SilverStream Software, Inc.

Verity, Inc.
Viador, Inc.
Vignette Corp.
webMethods, Inc.
WebTrends Corp.

E-commerce (9)
Bottomline Technologies, Inc.
Commerce One, Inc.
Entrade, Inc.
Healtheon/WebMD
i2 Technologies, Inc.
PurchasePro.com, Inc.
RoweCom, Inc.
S1 Corporation
VerticalNet, Inc.

E-tailing (7)
Amazon.com, Inc.
Barnesandnoble.com, Inc.
Drugstore.com, Inc.

eBay, Inc.
Fatbrain.com, Inc.
NextCard, Inc.
Priceline.com, Inc.

Media and Entertainment (4)
CNET, Inc.
InfoSpace.com, Inc.
MP3.com, Inc.
Net2Phone

Online Financial Services (4)
Ameritrade Holdings Corp.
CheckFree Holdings Corp.
E*Trade Group, Inc.
Knight/Trimark Group, Inc.

Internet Holding Companies (3)
CMGI, Inc.
Internet Capital Group
Wit Capital Group, Inc.

The 100 Best Internet Stocks by State/Country

State	Ranking
California	
Ariba, Inc. (Sunnyvale)	48
Ask Jeeves, Inc. (Emeryville)	98
Broadcom Corp. (Ervine)	6
BroadVision, Inc. (Redwood City)	5
Brocade Communications (San Jose)	33
Cisco Systems, Inc. (San Jose)	1
CNET, Inc. (San Francisco)	10
Commerce One, Inc. (Walnut Creek)	30
Concentric Network Corp. (San Jose)	20
Copper Mountain Networks, Inc. (Palo Alto)	42
Covad Communications Group (Santa Clara)	44
Critical Path, Inc. (San Francisco)	52
CyberSource Corp. (San Jose)	91
EarthLink Network, Inc. (Pasadena)	61
eBay, Inc. (San Jose)	19
E*Trade Group, Inc. (Menlo Park)	29
Excite@Home Corp. (Redwood City)	47
Exodus Communications (Santa Clara)	15
Extreme Networks, Inc. (Santa Clara)	60
Fatbrain.com, Inc. (Santa Clara)	70
Foundry Networks, Inc. (Sunnyvale)	65
Harmonic, Inc. (Sunnyvale)	31
Healtheon/WebMD (Santa Clara)	72
Inktomi Corp. (Foster City)	40
JDS Uniphase (San Jose)	18
Juniper Networks, Inc. (Mountain View)	59
Liberate Technologies (San Carlos)	62
Macromedia, Inc. (San Francisco)	93
Mercury Interactive Corp. (Sunnyvale)	11
MP3.com, Inc. (San Diego)	96

State	Ranking

California (continued)

Network Appliance, Inc. (Sunnyvale)	13
NextCard, Inc. (San Francisco)	78
Phone.com, Inc. (Redwood City)	63
Redback Networks, Inc. (Sunnyvale)	35
Sagent Technology, Inc. (Mountain View)	57
Scient Corp., Inc. (San Francisco)	83
Terayon Communications Systems (Santa Clara)	58
VeriSign, Inc. (Mountain View)	8
Verity, Inc. (Sunnyvale)	41
Viador, Inc. (San Mateo)	89
Yahoo! Inc. (Santa Clara)	2

Colorado

Carrier Access Corp. (Boulder)	12
TeleTech Holdings, Inc. (Denver)	56
Verio, Inc. (Englewood)	17

Connecticut

Priceline.com, Inc. (Stamford)	82

Georgia

CheckFree Holdings Corp. (Norcross)	25
InterCept Group, Inc., The (Norcross)	55
ISS Group, Inc. (Atlanta)	21
S1 Corporation (Atlanta)	26

Illinois

Entrade, Inc. (Northfield)	99

Kansas

National Information Consortium, Inc. (Overland Park)	69

Maryland

AppNet, Inc. (Bethesda)	88

State	Ranking

Massachusetts

Allaire, Inc. (Cambridge)	50
Art Technology Group (Cambridge)	87
CMGI, Inc. (Andover)	3
FirePond, Inc. (Waltham)	94
Lycos, Inc. (Waltham)	24
NetScout Systems, Inc. (Westford)	45
Open Market, Inc. (Burlington)	37
RoweCom, Inc. (Cambridge)	64
SilverStream Software, Inc. (Burlington)	68
Sycamore Networks, Inc. (Chelmsford)	75

Minnesota

Digital River, Inc. (Eden Prairie)	92
Net Perceptions (Eden Prairie)	51

Nebraska

Ameritrade Holding Corp. (Omaha)	23

Nevada

PurchasePro.com, Inc. (Las Vegas)	84

New Hampshire

Bottomline Technologies, Inc. (Portsmouth)	34

New Jersey

Knight/Trimark Group, Inc. (Jersey City)	9
Net2Phone (Hackensack)	77

New York

Barnesandnoble.com, Inc. (New York)	71
DoubleClick, Inc. (New York)	16
Interliant, Inc. (Purchase)	81
Mail.com, Inc. (New York)	95
Media Metrix, Inc. (New York)	67
Razorfish, Inc. (New York)	73
24/7 Media, Inc. (New York)	38
Wit Capital Group, Inc. (New York)	79

State	Ranking
Oregon	
WebTrends Corp. (Portland)	36
Pennsylvania	
Internet Capital Group (Wayne)	74
VerticalNet, Inc. (Horsham)	32
WorldGate Communications, Inc. (Trevose)	80
Texas	
Entrust Technologies, Inc. (Plano)	28
i2 Technologies, Inc. (Irving)	7
Vignette Corp. (Austin)	46
Virginia	
America Online Time Warner, Inc. (Dulles)	14
Cysive, Inc. (Reston)	76
Network Access Solutions Corp. (Sterling)	86
PSINet, Inc. (Herndon)	43
webMethods, Inc. (Fairfax)	85
Washington	
Amazon.com, Inc. (Seattle)	27
Drugstore.com, Inc. (Bellevue)	100
F5 Networks, Inc. (Seattle)	90
InfoSpace.com, Inc. (Redmond)	49
RealNetworks, Inc. (Seattle)	22
ShopNow.com, Inc. (Seattle)	97
Foreign	
BackWeb Technologies Ltd. (Ramat Gan, Israel)	54
Check Point Software Technologies, Inc. (Ramat Gan, Israel)	4
China.com Corp. (Hong Kong, China)	39
Global Crossing Ltd. (Hamilton, Bermuda)	66
Optibase Ltd. (Herzliya, Israel)	53

Index

Continental Airlines, 334
Convergence, 67
Copper Mountain Networks, Inc., 175–77
CopperNet, 307
Corel, 326
Corporate procurement processes, 193
Corporate suite, 128
Cotsakos, Christos M., 136
Covad Communications Group, 181–83
Cox Communications, 191, 235
Cox Enterprises, 338
Credit cards, 6, 283
Critical Path, Inc., 58, 205–7
Customer management, 346
Customer personalization, 254, 310, 331
Customer premises equipment, 6
Customer Relationship Management platforms, 22
Customer services, 217
Cyberian Outpost, 64
CyberSource Corp., 322
CyberStream, 143
Cysive, Inc., 28, 277–79

D

Dachis, Jeffrey A., 268
DaimlerChrysler, 277
Database(s), 220
    compatibility, 304
    corporate, 317
    information exchange, 188
    searches, 203
    security of, 112
Data communications management, 215
Data Mart Solution, 220
Data storage and retrieval, 88, 148
Data switches, 60, 274
Data/voice recognition, 85
Davis, Robert J., 121, 122
Dayton, Sky D., 232
Dedicated hosting, 293
Dedicated service, 30
Deja.com, 272
Dell Computer, 149, 293, 344
DellNet, 334
Demand collection system, 295
Denali Group, 332
Dennison, Jack, 265
Deshpande, Gururaj, 274
Deutsche Bank, 127
Deutsche Presse, 56
Digital certificates, 27, 32, 73, 133
Digital marketplace(s), 33–34, 35, 301
Digital media access devices, 85
Digital packet format, 1
Digital product delivery, 325
Digital River, Inc., 325–27

Digital Subscriber Line (DSL) technology, 12, 67, 155, 175–76, 181, 307
Digital video, 208
Digital Work, 302
Direct marketing, 164
Directory Engine, 169
Discount brokerages, 118
Discount pricing, 295
Disk farms, 14, 148
Document libraries, 293
Document Navigator, 173
Dodd, James B., 256
dot-com Solutions, 314
DoubleClick, Inc., 27, 32, 97–99
Dow Jones, 173
Dreamweaver, 328
Drivers, 254
Drugstore.com, Inc., 131, 349–51
DSL technology, 12, 67, 155, 175–76, 181, 307
Dun & Bradstreet, 241
Dynamic Advertising, Reporting, and Targeting (DART), 94–95
Dynamo, 310

E

E*Trade Group, Inc., 136–38, 205, 329
EarthLink Network, Inc., 14, 155, 232–34, 245, 334
eBay, Inc., 106–8
E-bill technology, 125
eBroker, 118
E-Chemicals, 272
E-commerce, 33–37, 40, 61, 65, 73, 182, 346
    Bottomline Technologies, Inc., 151–53
    business-to-business, 271
    Commerce One, Inc., 139–41
    customer personalization and, 331
    digital marketplaces, 35
    EDI, 34
    Entrade, Inc., 346–48
    Healtheon/WebMD, 265–67
    i2 Technologies, Inc., 70–72
    key technologies, 33–34
    management, 187
    market positioning, 36
    prospects and trends, 36–37
    PurchasePro.com, Inc., 301–3
    RoweCom, Inc., 241–43
    sites, outsourcing operation of, 100
    software, 125, 193
    S1 Corporation, 127–29
    transaction services, 322
    VerticalNet, Inc., 145–47
    Web site design/development, 298–99
Economic business models, 24
EDI software, 151
EDS, 28, 31